IMAGES
of America

UNION REVISITED

On the Cover: Janet Marie Ressler, Miss New Jersey 1957 and a native of Union, waves to the crowd from a 1958 Buick convertible supplied by Gaylin Buick. (Courtesy of the Union Township Historical Society.)

IMAGES
of America

UNION REVISITED

David Alan Johnson
Foreword by David Arminio

ARCADIA
PUBLISHING

ISBN 978-1-4671-3438-5

Published by Arcadia Publishing
Charleston, South Carolina

Printed in the United States of America

Library of Congress Control Number: 2015954747

For all general information, please contact Arcadia Publishing:
Telephone 843-853-2070
Fax 843-853-0044
E-mail sales@arcadiapublishing.com
For customer service and orders:
Toll-Free 1-888-313-2665

Visit us on the Internet at www.arcadiapublishing.com

To Laura, with sincere thanks for everything

Contents

Foreword

Whenever a presentation by the Union Township Historical Society is made to a senior citizens group in Union, the audience's favorite part of the session is comparing the old Union to the changing, "modern" Union. Those older than 75 who grew up in Union comment on their memories of what their hometown was once like. They remember Vauxhall Road not being paved. They remember the "dump" that was once located on the future site of Lowe's/Bradlee's/ Two Guys from Harrison. They remember Farcher's Grove. They remember Ma Durling, principal of Union High School. David Johnson's book will surely be a favorite for the seniors looking to reminisce and remember "when." It will also be compelling for younger generations who want to see how Union has developed over the years.

Union has long been a diverse town, with a history that goes back years before the American Revolution. As the war came to New Jersey and to Union—then known as Connecticut Farms—a significant role was played in that drama by some of our most important residents: Rev. James Caldwell and his wife, Hannah. During the war, Hannah became a martyr for the cause—having been shot and killed by a British soldier while standing by a window in the Caldwell Parsonage during the Battle of Connecticut Farms on June 7, 1780. From the start of the war, the Reverend Caldwell had been an ardent revolutionist and was not ashamed to proclaim so from the pulpit. He preached thunderous sermons, pleading for loyalty to the Patriots and the independent nation they were creating. In all, 31 officers and 52 enlisted men came out of his Elizabethtown Presbyterian Church congregation. Throughout the war, Caldwell served in the military as a chaplain and as assistant quartermaster. On November 21, 1781, Caldwell was shot and killed by James Morgan, who was hanged for that murder on Gallows Hill in Westfield, New Jersey.

Finally, 25 years after the end of the war, Union was established in 1808. The community has come a long way from that small farming village—growing into the vibrant town of 65,000 people that it is today.

—David Arminio, Past President
Union Township Historical Society

ACKNOWLEDGMENTS

"I can no other answer make but thanks," Sebastian says in Shakespeare's *Twelfth Night*. I would like to say thanks to any number of people who were generous enough to help me with this project, even though my thanks might not be as elegant as Shakespeare's.

Thanks go to Union Township Historical Society (UTHS) for allowing me access to its photograph collection, and especially to David Arminio for his help and support.

Many thanks are extended to Tom Haggerty for setting aside an evening just before Christmas to allow me to look at his collection of photographs. A large thank-you goes out to Tom Beisler for allowing me to borrow a large plastic bag full of photographs, some of which turned out to be absolutely priceless, and for patiently answering my many and persistent questions. Thanks go to my big brother Ralph H. Johnson (Union High School class of 1956) for helping me to date many of the photographs by identifying the make and model (and, most important, the year) of many of the cars in the images. I would also like to thank Kathy Ferguson Sinnes for sharing her photographs, along with Howie Frisch, who allowed me to use some first-rate images from his shoebox full of negatives. Richie Pisz was also a great help. Richie supplied several excellent pictures from his family's collection, almost all of which are included in this book.

Last, but certainly not least, many affectionate thanks go to Laura Libby for staying out of the way. After more than 20 years, she has learned to do this beautifully.

Introduction

Memory can play tricks with a person's mind, but photographs always tell the truth. Someone once remarked that memory might recall a long-ago picnic as being nothing short of undiluted joy, but nobody ever remembers the ants. My hope is that the accompanying photographs of the changes that have taken place in Union over the years will bring back a few pleasant memories but not ruin everyone's picnic by introducing too many ants.

Union Township has changed dramatically, almost overwhelmingly, since the 1950s. The town was still very rural in those days. A functioning farm, O'Mara's, sold fruit and vegetables at the far end of my street when I was in grammar school. Headley's Cider Mill on Stuyvesant Avenue sold homemade cider that tasted like real apples, and the Headley brothers made their own sausages that tasted like nothing I have eaten since.

Although the town was not really any smaller in those days than it was in later decades, it seemed that way. Neighbors really did know each other in those days and spoke to each other at length—sometimes a little too much at length. I knew the name of every family on my street: Mr. and Mrs. Hipp on the corner, and their Chow dog, Smokey; Mr. and Mrs. Kropp lived next to them; then Mr. and Mrs. Falk; then us; the Stahls; then the Schneiders, then old Tilly Fuchs; and so on up the street. On summer evenings, everyone sat on their front steps and would say "hello" as you walked past. When my father and I took our dog, a white German shepherd Chow mix named Pete, for his constitutional, it would take the better part of an hour just to go a few streets—everyone wanted to talk, so we stopped to talk.

Over the years, things changed—for better or worse, depending upon a person's point of view. The O'Mara farm was sold to a developer, who built houses on the land. Headley's Cider Mill was pulled down and replaced by the editorial offices of the *Union Leader* newspaper (now the *Local Source*). Neighbors either moved away or passed away, and new neighbors moved in. Union landmarks disappeared, including Haines Farms, a familiar sight on Chestnut Street for decades. Union High School moved from Caldwell Avenue, where it had been a landmark for many years, to North Third Street. Newark State College became Kean College and then Kean University. Long-established businesses in Union Center were either sold or went out of business: Woolworth's, Whitney's Fashions, Stan Sommer, Nawrocki's Pharmacy. It was not the same town anymore.

But the new neighbors turned out to be sociable when you got to know them, even if they did not sit on their front steps and say hello anymore. New businesses took the place of the old departed establishments, and quite a few of the older places are still around and probably will be for years to come. And the kids from Union High School and Kean University still go to classes every morning, just as they did in years gone by.

I had a history teacher at Burnet Junior High School—that is gone, as well—who once told the class, "Man hates change, but change is constant." I have always remembered that line. Whether all the changes that have taken place in Union since the 1950s are welcomed, hated, or just tolerated, they are facts of life—and more changes are on the way, rest assured. As I mention in my first book on Union, which dates from 1994, "Photographs from many sources illustrate this change, like fragments of a glass mosaic. Whether or not the change is for better or worse is for the reader—or viewer—to decide." I suppose the theme of this book is that the past is a nice place to visit, but it would be too impractical—and probably too painful—to live there. (French actress Simone Signoret called her autobiography *Nostalgia Isn't What It Used to Be*.) And as my landlady used to say when I lived in Brentford, England, we probably could not afford the rent, anyway.

In his play *The Glass Menagerie*, Tennessee Williams writes, "In memory everything seems to happen to music." Since this is a book of photographs and not a video, I am afraid that the reader will have to supply his or her own music. But maybe you already have something suitable in mind?

One

ALL AROUND THE TOWN

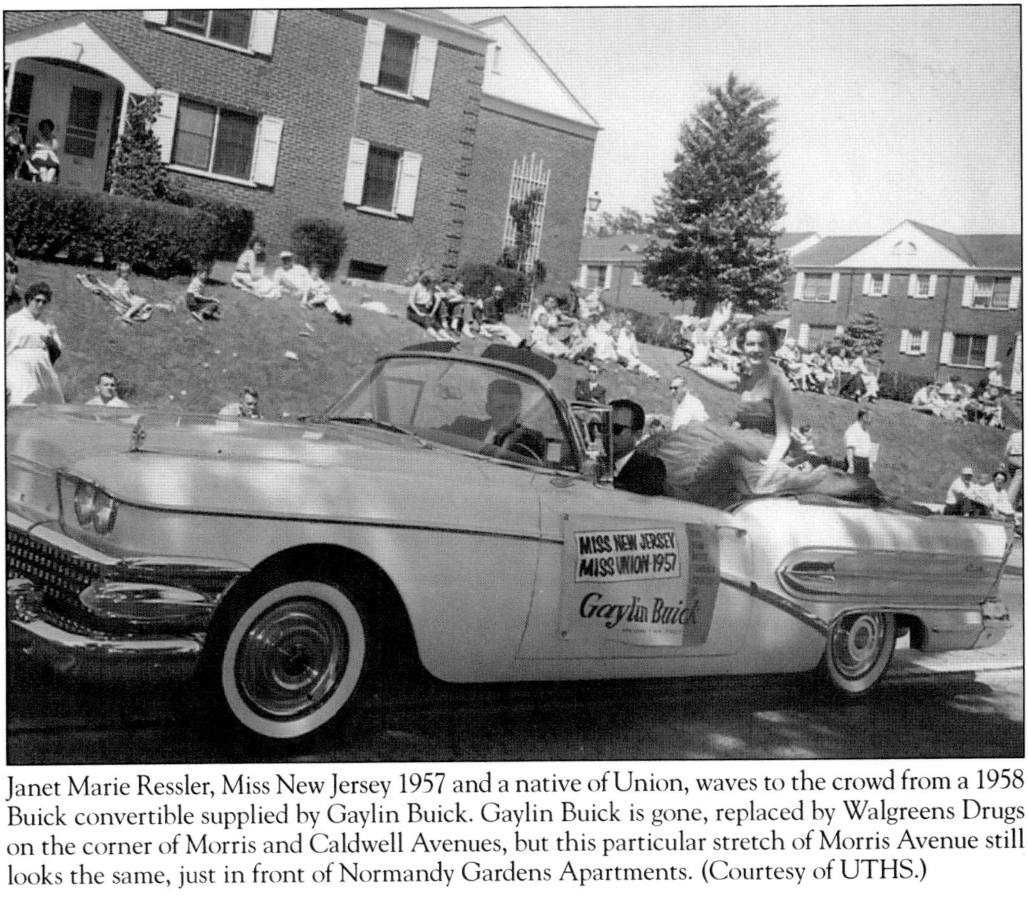

Janet Marie Ressler, Miss New Jersey 1957 and a native of Union, waves to the crowd from a 1958 Buick convertible supplied by Gaylin Buick. Gaylin Buick is gone, replaced by Walgreens Drugs on the corner of Morris and Caldwell Avenues, but this particular stretch of Morris Avenue still looks the same, just in front of Normandy Gardens Apartments. (Courtesy of UTHS.)

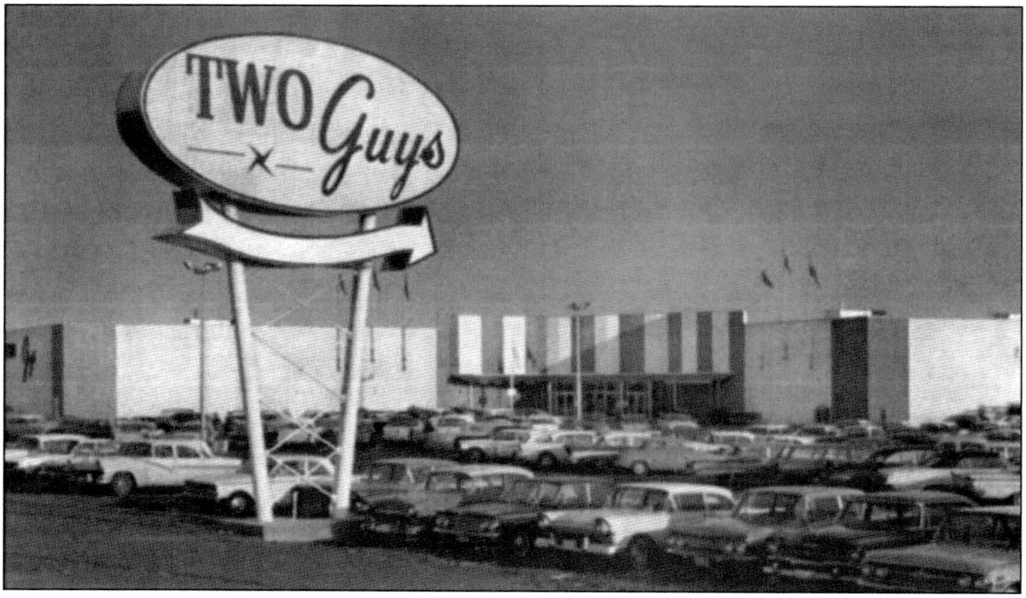

Pictured here is Two Guys from Harrison, known as Two Guys, in the early 1960s. Shop owners in Union Center feared that Two Guys would put them out of business—fears that turned out not to be justified. The big discount department store sold everything from clothing to groceries and appliances and really did sell them cheaper. It was a great place to do Christmas shopping—everything one needed for everyone on the list was available in one stop: books, records, perfume, cigars, pipe tobacco, Two Guys had it. (Courtesy of UTHS.)

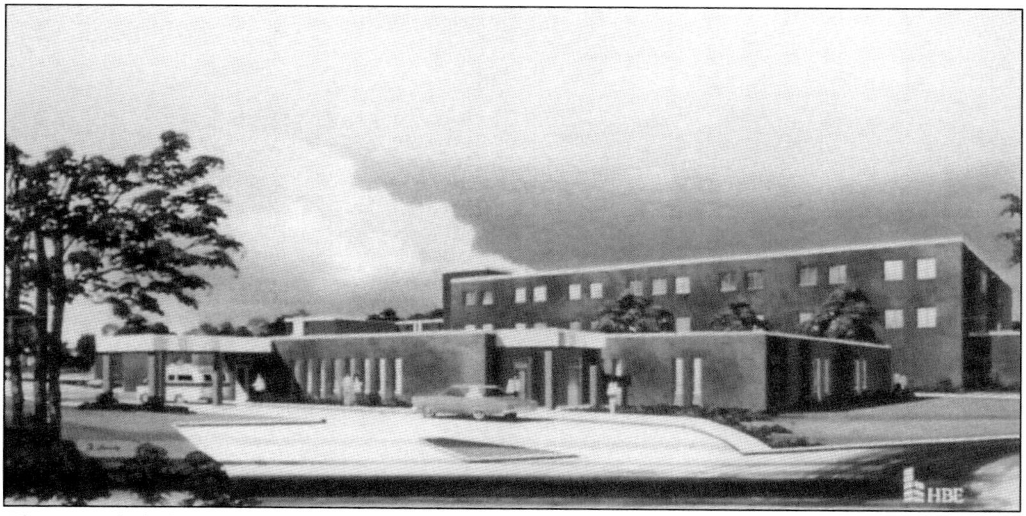

This is a slightly truncated postcard showing the Galloping Hill Road entrance of Memorial General Hospital, which was later renamed Union Hospital. Only the emergency ward of the hospital remains in service. The rest of the building was vacant for several years, but has since been occupied by other facilities. Part of the building has been acquired by Overlook Hospital as an outpatient facility. (Courtesy of UTHS.)

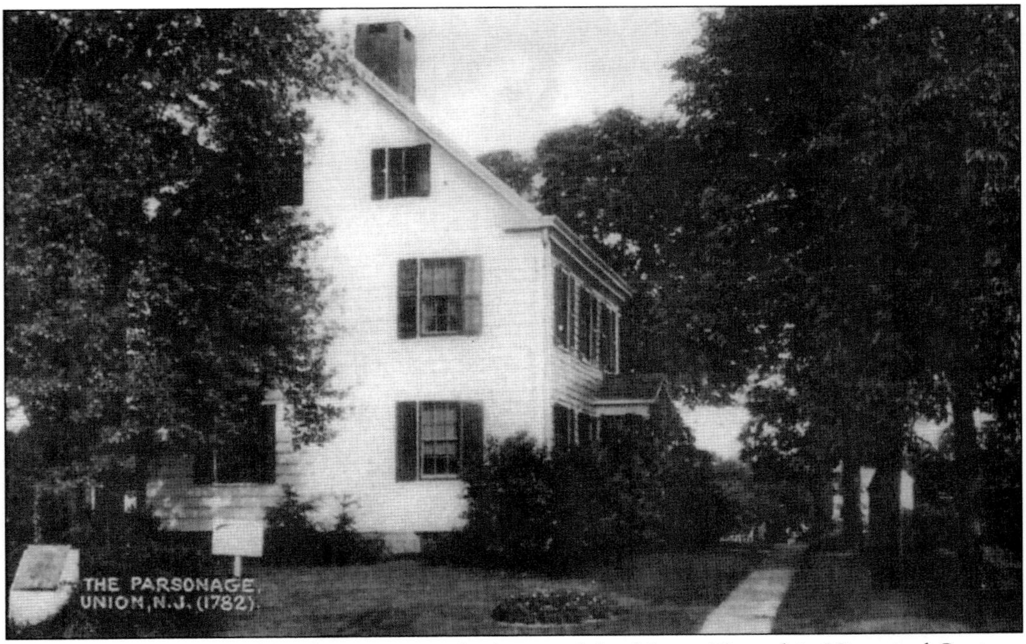

Pictured here is the Caldwell Parsonage, the home of the Union Township Historical Society. It served as the residence of the pastor of Connecticut Farms Church from the 1780s until the beginning of the 20th century. The old parsonage became a museum in the 1960s and is filled with artifacts from Union Township's past. (Courtesy of UTHS.)

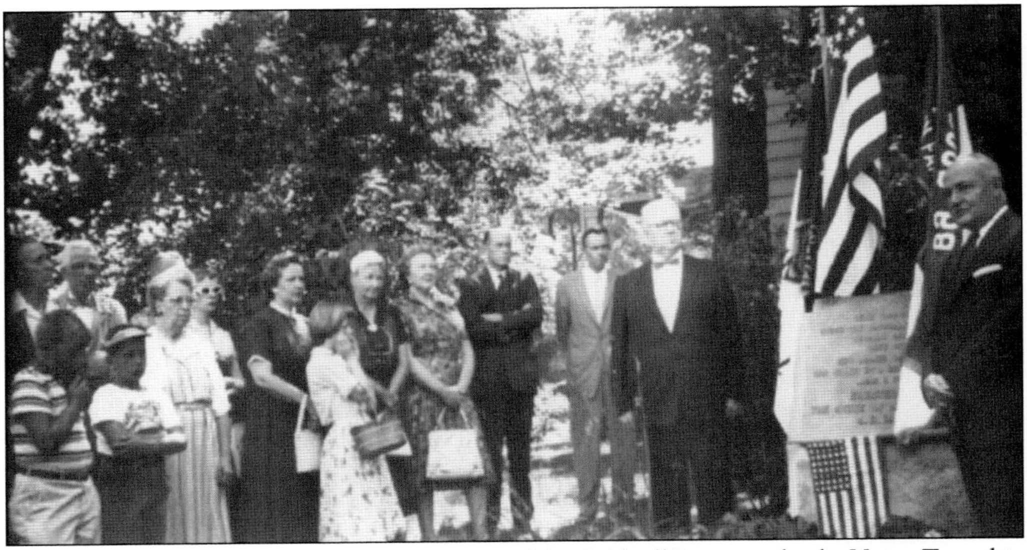

Rev. Fred Druckenmiller speaks at the acquisition of the Caldwell Parsonage by the Union Township Historical Society on July 4, 1959. Before the historical society acquired the property, the house had been a private residence—a two-family rental, according to one source. Soon afterward, some of the local residents sued both the historical society and Union Township to prevent the opening of the parsonage as a museum. Neighbors feared that a museum in the area would lead to crowds as well as traffic congestion, a fear that turned out to have absolutely no foundation. The suit was dismissed in December 1960, and the Caldwell Parsonage Museum opened in 1961. (Courtesy of Tom Haggerty.)

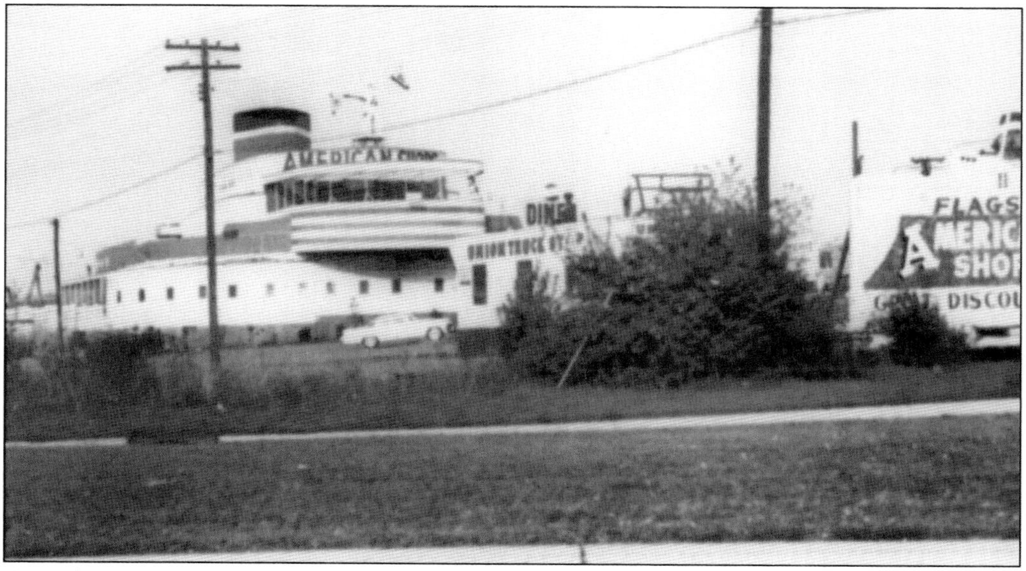

One of Union Township's most familiar landmarks is the Flagship, on the center island of Route 22. This photograph is undated, but it is probably from the early 1960s. Over the years, the Flagship has been occupied by any number of businesses, including a nightclub in the 1930s. At the time this photograph was taken, it was the home of American Shops, a clothing shop for men. American Shops was famous for having a going out of business sale that went on for years—it seemed like forever. This protracted sale has been called a brilliant marketing ploy, along with the longest-running practical joke in living memory. Possibly, it was meant as both. (Courtesy of UTHS.)

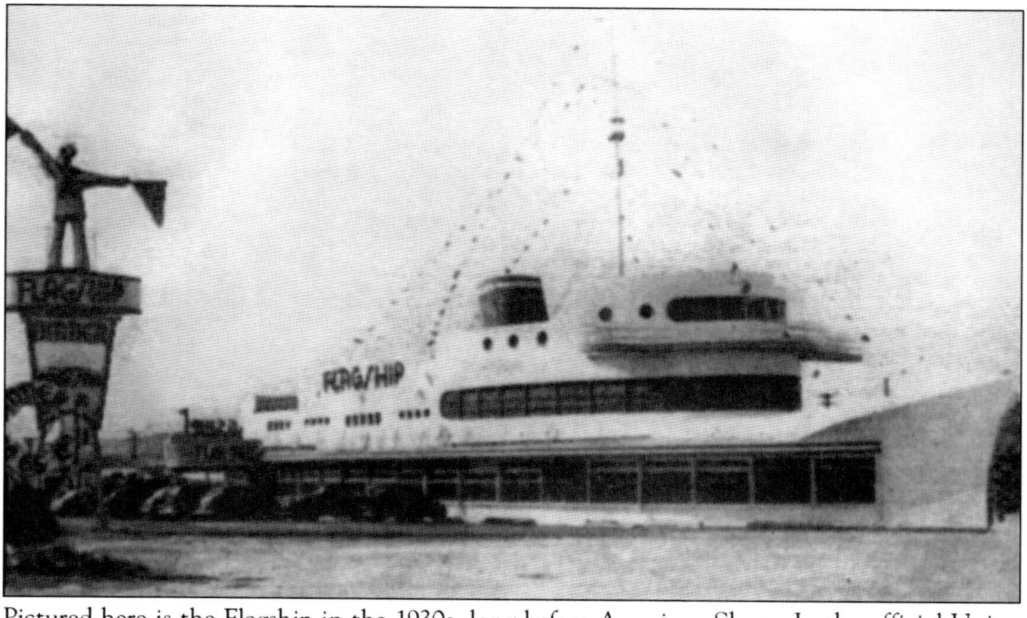

Pictured here is the Flagship in the 1930s, long before American Shops. In the official Union Township Directory, the listing for the Flagship reads, "On 29 Highway, Dining and Dancing, Entertainment Nightly. Telephone: Unionville 2-3107." (Courtesy of UTHS.)

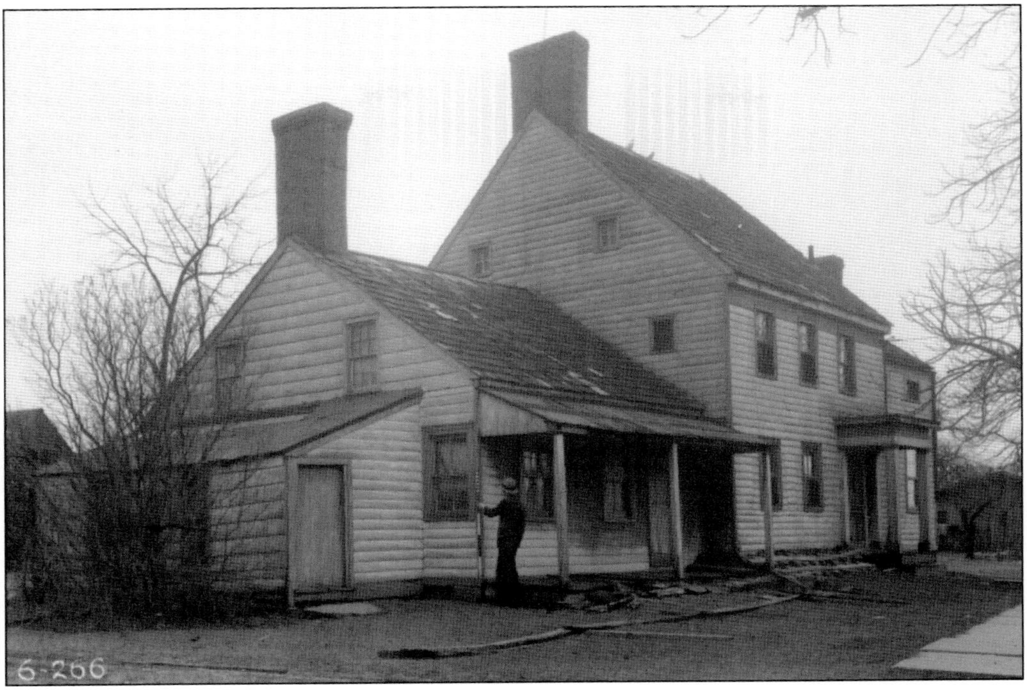

The Headley family has been in the area for many generations and was part of the original town known as Connecticut Farms. This image of the Brandt-Headley farmhouse at 1827 Vauxhall Road was taken on March 19, 1936, by R. Merrit Lacey for the Historic American Buildings Survey. (Both, courtesy of the Library of Congress.)

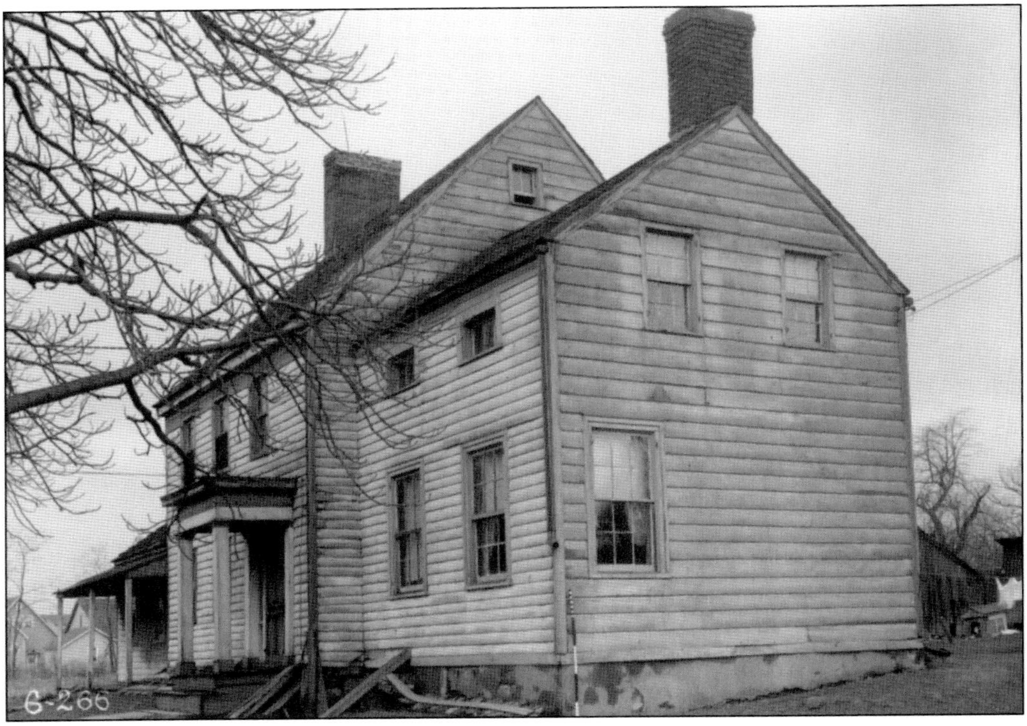

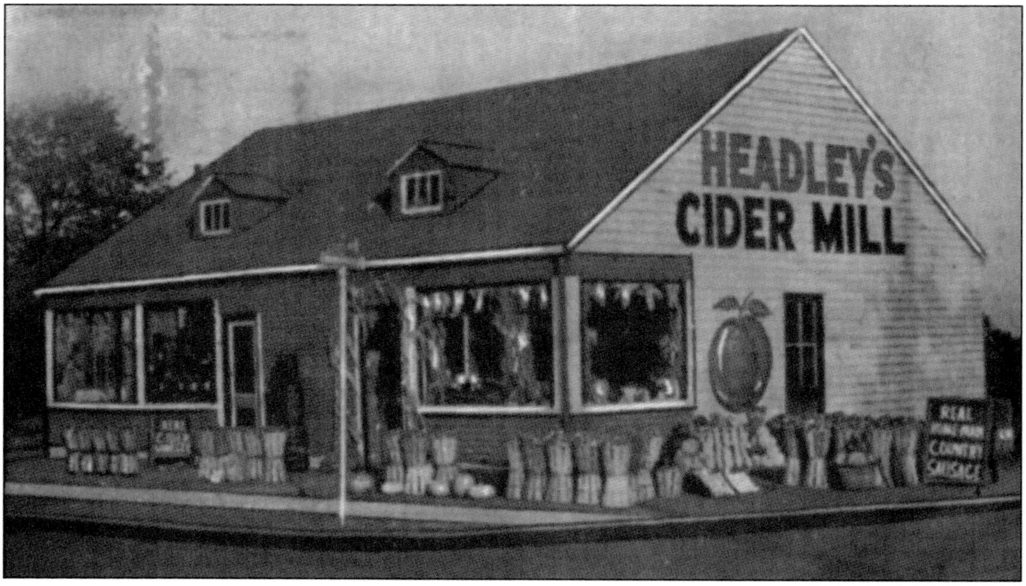

This is a postcard from the 1950s of Headley's Cider Mill. Headley's was situated on the corner of Stuyvesant and Mountainview Avenues, at 1291 Stuyvesant Avenue, which is the current site of offices for the *Union County Local Source* newspaper, formerly the *Union Leader*. Chalkboards outside the cider mill advertise "Real Cider Vinegar" and "Real Home-Made Country Sausage." Headley's apple cider tasted like real apples, and its homemade sausage was a thousand times better than anything from any supermarket. At Halloween, trick-or-treaters were treated to a glass of Headley's famous cider. (Courtesy of UTHS.)

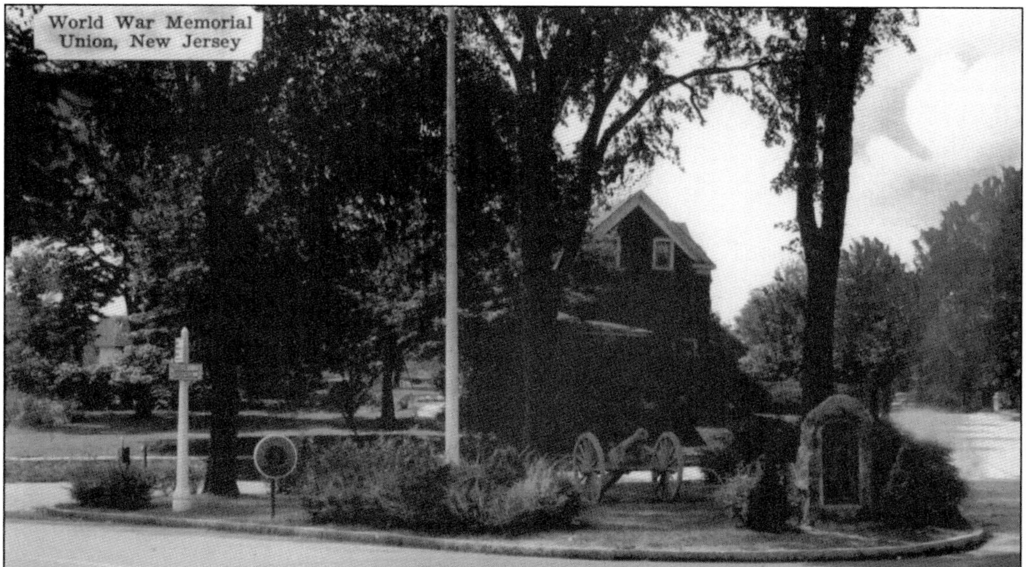

The Stuyvesant Avenue/Elmwood Avenue island was known as the war memorial in the 1950s. The street trailing off into the distance on the right-hand side of the photograph is Johnson Place. The famous cannon has occupied that particular spot since about 1900, when the island was known as the triangle and both Stuyvesant Avenue and Elmwood Avenue were dirt roads. The cannon dates from the time of the American Revolution, but the gun carriage is not quite as old; it dates from the Civil War era. (Courtesy of UTHS.)

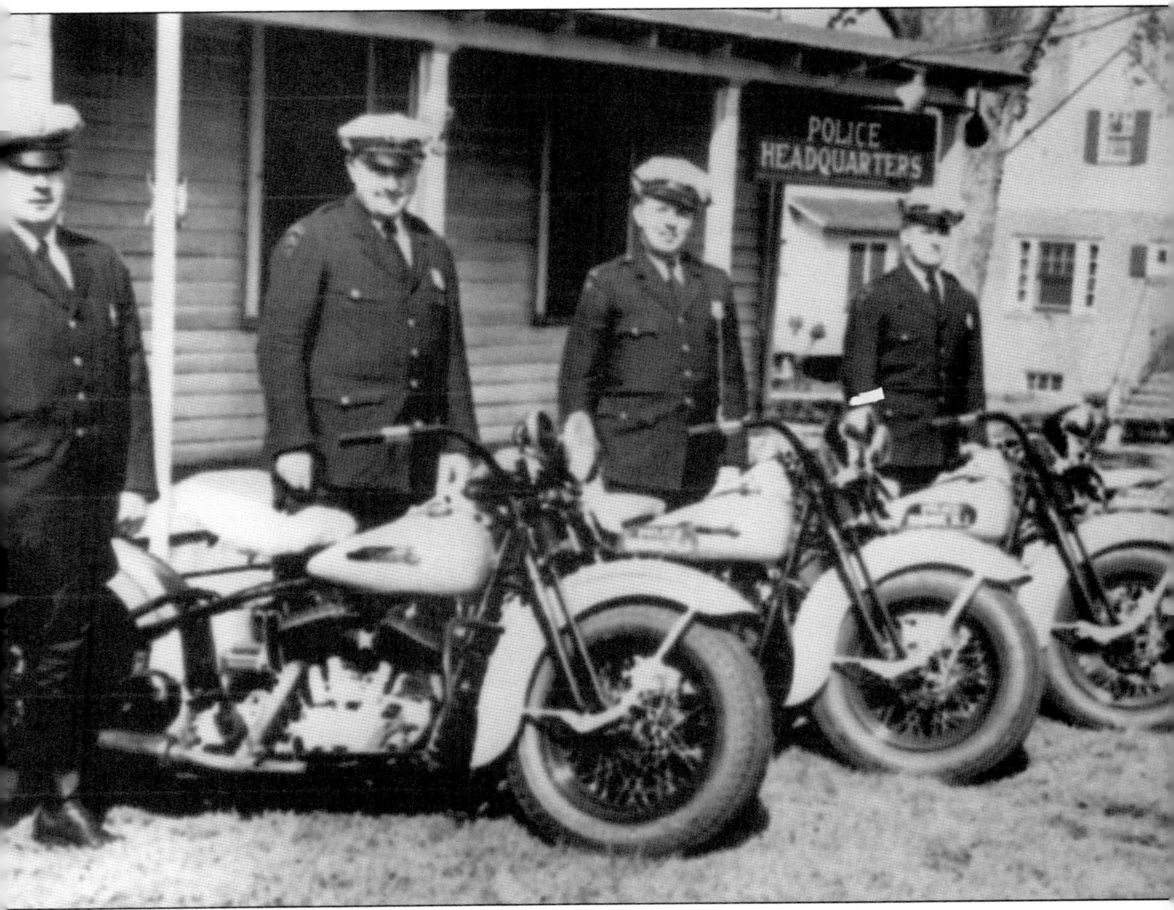

Four of Union Township's finest pose with their motorcycles in front of police headquarters on Caldwell Avenue. At the time, which was sometime during the 1930s, motorcycle police were a fairly common sight around Union. Policemen on motorcycles disappeared from Union's streets for a while but have made a comeback in recent years. In the 1930s, Union Township was still fairly rural, with a population of about 16,000, and crime was not a major concern. (Courtesy of UTHS.)

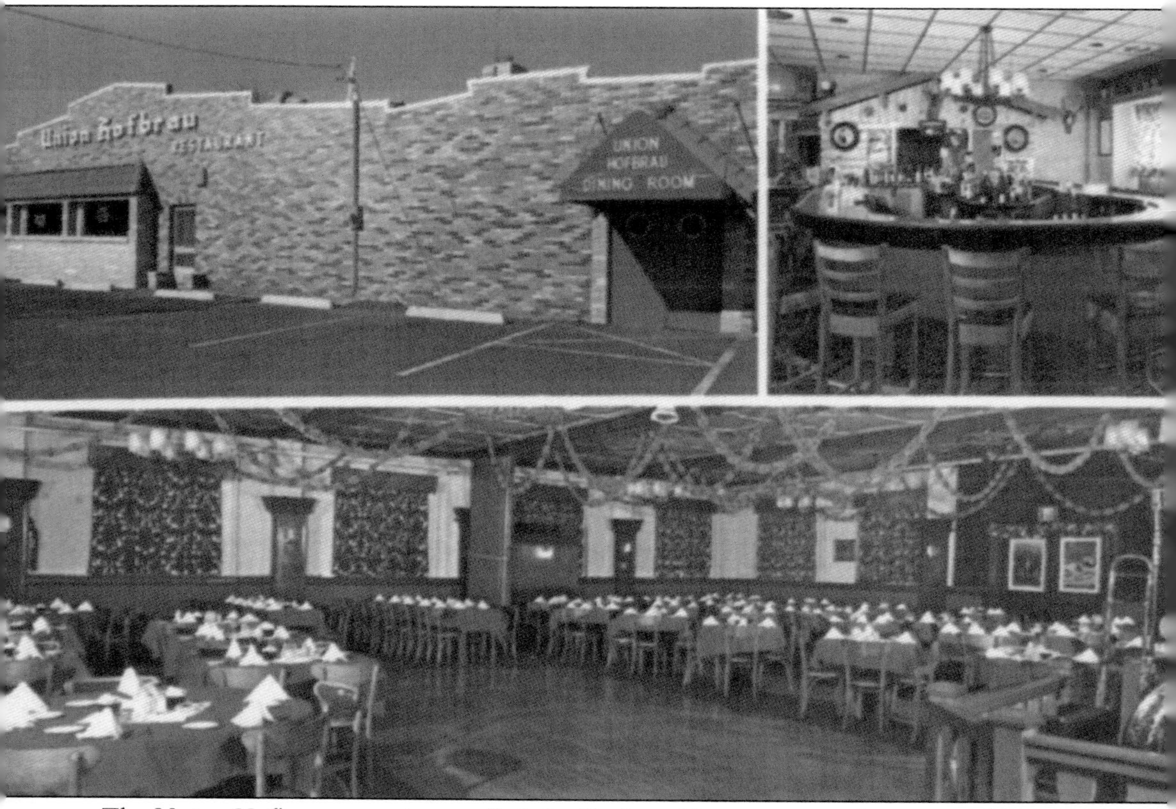

The Union Hofbrau, sometimes called the Hofbrau House, was on the corner of Stuyvesant Avenue and High Street. The Hofbrau served either the best German cuisine in town or the most fattening food in the world, depending upon who was giving his opinion. The restaurant also had the reputation for dishing out the world's best coleslaw and German potato salad. Max Ecstein, the owner, performed songs like "Hello, Dolly" for his clientele during supper. A Portuguese restaurant now occupies the site. (Courtesy of UTHS.)

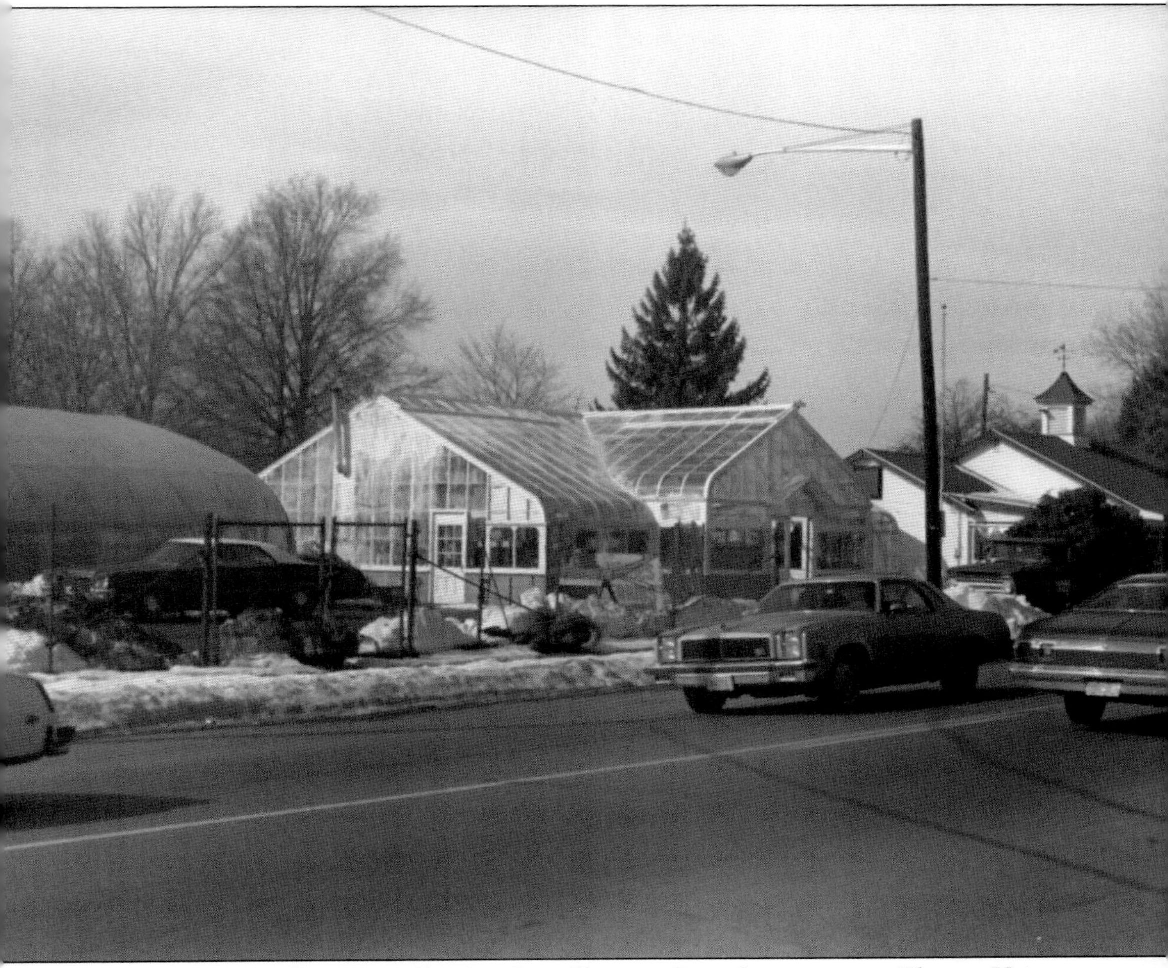

Haines Farms was a well-recognized landmark on Chestnut Street for many years. The two Haines brothers, Raymond and Wilfred, started the business as a vegetable stand and a chicken- and egg-delivery service before World War II. Some local schools used to organize visits to Haines Farms so that the students could take a look at some real live turkeys around Thanksgiving time. The greenhouse was displayed at the New York World's Fair in 1939 and donated to the Smithsonian Institution in Washington, DC, after the business closed in the 1980s. (Courtesy of Union Township.)

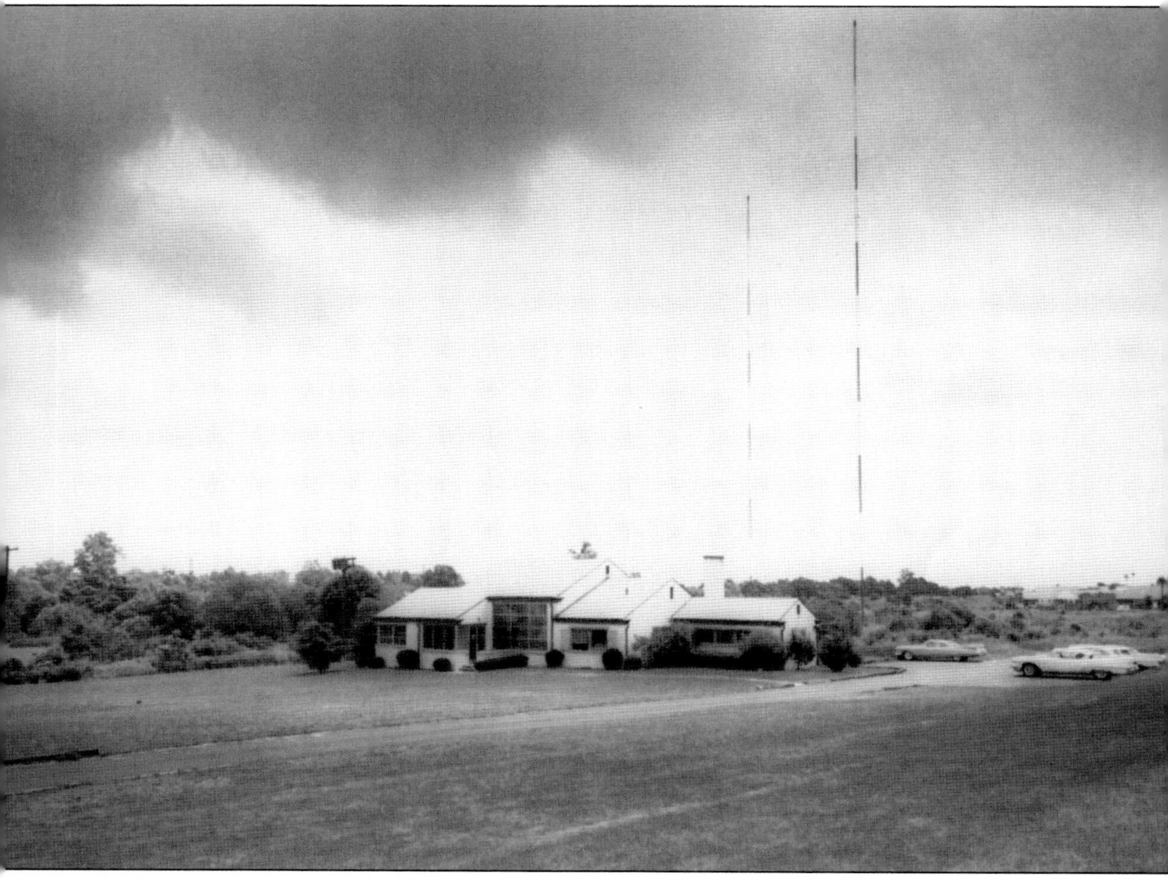

Radio Station WNJR, 1440 on the AM dial, used to broadcast from its studios on Union Avenue, just a short walk from Franklin School. WNJR was the perfect radio station for the hard of hearing. Because it was right in Union, an average WNJR broadcast signal could shatter every window—and eardrum—in town, even at low volume. The station's twin broadcast towers were a familiar sight to township residents and were visible even at night because of their flashing red lights. The photograph has no date, but it is probably from about 1960, as one of the cars parked next to the building is a 1959 Cadillac. (Courtesy of Union Township.)

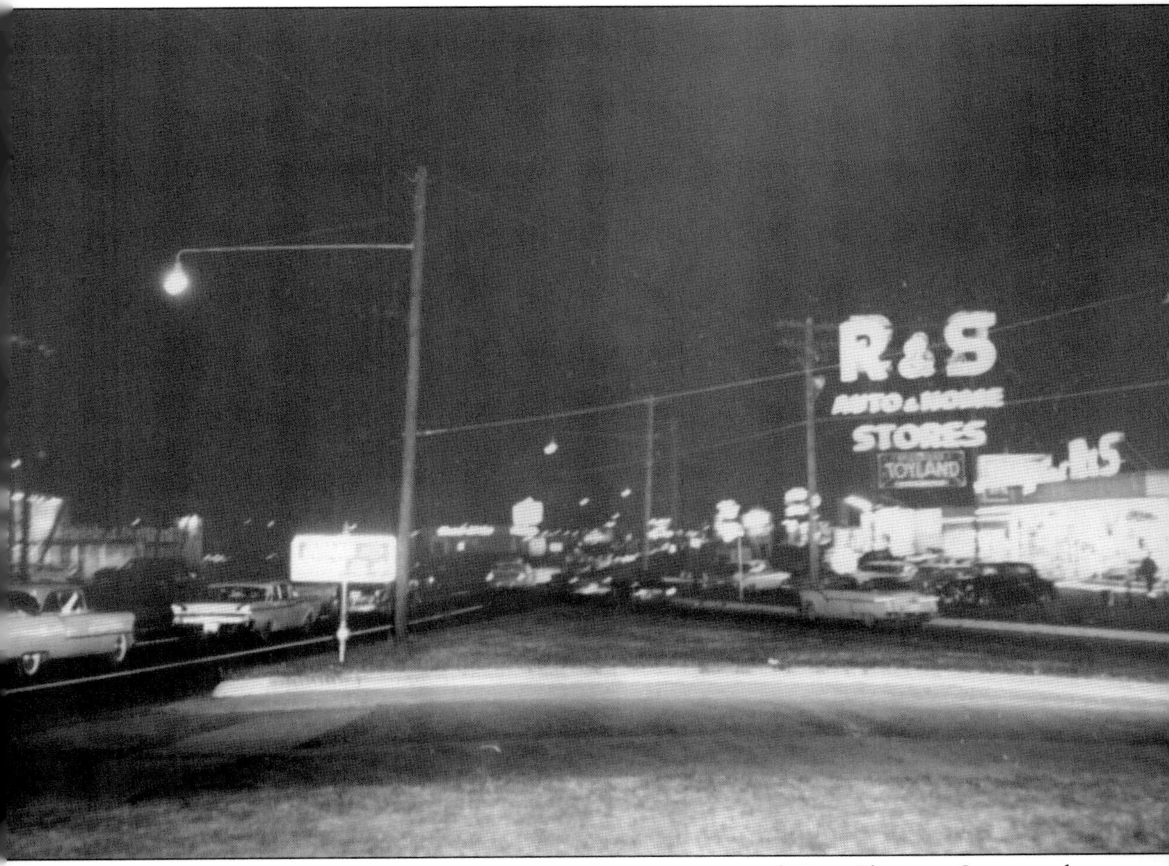

Pictured here is R&S Auto and Home Stores, at the intersection of West Chestnut Street and Route 22 West. By the late 1960s, R&S sold a lot more than just automobile parts and home appliances. One could buy everything from toys to radios and cameras. The store's slogan used to be "Buy for less at R&S." Employees used to say, "Work for less at R&S," as many of the firm's employees were paid only minimum wage. Only Route 22's heavy traffic, which will remain into infinity, is the same today. To the left of the photograph is Union's famous Flagship, which was probably still the home of American Shops when this photograph was taken in the 1960s. (Courtesy of Union Township.)

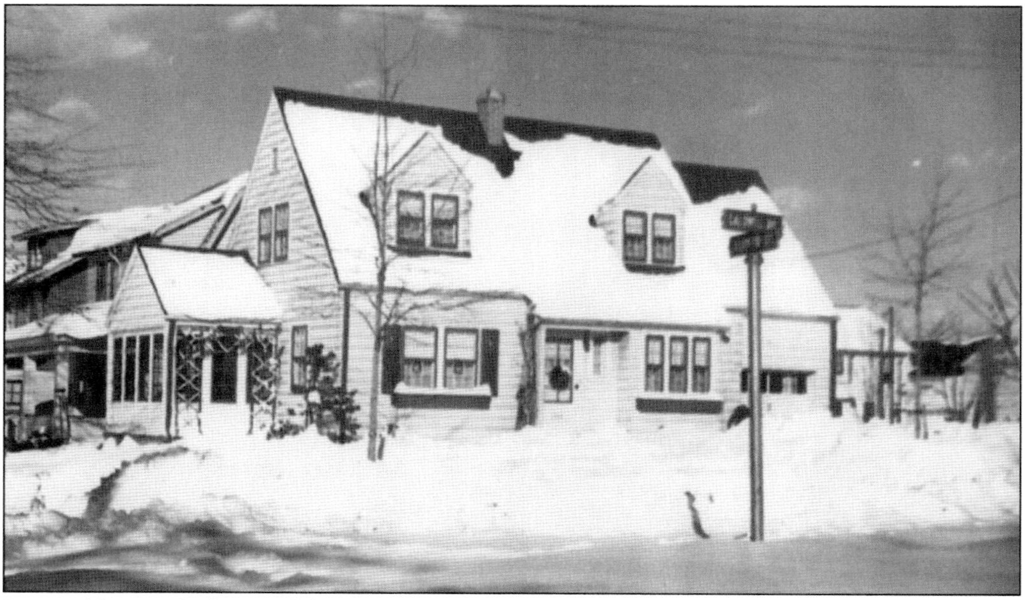

Pictured here is the home of the Pisz family, on the corner of Berwyn Street and Caldwell Avenue, following the blizzard of 1947. Just next door to Union High School, the home was designed and built in 1941 by Frank A. Pisz Sr. and Frank A. Pisz Jr. Note the old-style street signs. What was then Union High School is just across Berwyn Street, to the left, out of the photograph. The house is still there and still looks the same, but the old high school is now Burnet Middle School. (Courtesy of Richard Pisz.)

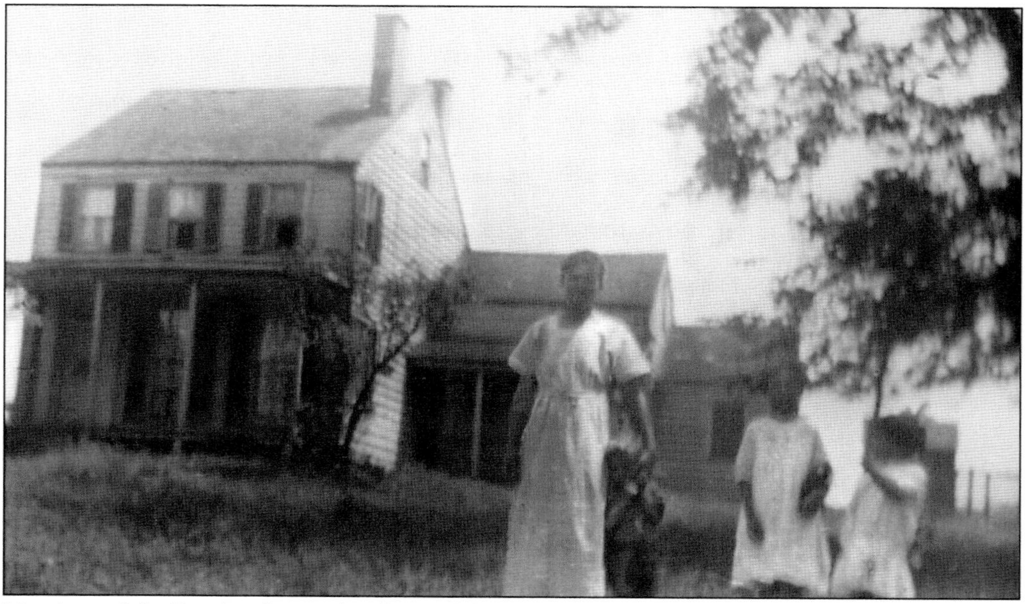

Members of the Pisz family stand in front of their farmhouse in 1923. The Pisz farm was at the end of Chestnut Street near Route 22, which was Highway 29 in those days, close by the site of the old R&S Stores. Among the things they grew were strawberries; theirs was said to be the largest strawberry farm in Union County. The family lost everything in 1936, during the Great Depression, when Grandfather Pisz could not pay the taxes on the property. The boy in the photograph is Frank A. Pisz Jr., the father of the photograph's contributor. (Courtesy of Richard Pisz.)

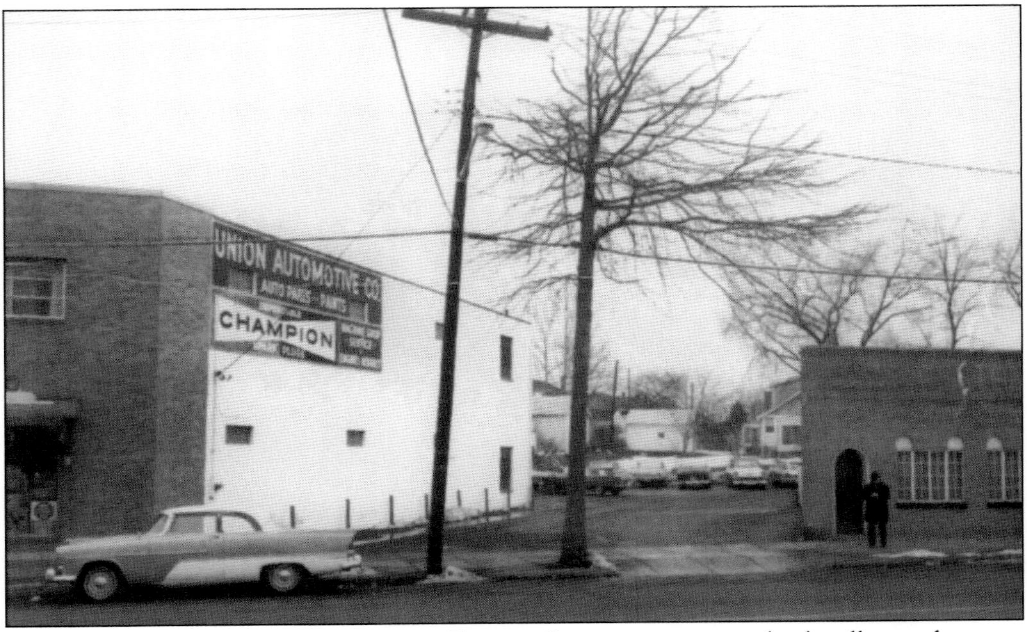

Pictured here is the Chestnut Tavern on Chestnut Street or, more exactly, the alleyway between the Chestnut Tavern and the Union Automotive Company. Although the Chestnut Tavern has been replaced by the Chestnut Chateau, the current resident of the building, the alleyway is still there. Judging from the vintage of the cars, the photograph dates from the early 1960s. (Courtesy of UTHS.)

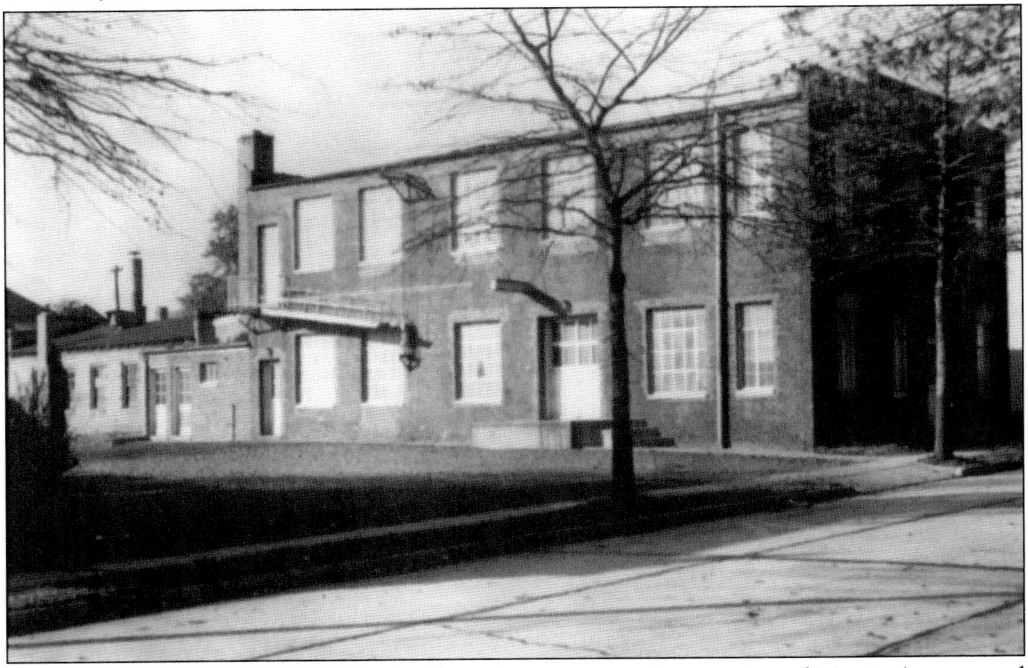

Pictured here in the early 1940s is the Kratt factory, at the intersection of Morris Avenue and Johnson Place. The William Kratt Company manufactured its famous pitch pipe at this site for many years, beginning in the mid-1920s. The building has not changed very much, except that it is now covered by a coating of white paint. (Courtesy of UTHS.)

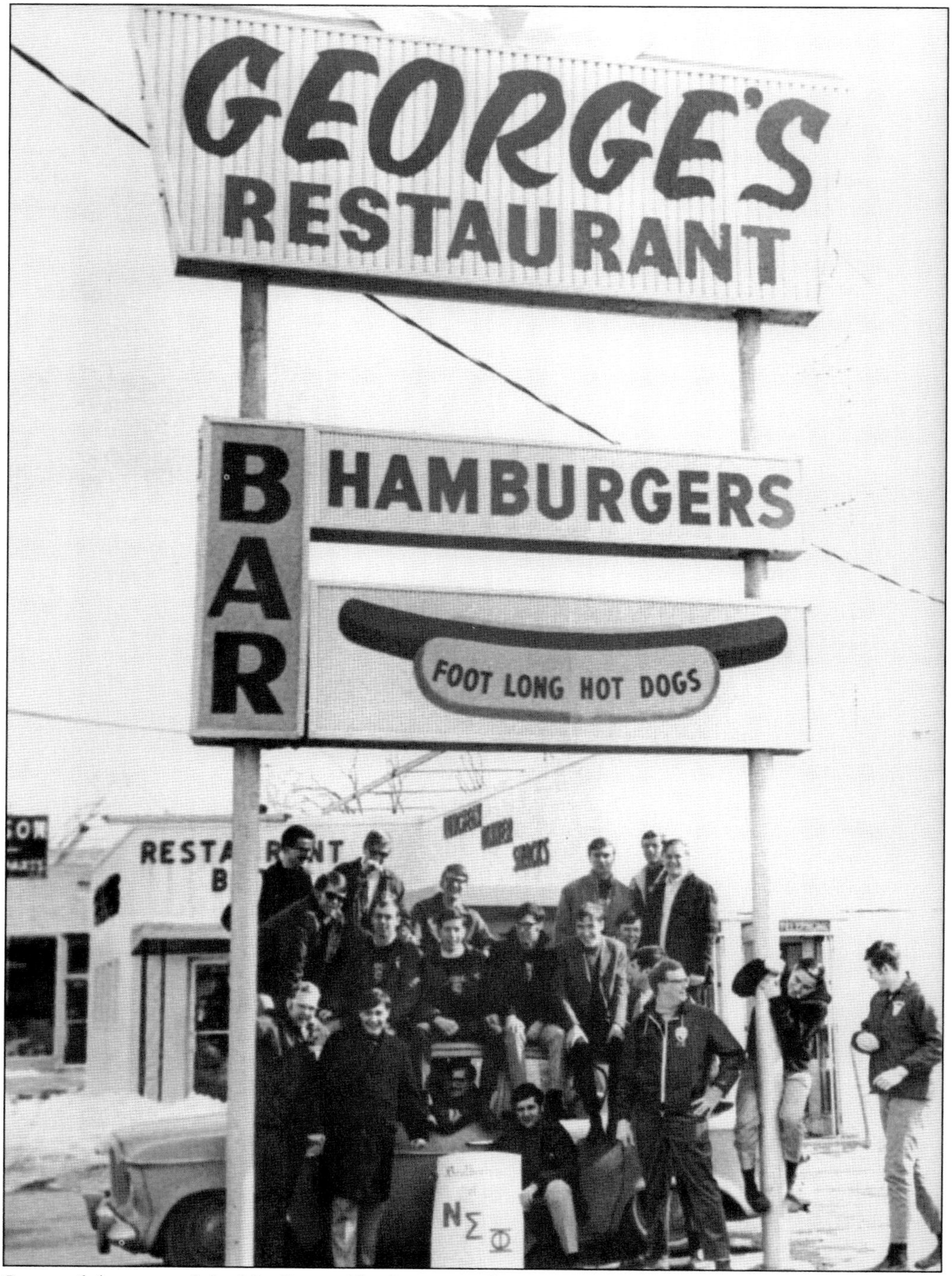

Some of the guys of the Nu Sigma Phi fraternity from Newark State College congregate outside George's Restaurant on Morris Avenue during the late 1960s. George's, the home of the foot-long hot dog, has been gone for years. During the 1950s and 1960s, being taken to George's by a fellow's parents (or a girl's) was considered to be a huge treat. Newark State College has been subsumed by the infinitely expanding Kean University, where Nu Sigma Phi might very well still exist. (Author's collection.)

Newark State College graduated its last class in 1973 and changed its name to Kean College of New Jersey. The institution began as Newark Normal School in 1855, became Newark State Teacher's College, and moved to Union Township in the late 1950s. The institution took the word "Teacher's" out of its name to attract potential students who had no intent of entering the teaching profession. It is now Kean University, which has a sprawling campus that bears little resemblance to its ancestors. (Author's collection.)

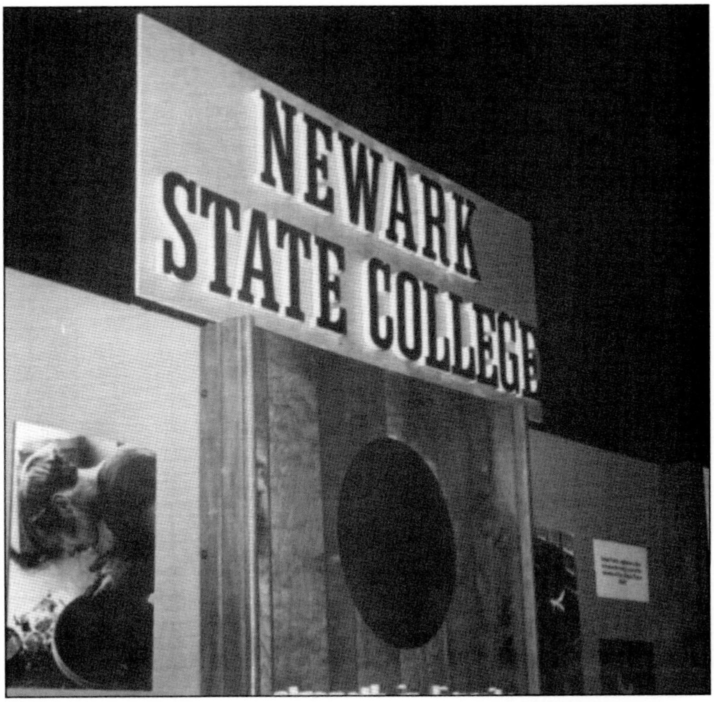

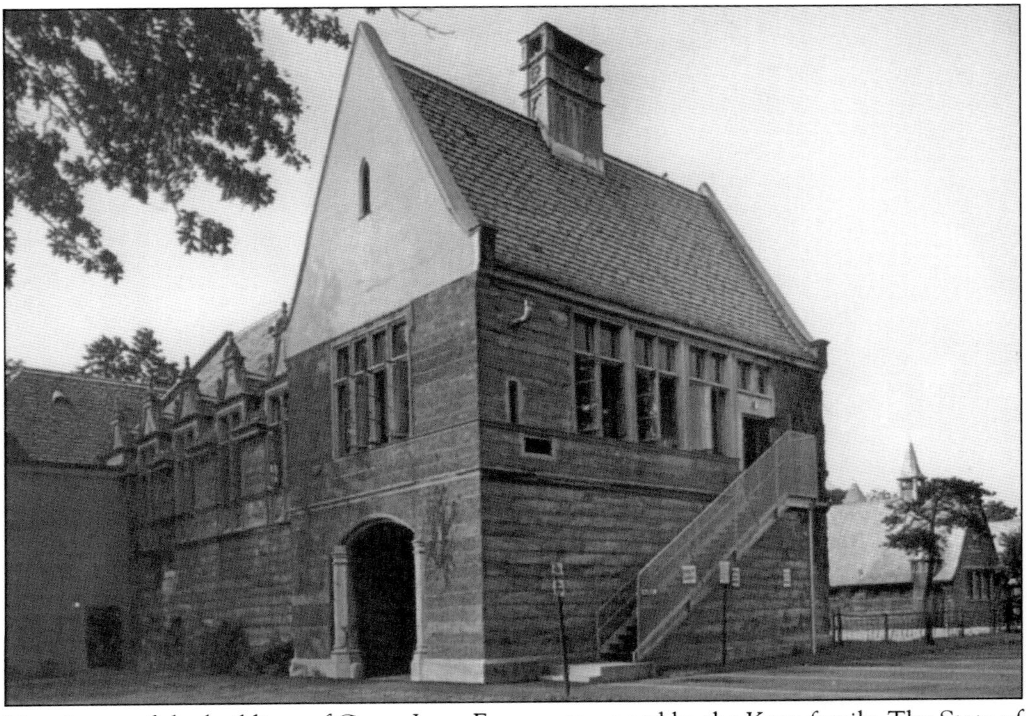

Here is one of the buildings of Green Lane Farm once owned by the Kean family. The State of New Jersey acquired the land in the 1950s, and Newark State Teacher's College moved to the site in 1958 from its original home in Newark, New Jersey. Since that time, the institution has changed almost beyond recognition. But many of the old buildings remain and still serve a useful purpose as offices or administrative centers, like this one. (Courtesy of UTHS.)

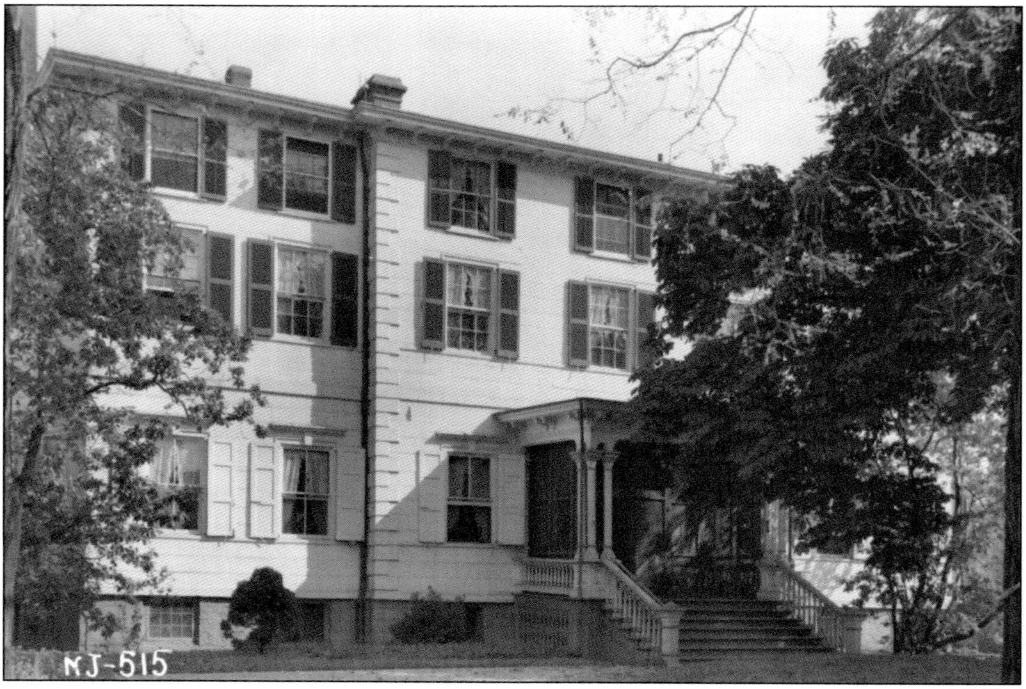

Liberty Hall is a National Historic Landmark located on Morris Avenue that opened as a museum in 1973. The estate was built in 1760 and has been home to many prominent figures of American history. Capt. John Kean inherited the home in 1932 and after his death, his wife began to preserve the house as a museum. (Both, courtesy of the Library of Congress.)

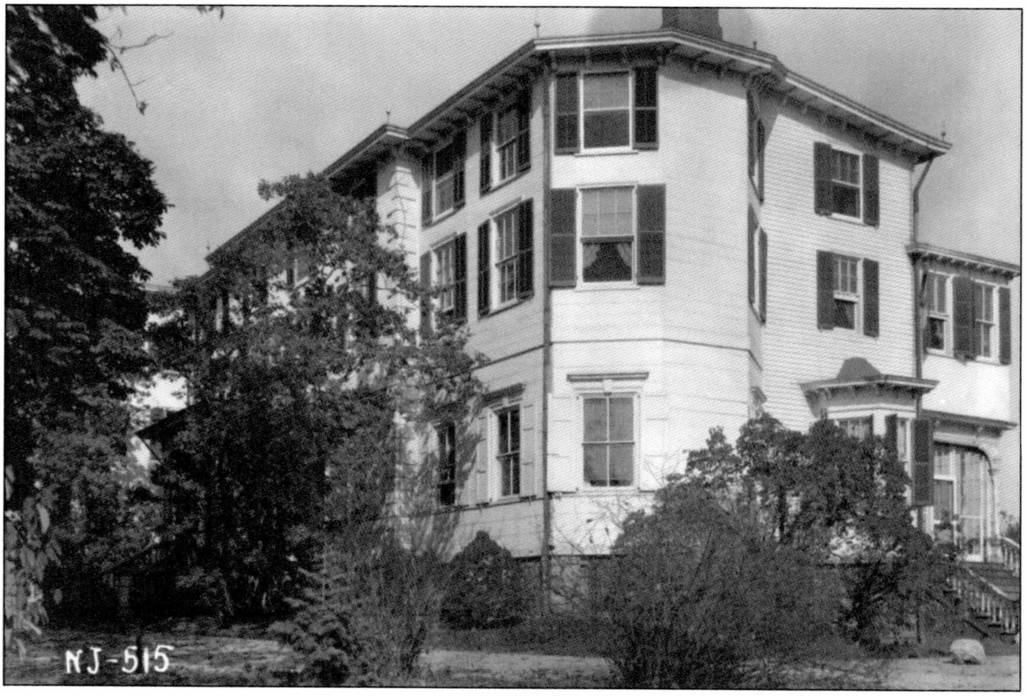

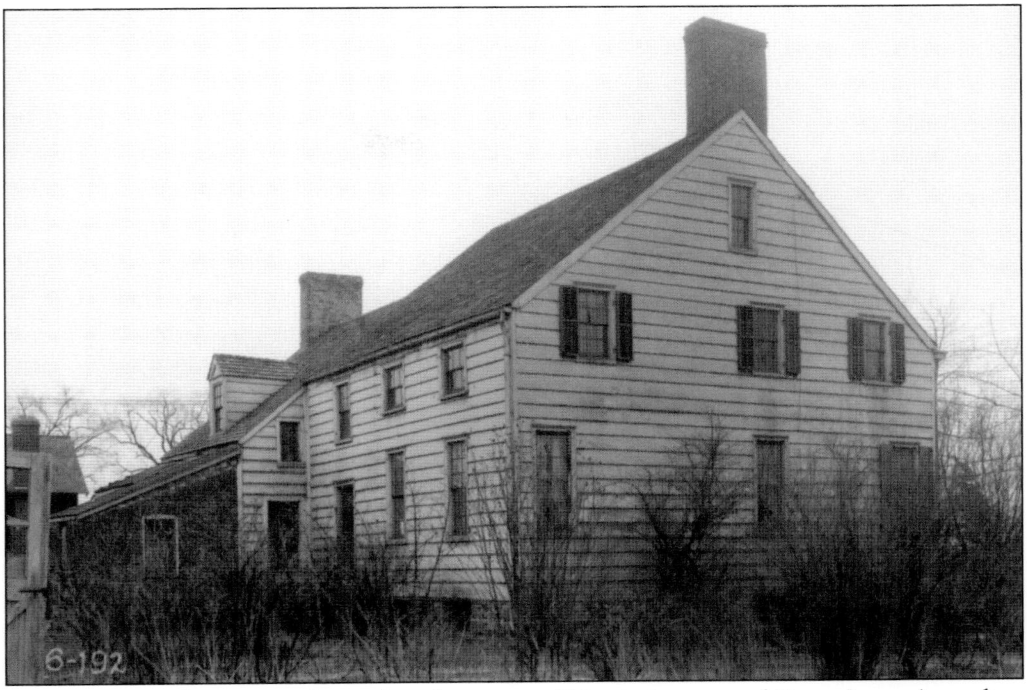

The James Townley House is located on the corner of Morris Avenue and Green Lane. According to the Historic American Buildings Survey, it was built before 1796 by William Townley, and additions to the home were made by his son James Townley. The above exterior image was taken by photographer R. Merrit Lacey on March 23, 1936. The house foundation is of stone masonry, and the exterior walls are timber framing and clapboard siding. The below exterior image was taken by photographer Nathaniel R. Ewan on March 7, 1939. (Both, courtesy of the Library of Congress.)

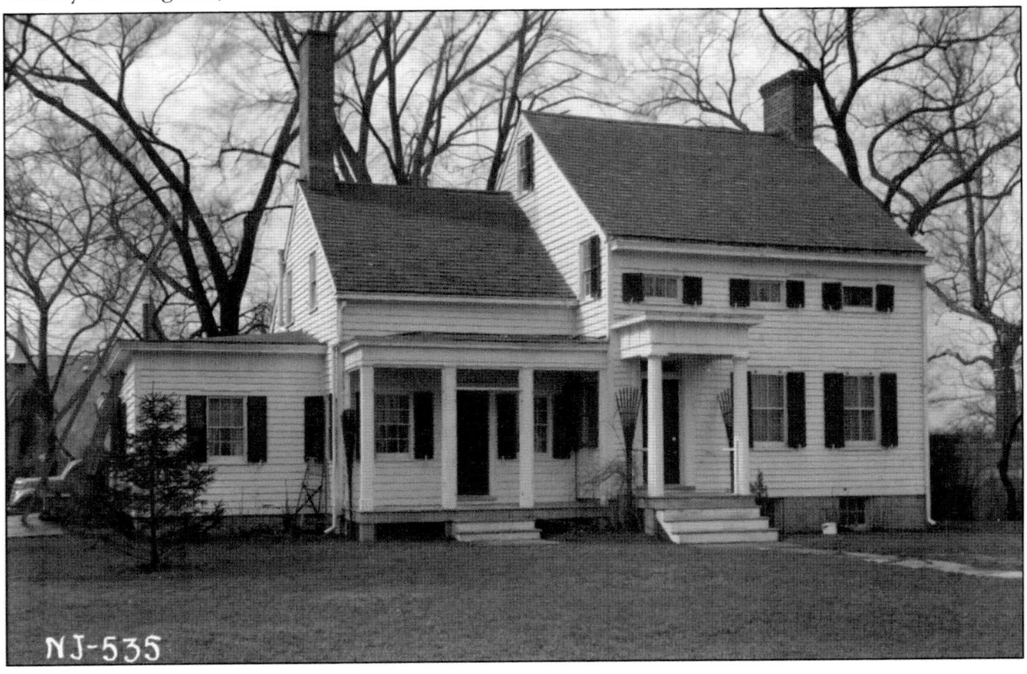

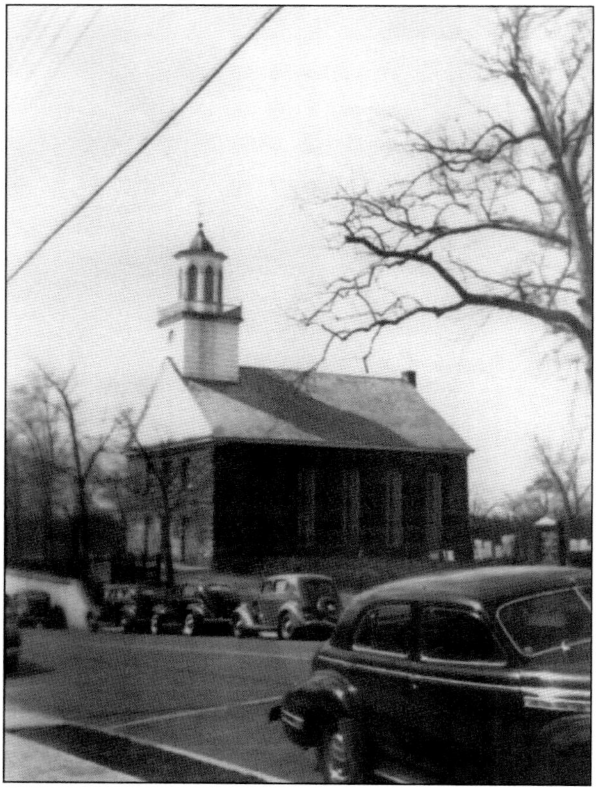

Connecticut Farms Presbyterian Church, on Stuyvesant Avenue, is pictured here in the early 1940s. The car featured in the lower right-hand corner of this photograph is a 1941 Buick. The congregation dates from 1730, but the original church building was destroyed during the Revolutionary War. The photograph captures the rebuilt church as it would have looked since the 1780s, plain and box-like, with a churchyard that dated from Colonial times. Below is a photograph of the church on March 7, 1939, by Nathanial R. Ewan for the Historic American Buildings Survey. By the end of the 1940s, the church building would be enlarged by an extensive new addition that would completely change its appearance. (Left, courtesy of UTHS; below, courtesy of the Library of Congress.)

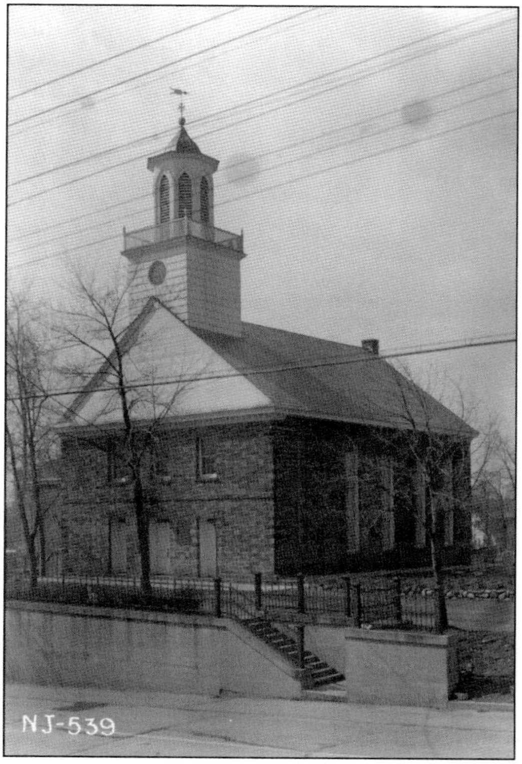

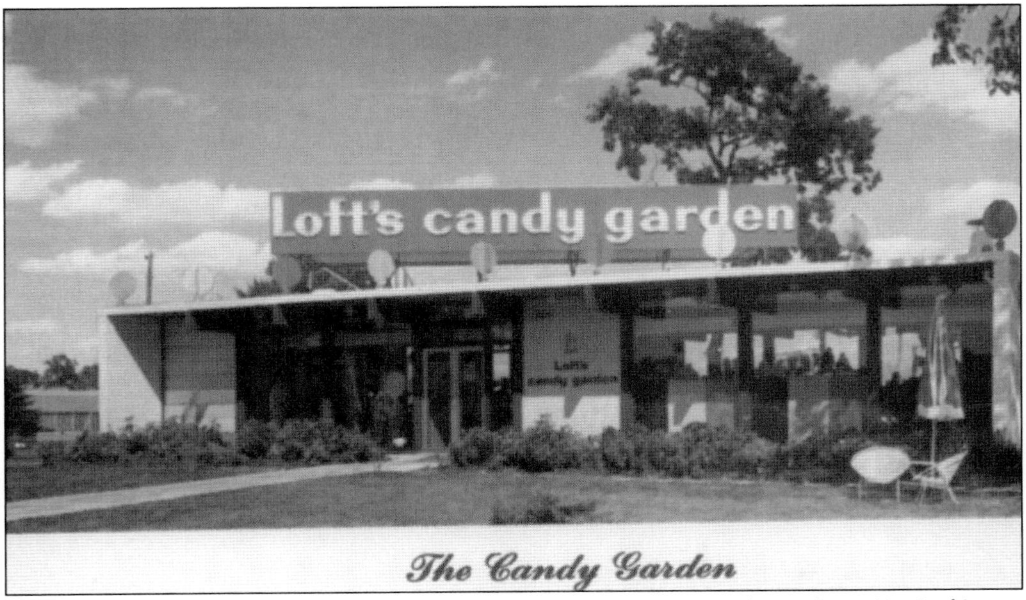

Pictured here is a Loft's Candy Garden advertisement dating from the early 1960s. Loft's was situated in the center island of Route 22. According to those who remember the place—mostly old-time chocoholics—the shop sold very good chocolate and other sweets, but many chocolate lovers preferred Helen Elliott and Fanny Farmer's chocolates. There were also many who preferred shopping in Union Center, as opposed to driving out to Route 22. A Wendy's fast-food restaurant now occupies the site. (Courtesy of UTHS.)

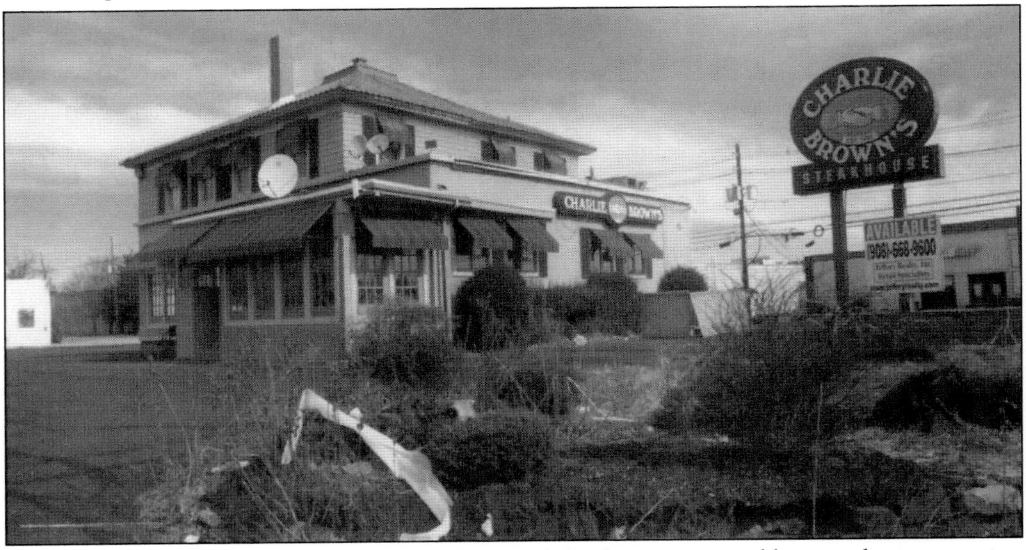

Charlie Brown's Restaurant—or at least what was left of it—is pictured here at the intersection of Route 22 West and Springfield Road. When this undated photograph was taken, the building was vacant, and the property was for sale. According to a customer who used to frequent Charlie Brown's on a regular basis, it was "the sort of place where you went for a drink and wound up having a meal." It was also famous for its large bar, as well as for its sandwiches, which were "very generous." Before Charlie Brown's, Oscar's occupied the site. Charlie Brown's was more of a family-oriented restaurant, with a salad bar. An auto-parts store occupies the location these days. (Courtesy of UTHS.)

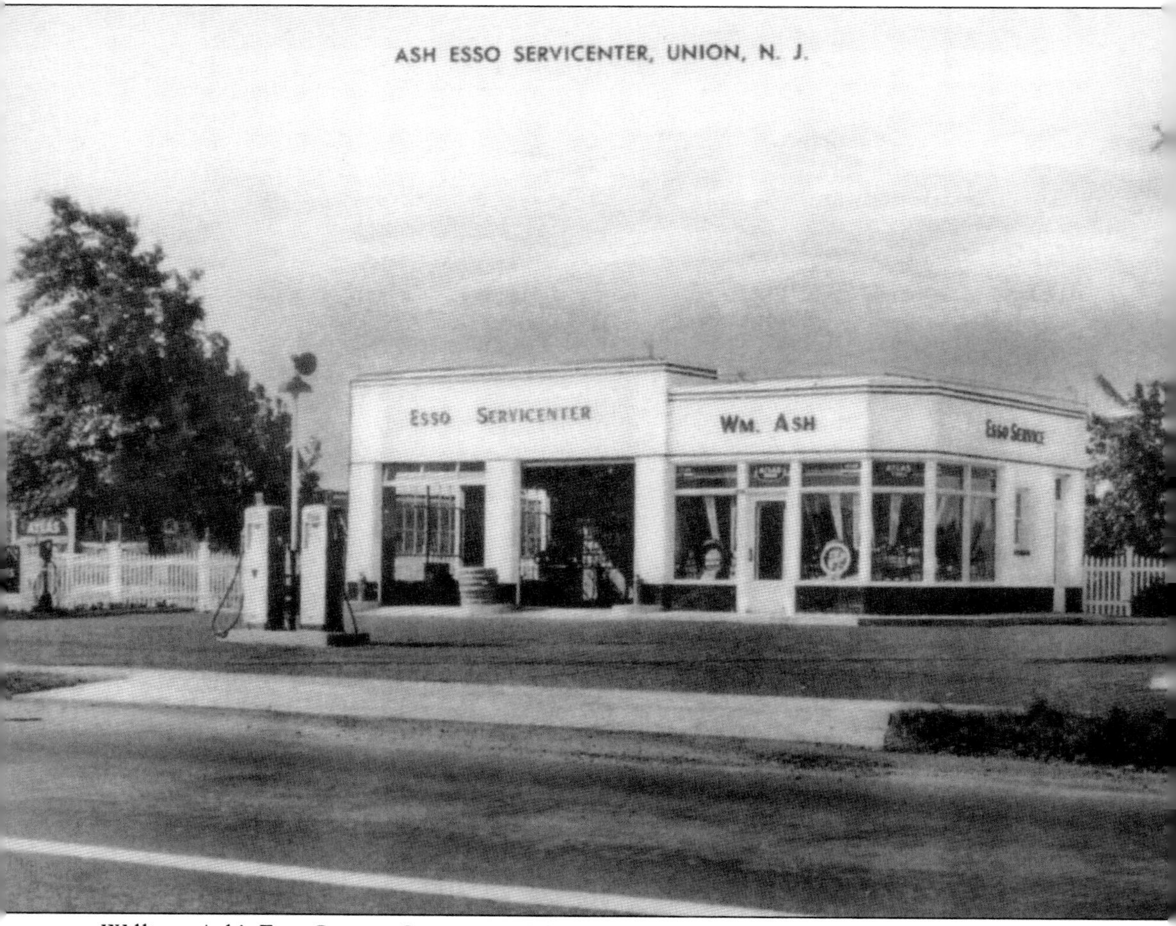

William Ash's Esso Service Station, on Morris Avenue, is pictured here in the days before Esso became Exxon and when gasoline sold for about 20¢ per gallon. (A team in one of the local bowling leagues called itself the Esso Bees. This nice little play on words would not work with Exxon.) This photograph must have been taken on a Sunday. Even in the late 1940s, traffic on Morris Avenue was never as light as it is in this image. A service station still occupies the site—a BP station, across the street from Holy Spirit Church. (Courtesy of UTHS.)

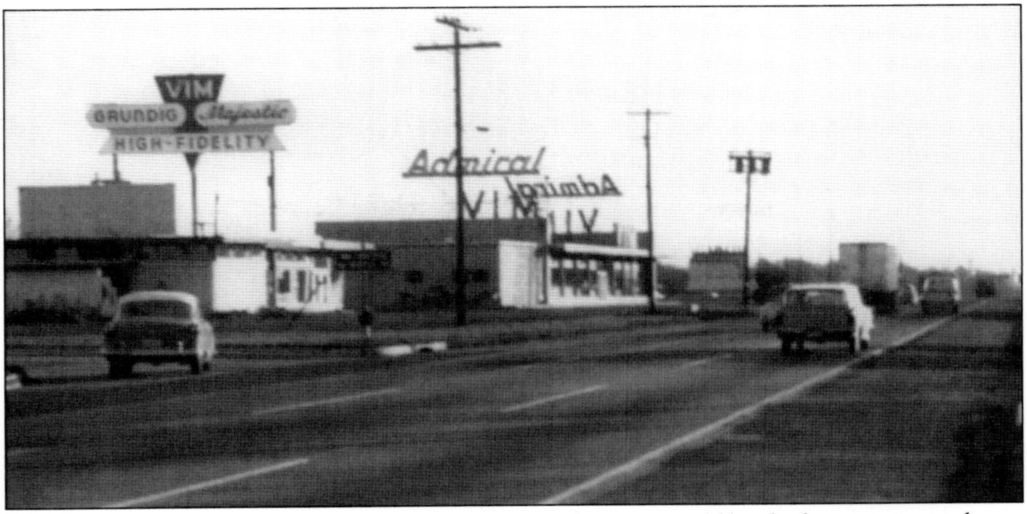

VIM Appliances, in the center island of Route 22, was where one could buy hi-fi equipment and even an Admiral television, all made in the USA. VIM had a catchy radio jingle: "VIMMMMMMMM for value." This photograph must also have been taken on a Sunday afternoon—traffic on Route 22 is not only light, but actually seems civilized, which it never was on any other day of the week. The car in the right-hand lane is a 1961 Rambler, which places the scene sometime in the 1960s. (Courtesy of UTHS.)

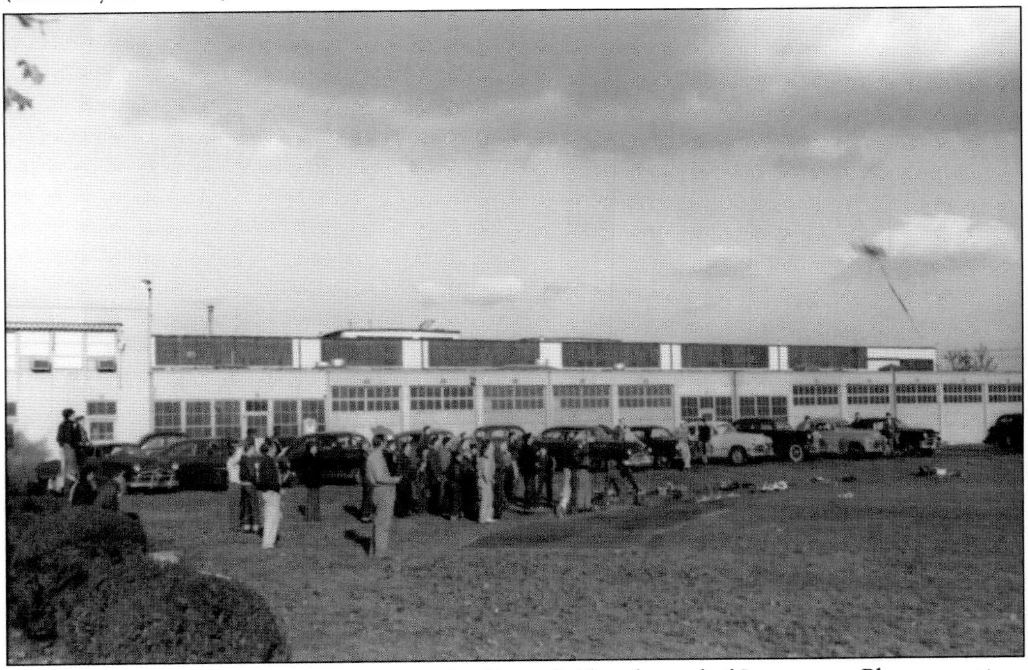
Model airplane enthusiasts congregate at the flying field at the end of Swanstrom Place sometime in the mid-1950s. Behind all the parked cars are the garages of Union Township's department of public works. Behind the garages are the windows of the Elastic Stop Nut Corporation of America's factory. Elastic Stop Nut closed in the mid-1990s and has been replaced by housing. Burnet Junior High School would make its appearance on the far side of the field, about a quarter of a mile in back of where the photographer is standing, in the late 1950s. The junior high would be replaced by the new Union High School in September 1969. (Courtesy of UTHS.)

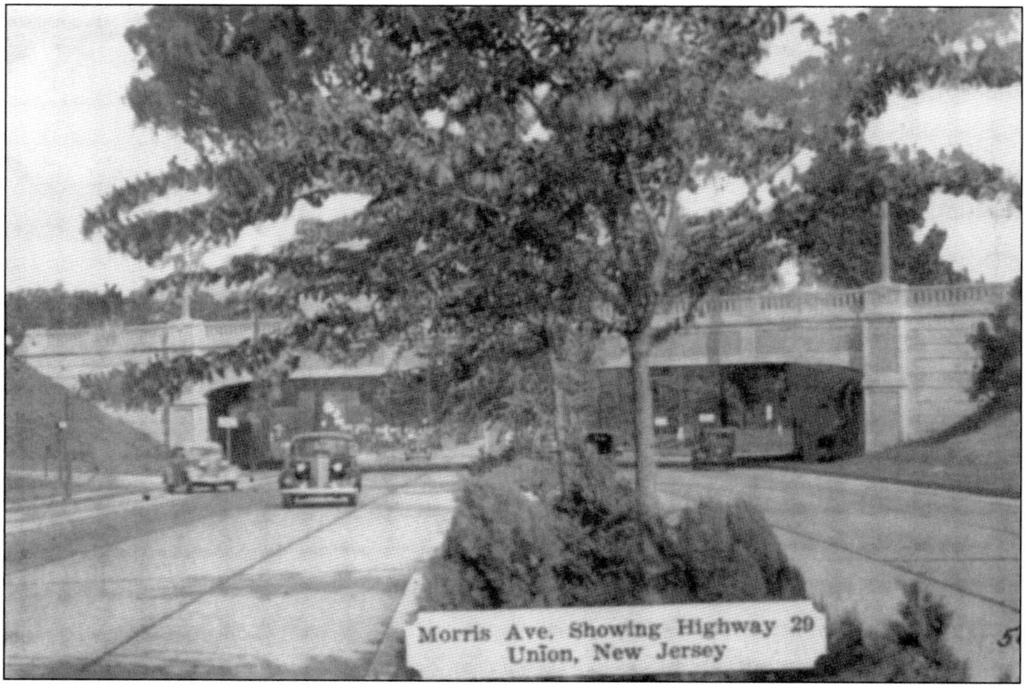

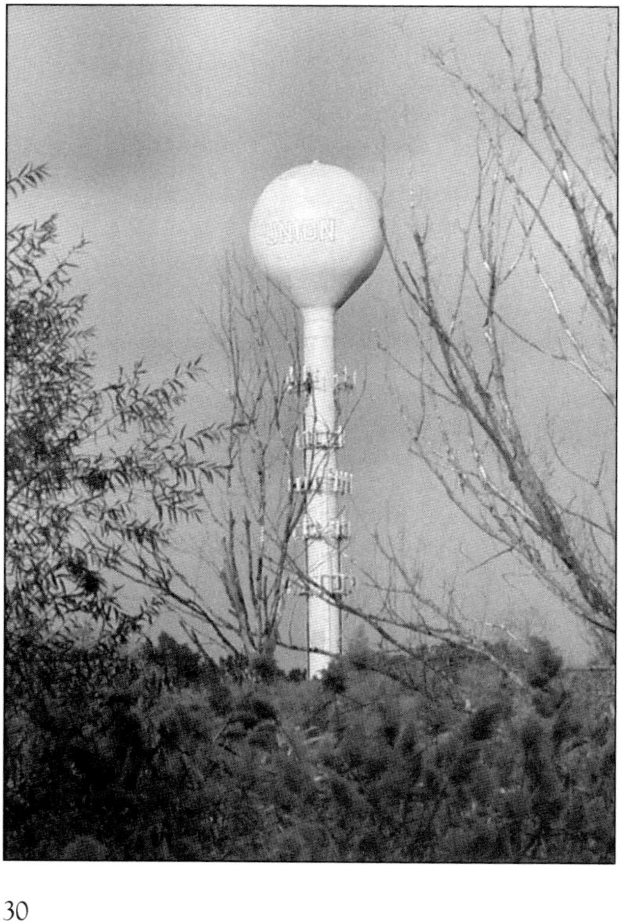

This is a 1940s photograph of Morris Avenue with a view looking toward Elizabeth. All the trees in the center island are gone and have been replaced by maintenance-free concrete, and the cars are newer and faster these days, but the view remains pretty much the same. The Union Watersphere had not yet been built when the photograph was taken, and Highway 29 has become Route 22. Morris Avenue itself was still concrete at the time; it had not yet been covered by asphalt. (Courtesy of UTHS.)

The Union Watersphere was constructed in 1965 adjacent to Route 22. At 211 feet tall, it has been hailed the "world's tallest watersphere." (Courtesy of the Library of Congress.)

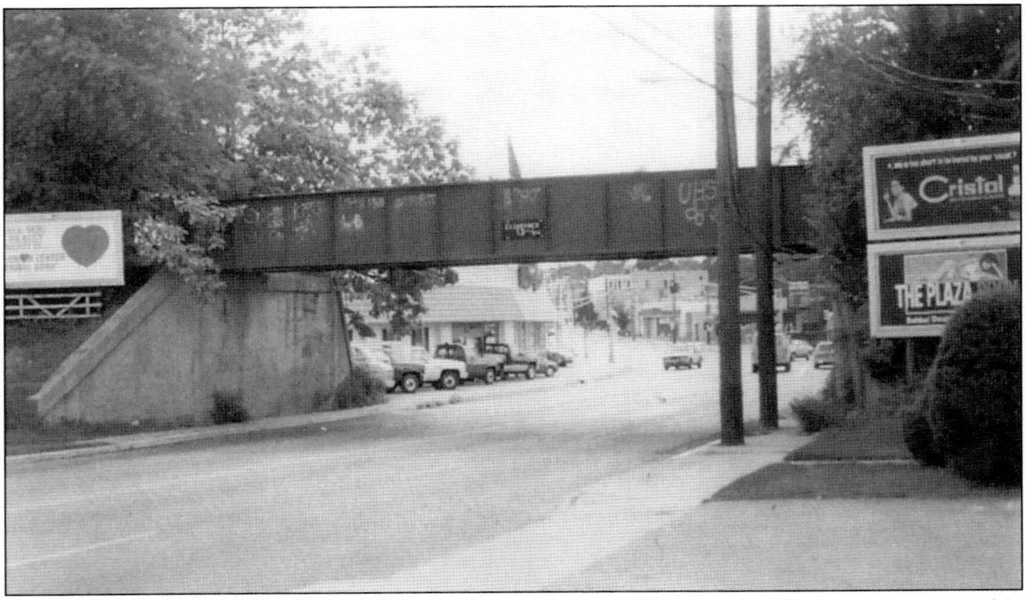

This is the Rahway Valley Railroad trestle crossing Morris Avenue near Elmwood Avenue. This photograph was taken in the 1980s—some Union High School graduate has scrawled "UHS 80" in white paint on the right side of the bridge. Union residents did not object to the removal of the bridge; it was considered more of an eyesore than a landmark. Union Center National Bank, "The Bank with a Heart," has an advertisement just to the left of the trestle. (Courtesy of UTHS.)

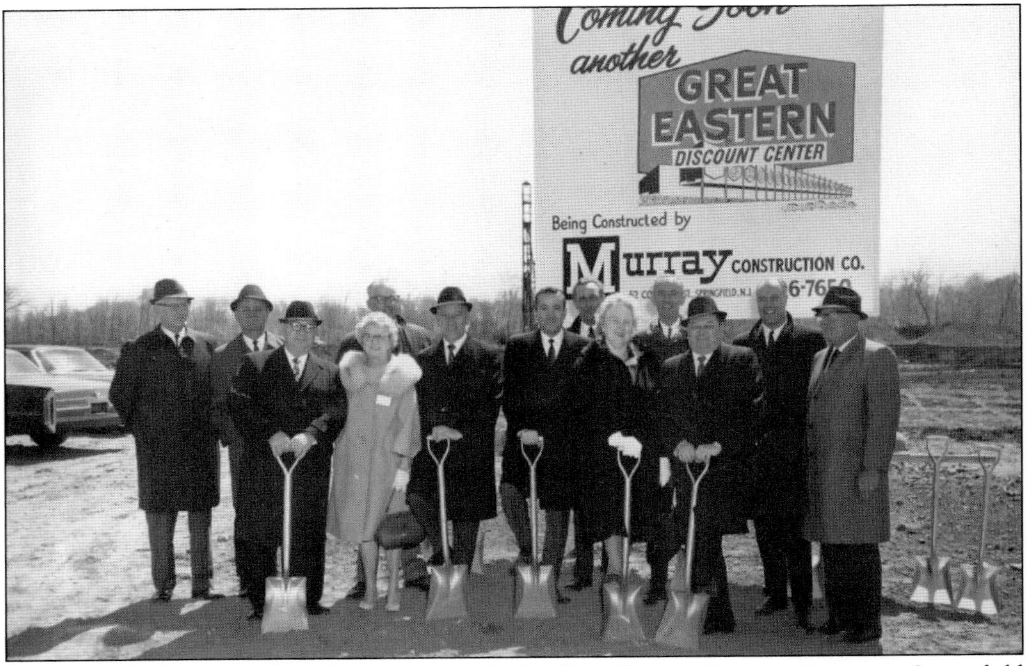

Pictured here is the ground-breaking ceremony for the Great Eastern Discount Center on Springfield Avenue in the 1960s; the car on the left is a 1966 Cadillac. Great Eastern was not the first discount store to come to Union; Two Guys was already open, over on Morris Avenue. Among the township officials in the photograph is Mary E. Miller, fifth from the right. The Miller family lived in Union since the early 1700, when the town was still called Connecticut Farms. (Courtesy of UTHS.)

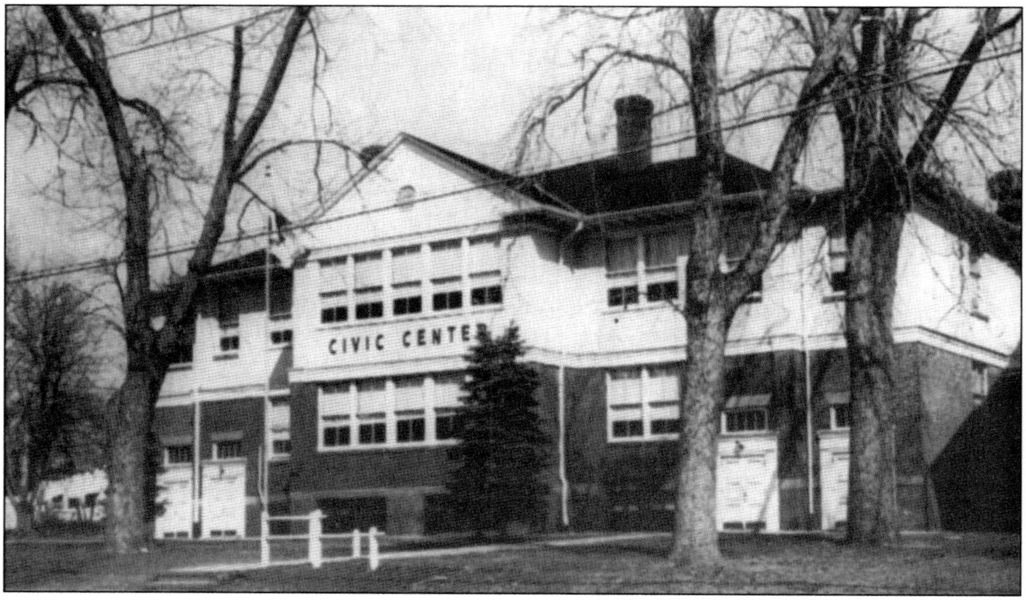

Pictured here in the 1950s is the Union Civic Center. The building began life as a school, a combination grammar school and high school, later became Union High School, and ended its days as a place for young people to gather, listen to records, and play pool and other games. The building was also known as the recreation center. It was demolished in 1988, eight decades after it was built. (Both, courtesy of UTHS.)

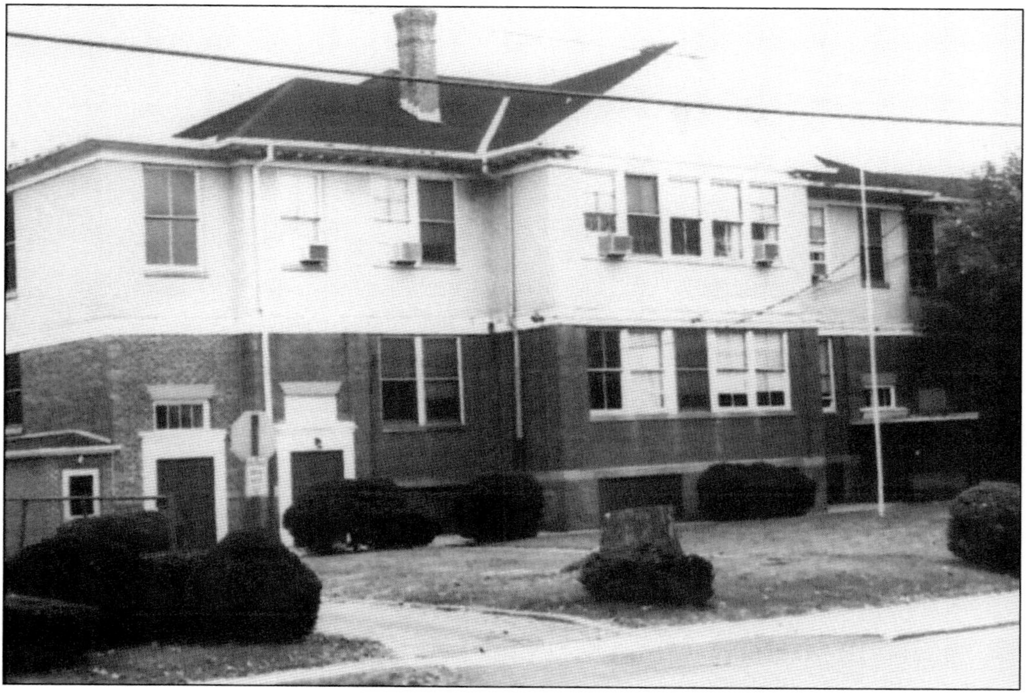

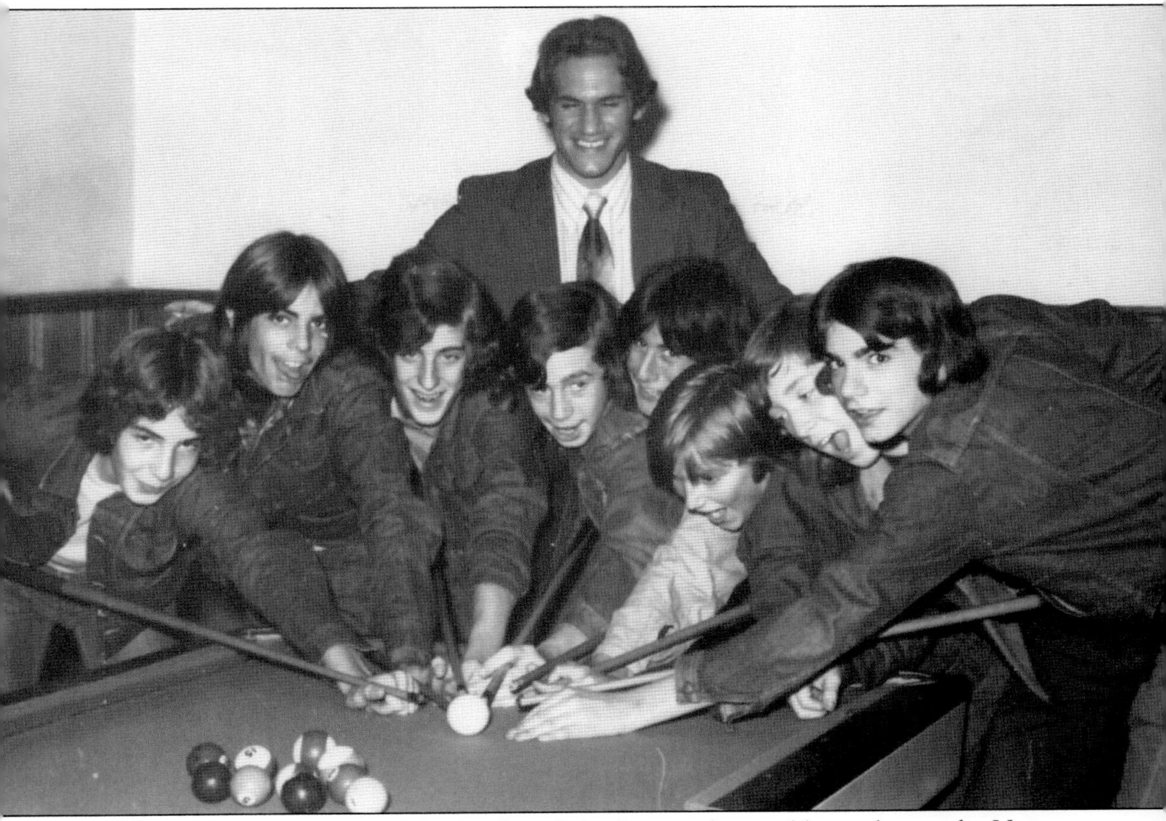

Richard Pisz (adult) and some of the local pool sharks pose for a publicity shot at the Union Civic Center sometime between 1972 and 1974. At about the time this photograph was taken, attendance at the recreation center's Youth Club was falling off sharply, and it continued to decline during the 1970s. But the building was also used by the town's senior citizens, the Golden Age Club, who attended meetings on a "regular and heavy" basis. It was finally pulled down in 1988 to make room for condominiums. (Courtesy of Union Township.)

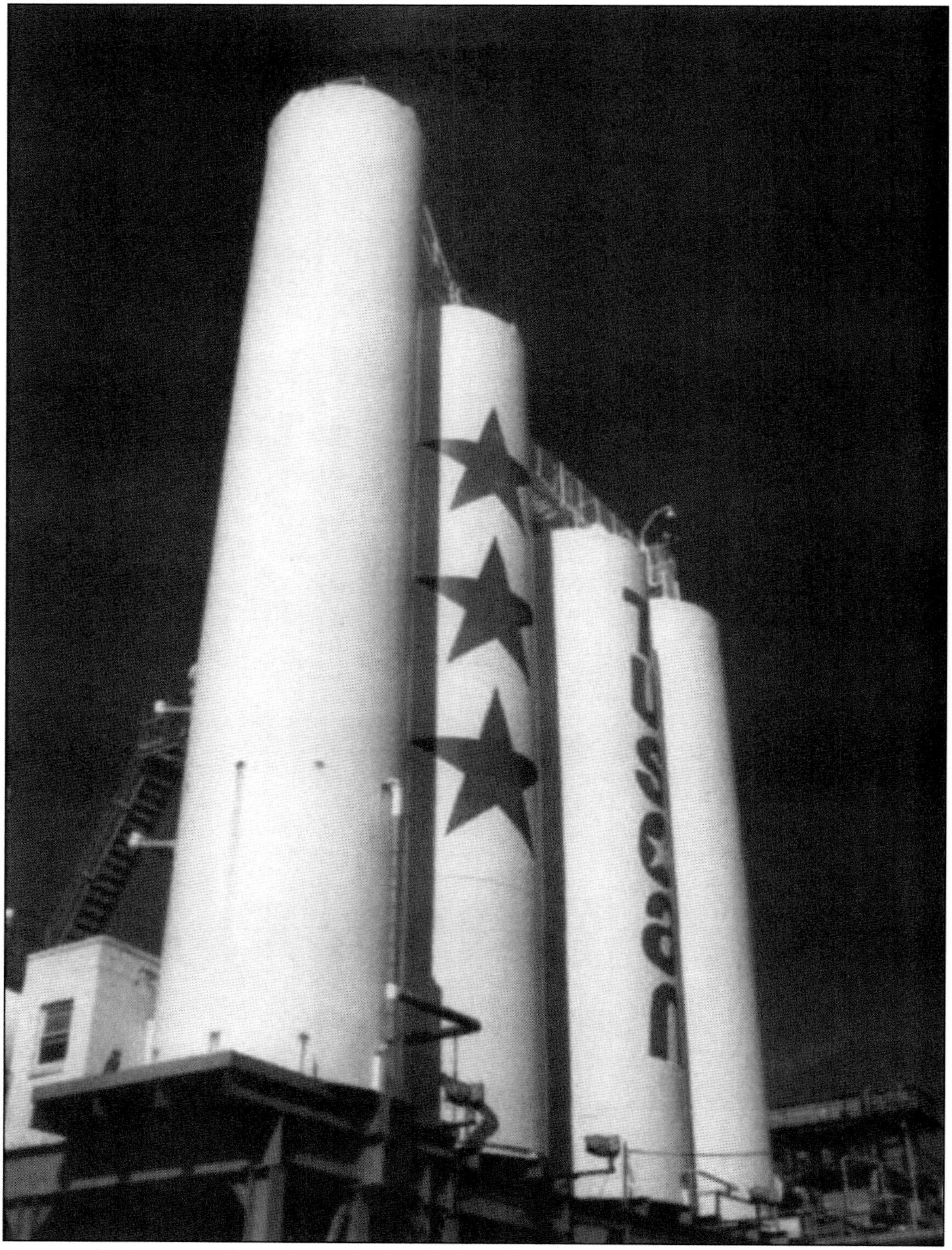

Anyone driving, or walking, down the long hill on Union Avenue, past the transmitters of radio station WNJR, would come to Tuscan Dairy and its sprawling facilities. Pictured here are the dairy's towers, actually called silos. The dairy closed its milk-processing and ice-cream plant in the early 2000s; much of its equipment was auctioned off in February 2006. The property known as the old Tuscan Dairy site has reportedly been acquired by developers. The new owners are said to be planning to build 260,000 square feet of warehouse space on the property. (Courtesy of UTHS.)

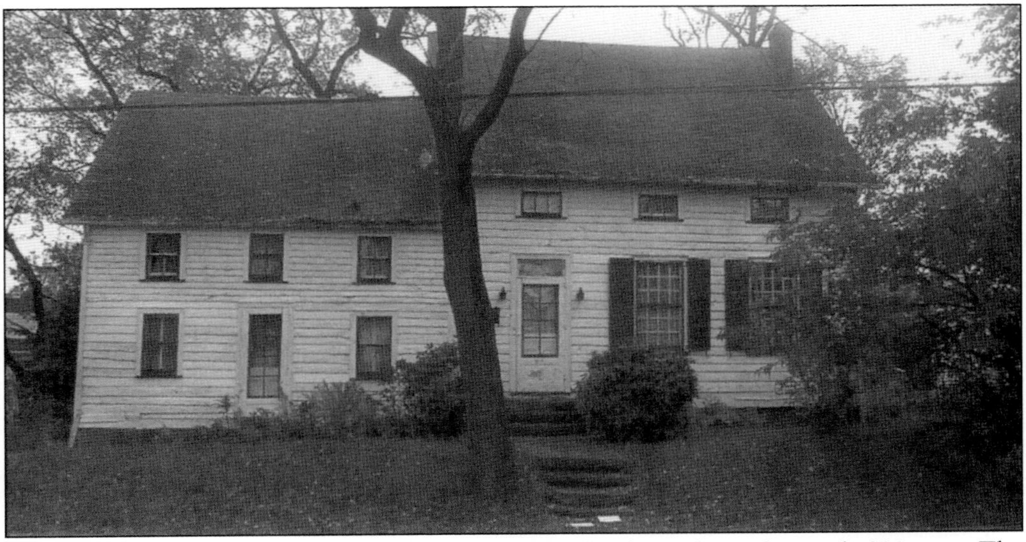

The Miller house on Colonial Avenue was the Miller family residence for nearly 300 years. The Millers settled in what was then called Connecticut Farms in the 1660s—the name of the town was not changed to Union until the early 1800s—and built this house in the early 1700s. The property was fairly extensive; a dairy and a wheelwright's shop were also built on the Miller estate. But by the time this photograph was taken, in the early 1990s, only the house remained. (Courtesy of UTHS.)

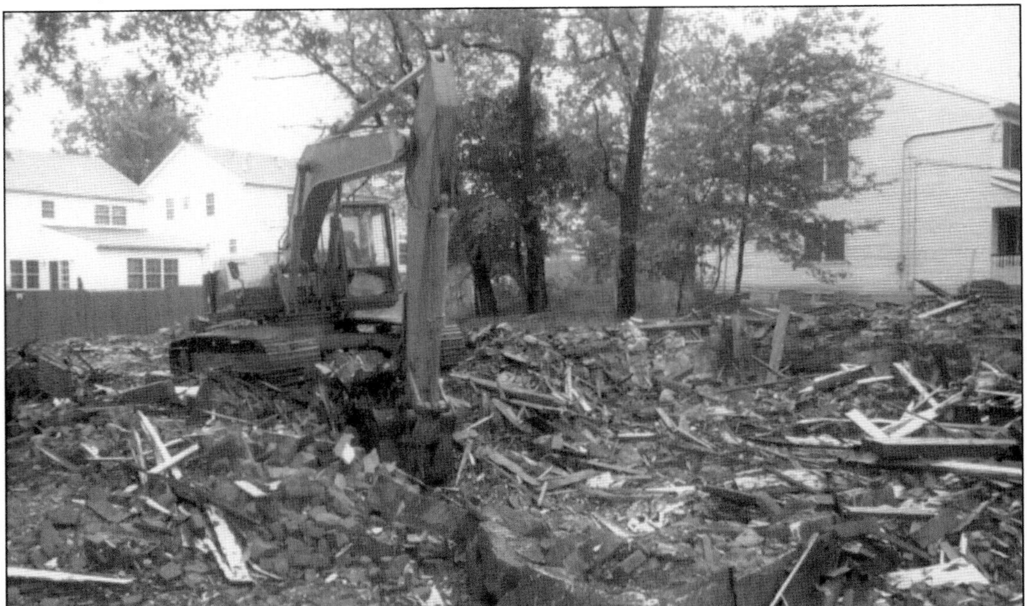

Following Mary Miller's death in 2002, the Miller house was sold to a developer. The house was situated on a double lot; the developer proposed moving the original house to one of the lots and building a new house on the adjoining lot. But an engineer and an architect performed a study of the Miller house and determined that the 275-year-old structure would never withstand the stress of such a move. Next, the developer applied for a subdivision of the lot, along with the demolition of the Miller house. This application was granted. In 2006, the Miller house was pulled down, and an irreplaceable piece of Union Township history disappeared. (Courtesy of Tom Haggerty.)

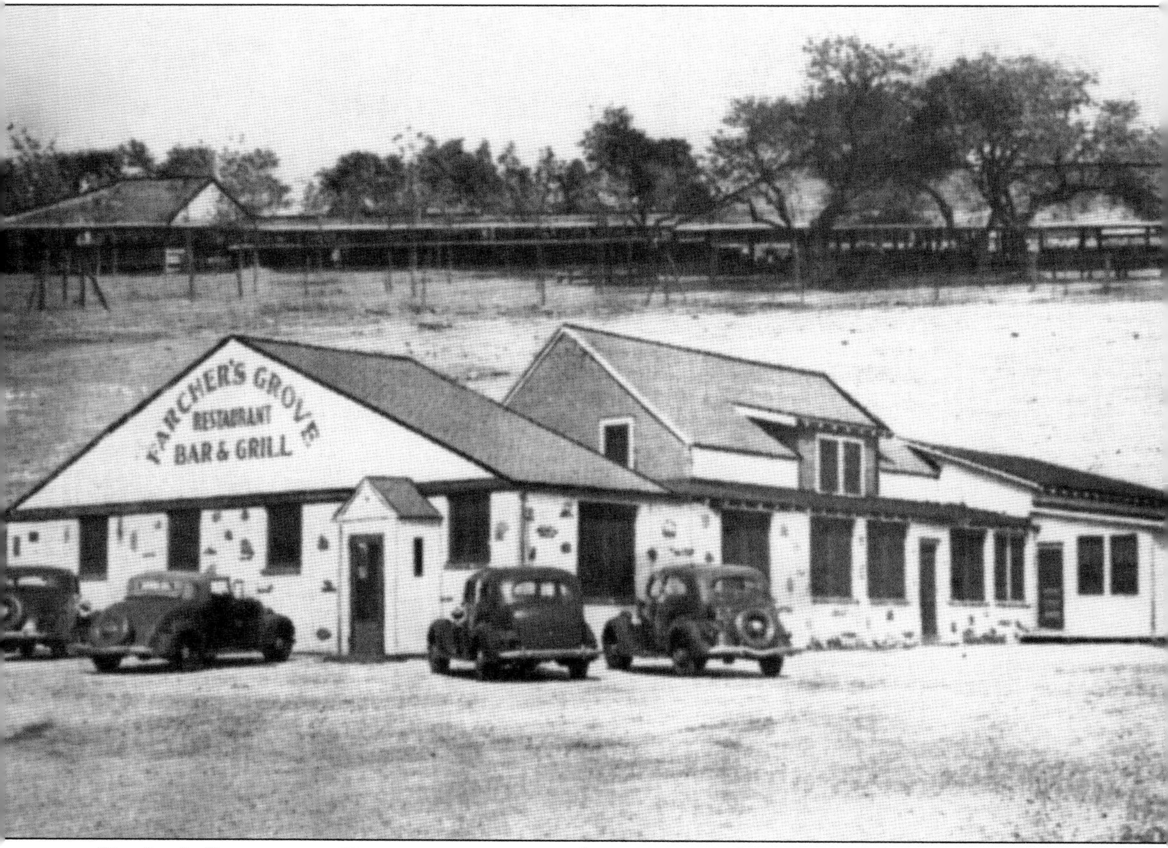

Farcher's Grove was a German restaurant and picnic ground on Springfield Road, just off Route 22. It was "a nice place to eat," according to a Unionite who used to eat there frequently. It was also the home of the Elizabeth SC, which was part of the German American Soccer League. They used the Grove's playing field and clubhouse for their soccer matches. The Elizabeth SC won the National Challenge Cup in 1970 and again in 1972. Farcher's Grove was sold in 1999. The photograph dates from the late 1930s, when Route 22 was still 29 Highway. The car on the far right is a 1936 Ford. (Courtesy of UTHS.)

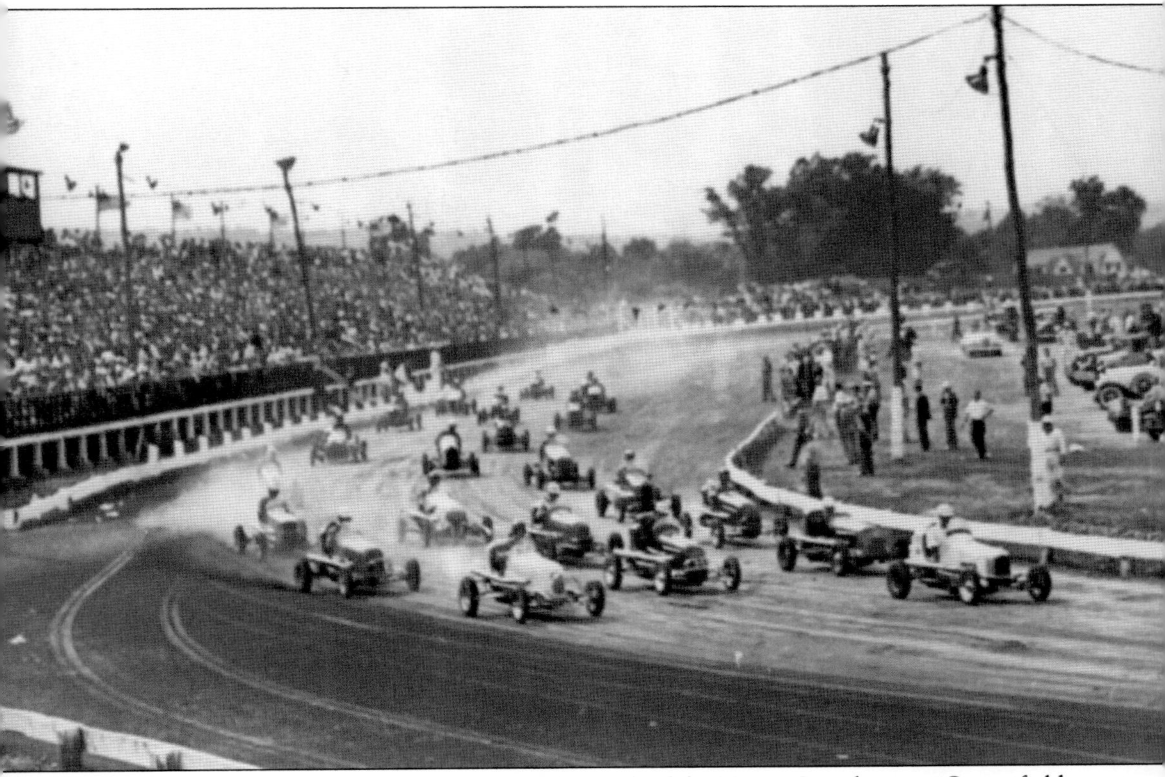

The miniature racing cars go round and round the track of the Union Speedway, on Springfield Road, around 1938. Union Speedway only existed for four years, from 1936 to 1940, and was apparently quite popular—the grandstand is completely packed. The half-mile dirt track was situated between Farcher's Grove and 29 Highway (Route 22), in the vicinity of Iorio Street. It was demolished in the 1940s to make room for factories. (Courtesy of UTHS.)

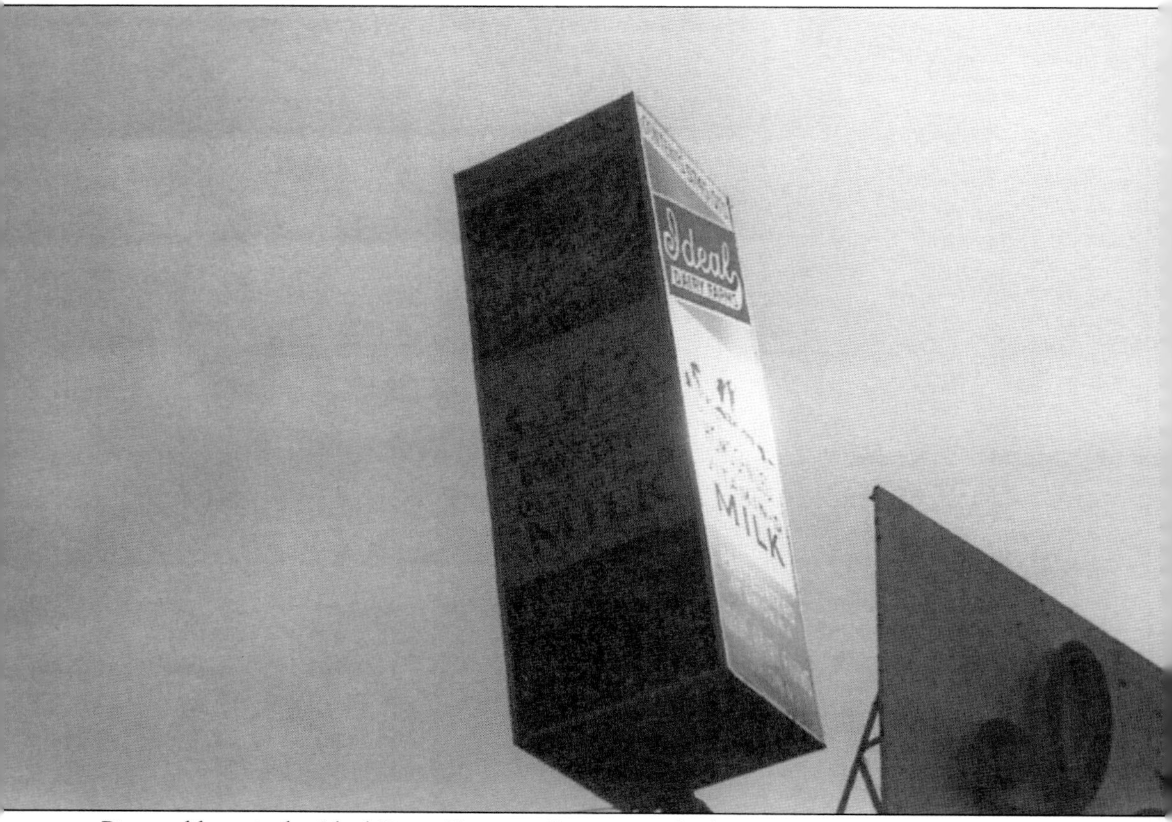

Pictured here is the Ideal Dairy Farms milk carton, which was not nearly as well known as the famous cows' heads on Morris Avenue, near Lousons Road. The two Ideal Dairy cows were among Union's most recognizable and memorable landmarks—anyone who lived in Union or drove through town on Morris Avenue has vivid memories of the Ideal Dairy sign. In the early 1980s, the sign—the milk carton and the two Morris Avenue cows—came down when Ideal Professional Office Park was built, with offices for doctors, lawyers, and businesses. (Courtesy of Singer Media.)

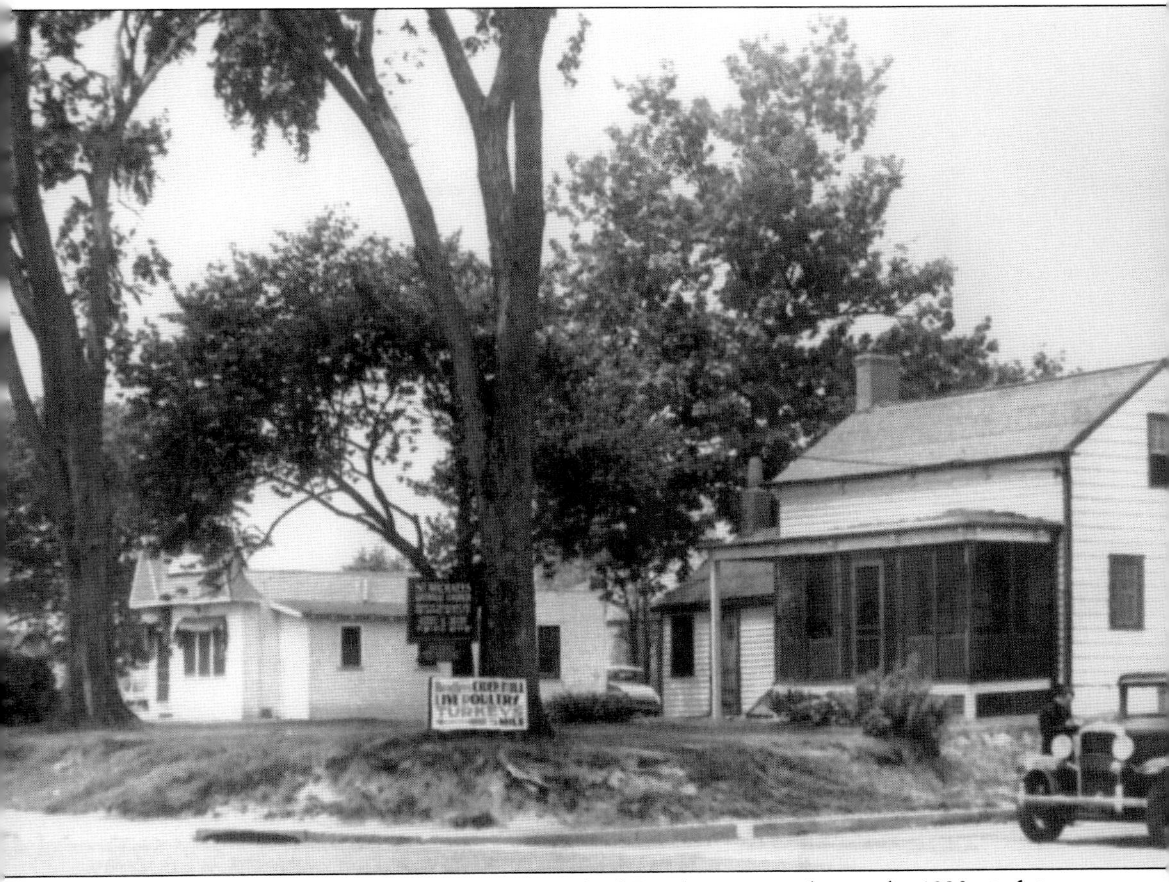

This is the corner of Stuyvesant Avenue and Vauxhall Road sometime during the 1920s, judging from the vintage of the automobile. The building on the left, half hidden by trees, is Corrigan's Tavern, owned by Peter and Marty Corrigan, who also owned the house on the right side of the photograph. (This made for a nice easy commute to work for the Corrigans.) The larger of the two signs points the way to "Live Poultry: Turkeys – 1/2 Mile." The other sign gives the mass schedule at St. Michael's Church, which is just down the street on Vauxhall Road. (Courtesy Kathy Ferguson Sinnes.)

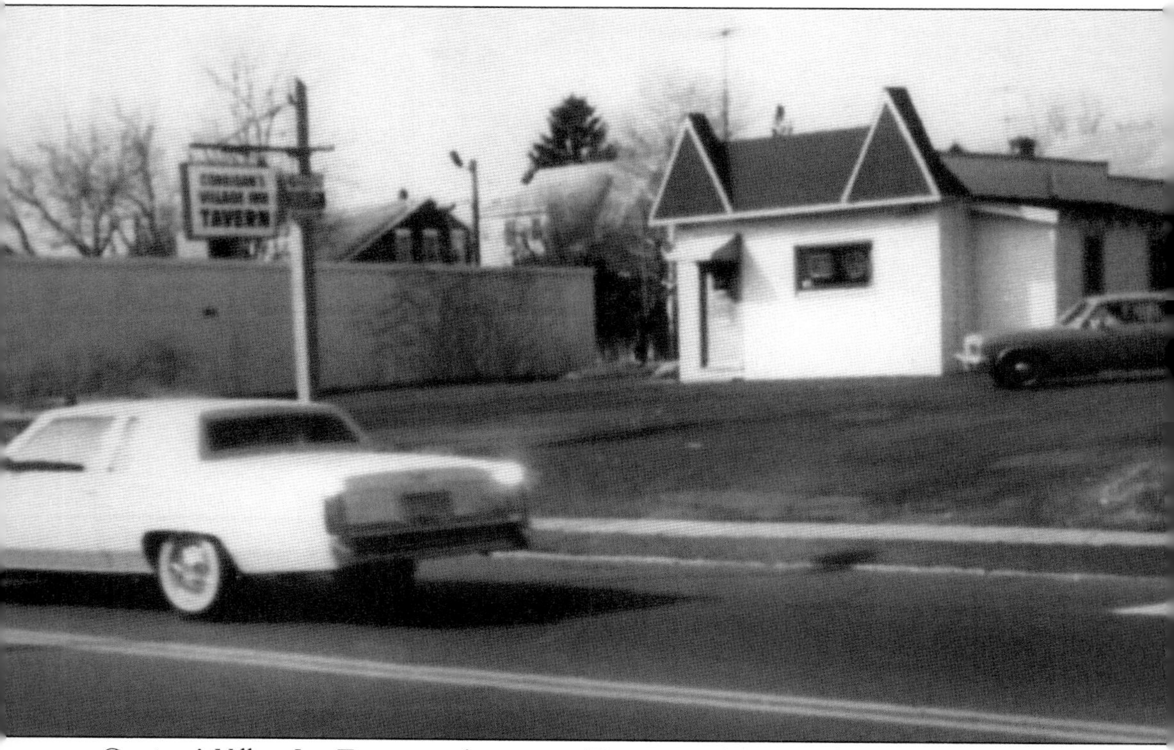

Corrigan's Village Inn Tavern, on the corner of Stuyvesant Avenue and Vauxhall Road, is pictured here many years after the image on the previous page. Locals described Corrigan's as a saloon, bar, or gin mill, but it was a nice little place to have a quiet drink after work. The television may have been turned on, but it was usually at low volume—the atmosphere could accurately be described as mellow. The building has since been demolished and replaced by a QuickChek; there is also a 7-Eleven just up the street on Stuyvesant Avenue. Corrigan's will be missed by its many customers, or, as a literary critic once said, by its habitués and sons of habitués. (Courtesy of UTHS.)

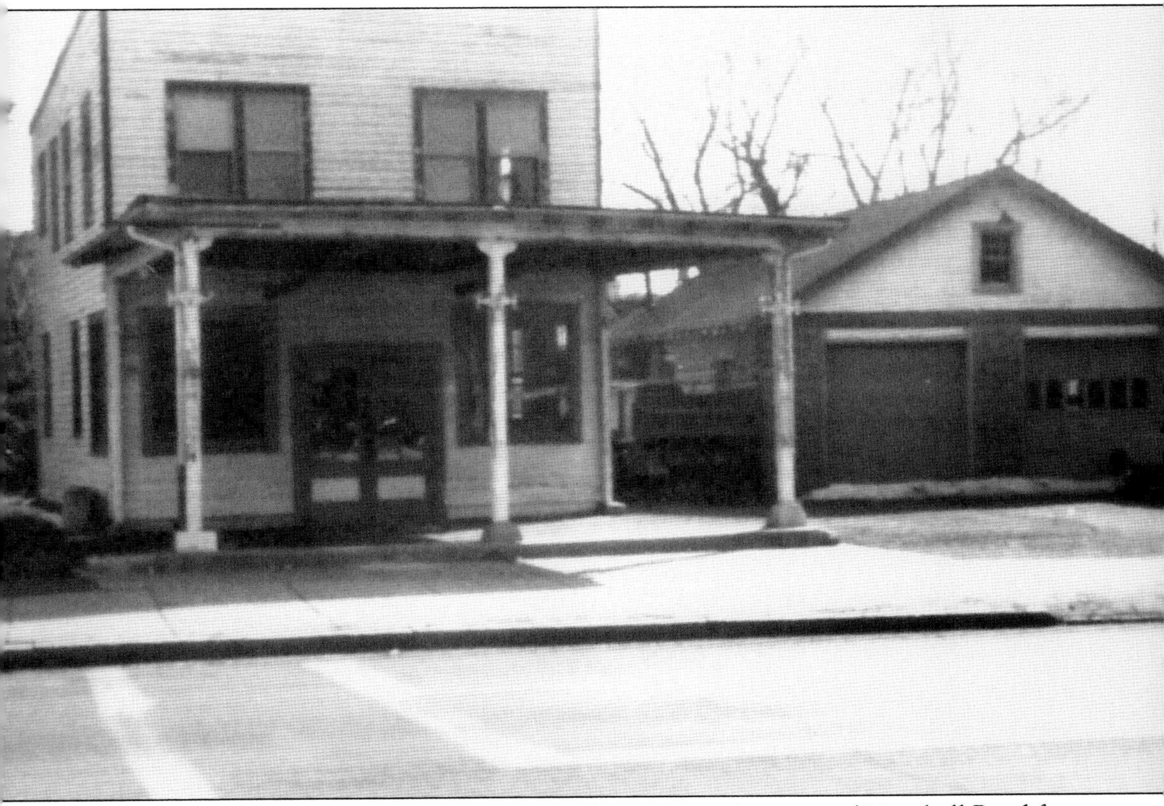

There was an Esso service station on the corner of Stuyvesant Avenue and Vauxhall Road for many years; it stood just across the street from Corrigan's Village Inn Tavern, on the opposite side of Stuyvesant Avenue. On the other side of Vauxhall Road, which would be to the left of the Esso station, a Food Fair supermarket was situated. (This supermarket has since changed hands many times.) A Magic Fountain ice cream and yogurt stand now occupies the site. Irving "Slim" Trimmer's Shell station was located on the on the other side of Union Center, on Stuyvesant Avenue at Elmwood Avenue, diagonally across from the cannon. (Courtesy of UTHS.)

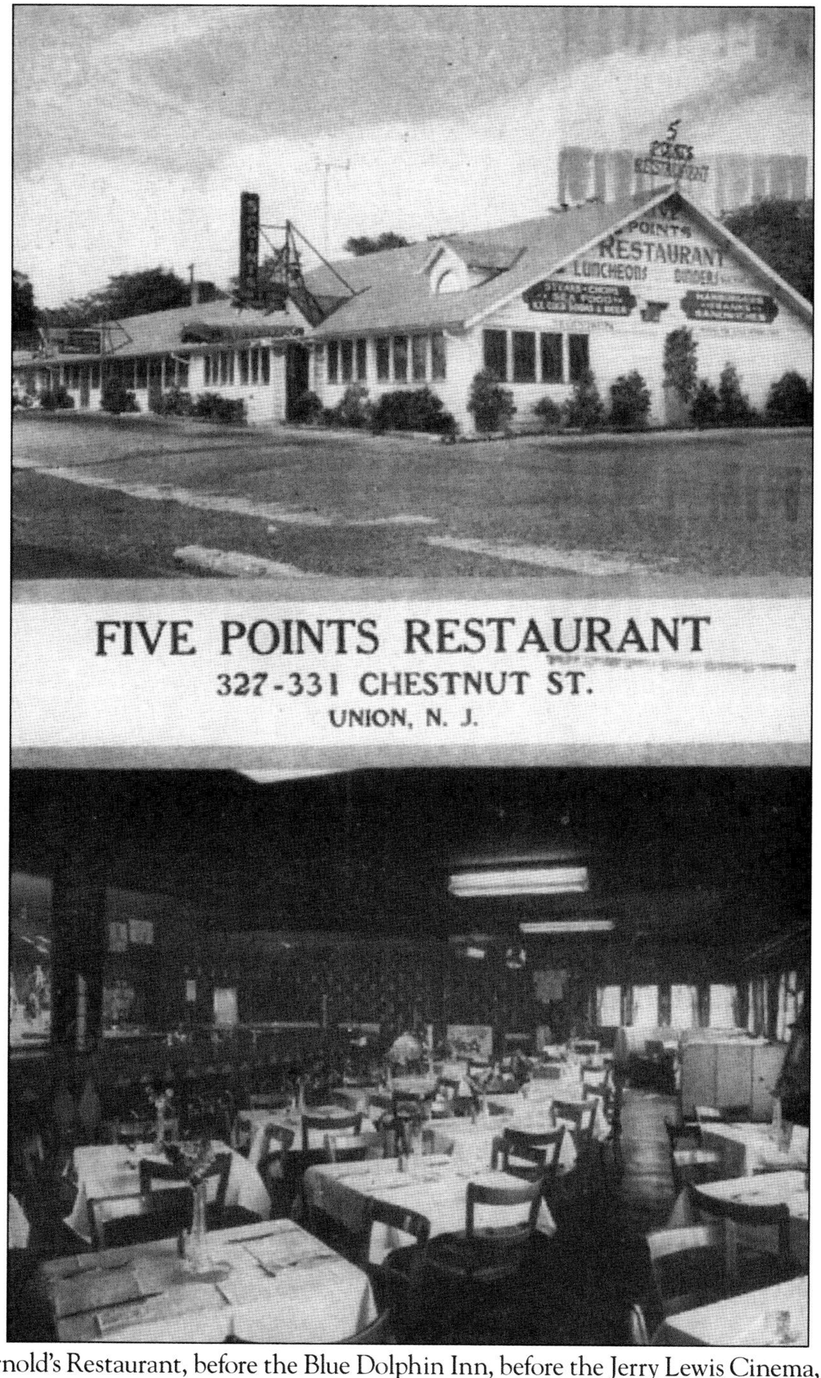

Before Arnold's Restaurant, before the Blue Dolphin Inn, before the Jerry Lewis Cinema, and long before Rite Aid, the Five Points Restaurant occupied the location at the corner of Chestnut Street and Delaware Avenue. Peterson's, which would later become the Galloping Hill Inn, occupies the other side of Delaware Avenue, just out of the photograph. This advertisement for Five Points Restaurant dates from the early 1950s. Those who remember the restaurant say that the food was "better than average," and the interior was cozy and comfortable. (Courtesy of UTHS.)

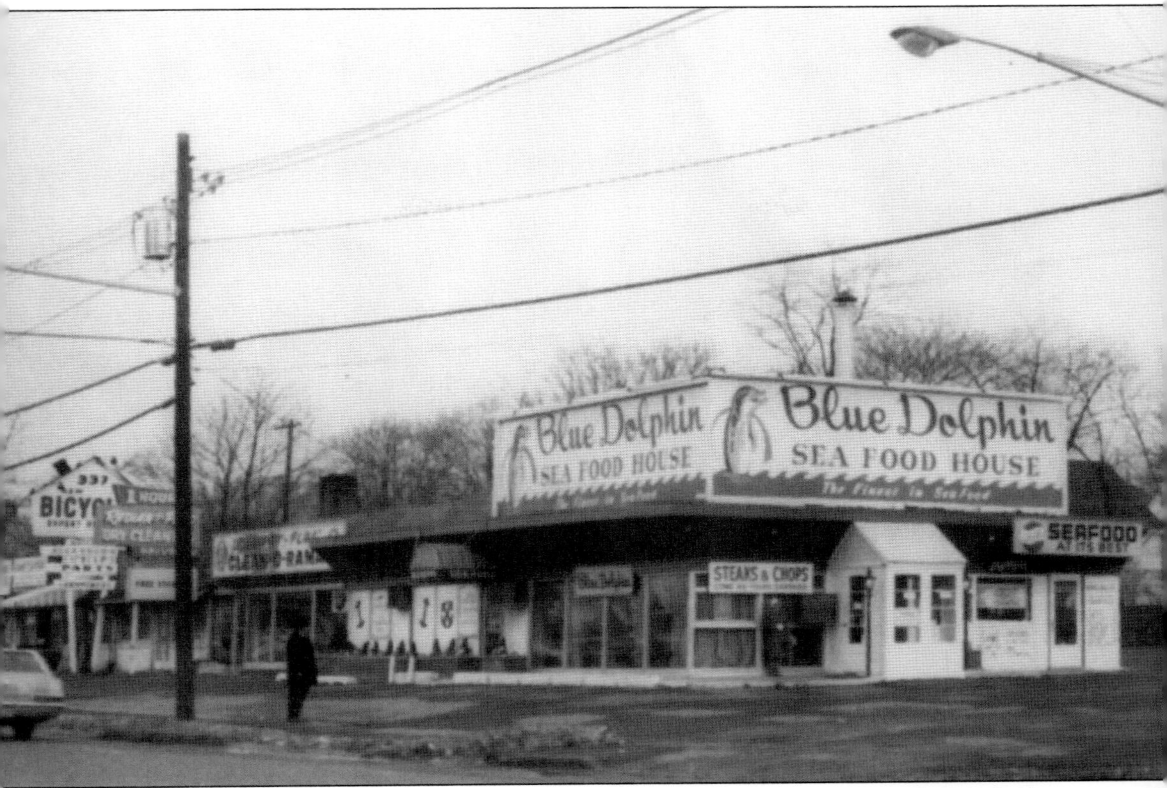

Pictured here is the Blue Dolphin Sea Food House on Chestnut Street, sometime during the late 1960s. (That is a 1966 Chevrolet station wagon parked next door, in front of Clean-O-Rama 1-Hour Dry Cleaning Service.) Five Points Restaurant, followed by Arnold's Ice Cream, occupied the site before the Blue Dolphin. Eventually, when the Blue Dolphin was pulled down, the site became home to a Jerry Lewis Cinema, and it is currently the location of a Rite Aid drugstore. (Courtesy of UTHS.)

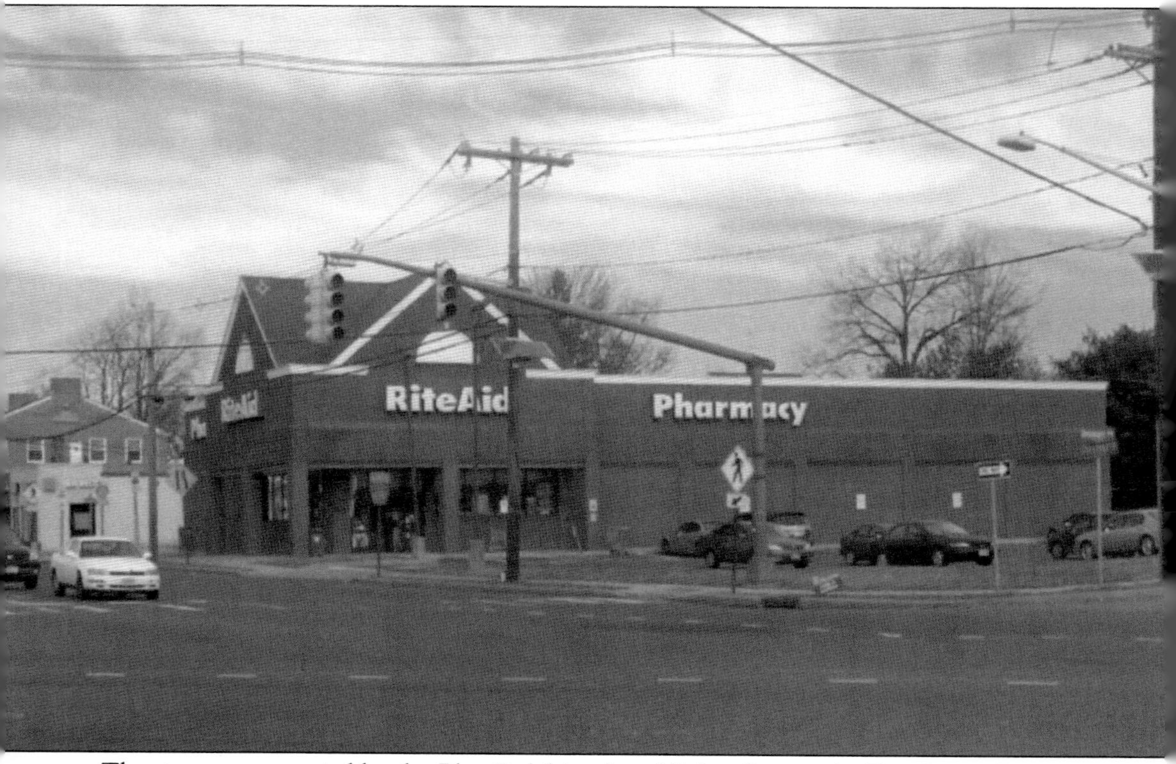

The site once occupied by the Blue Dolphin, Arnold's Ice Cream, the Five Points Restaurant, and the Jerry Lewis Cinema is currently the home of a Rite Aid. Residents of Union complain that the town needs another pharmacy —to go along with the Rite Aid in Union Center, as well as the Walgreens and CVS pharmacies all around the town—about as desperately as it needs higher taxes. In all likelihood, Union is going to get more of both in the not-too-distant future. (Courtesy of UTHS.)

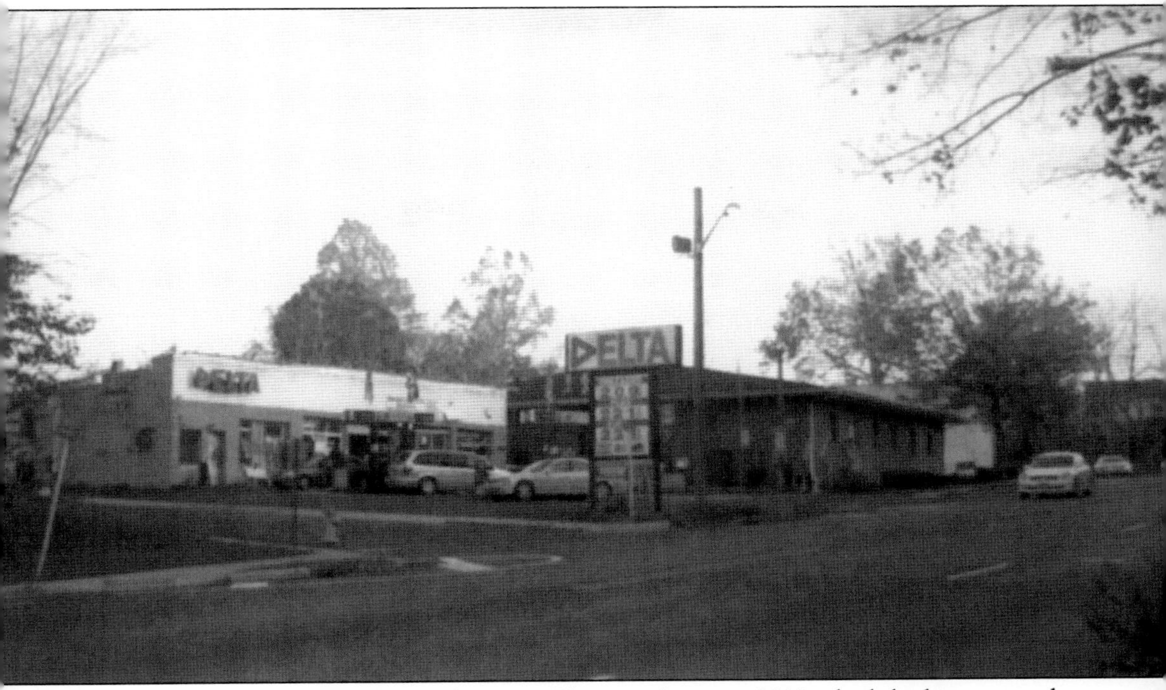

This photograph is a change of pace, featuring Chestnut Street in 2010, which looks very much the same, except for the price of gasoline, of course. (Courtesy of UTHS.)

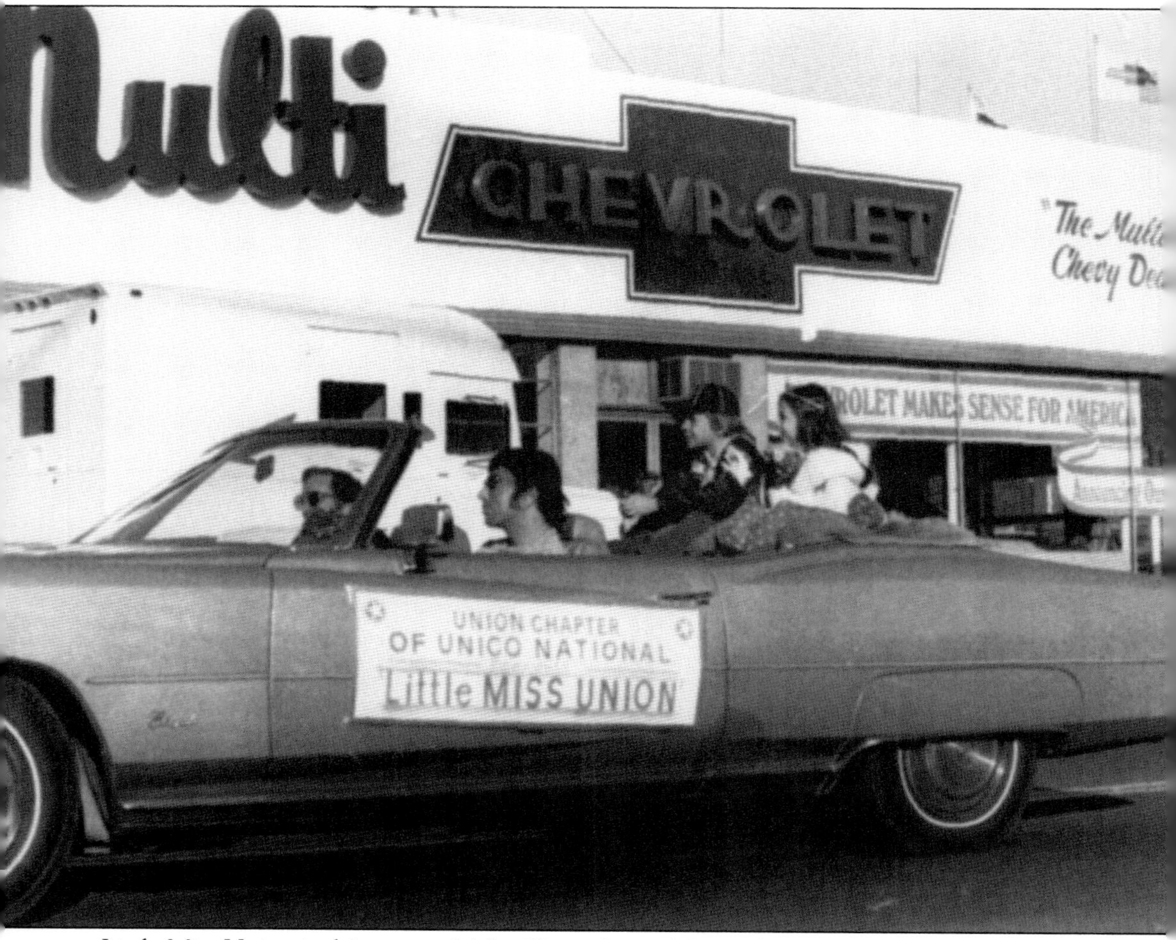

Little Miss Union is driven past Multi Chevrolet on Morris Avenue sometime during the mid-1970s. The driver of the car, which is a Buick, not a Chevrolet, wears fashionable long hair and sideburns. The advertisement in Multi's window tells the world, or at least the residents of Union Township, that "Chevrolet Makes Sense for America." In a previous era, Dinah Shore used to sing, "See the USA in your Chevrolet." The boy in the Cub Scout uniform in the backseat, presumably the brother of Little Miss Union, seems to be enjoying the ride as much as his sister. (Courtesy of Howie Frisch.)

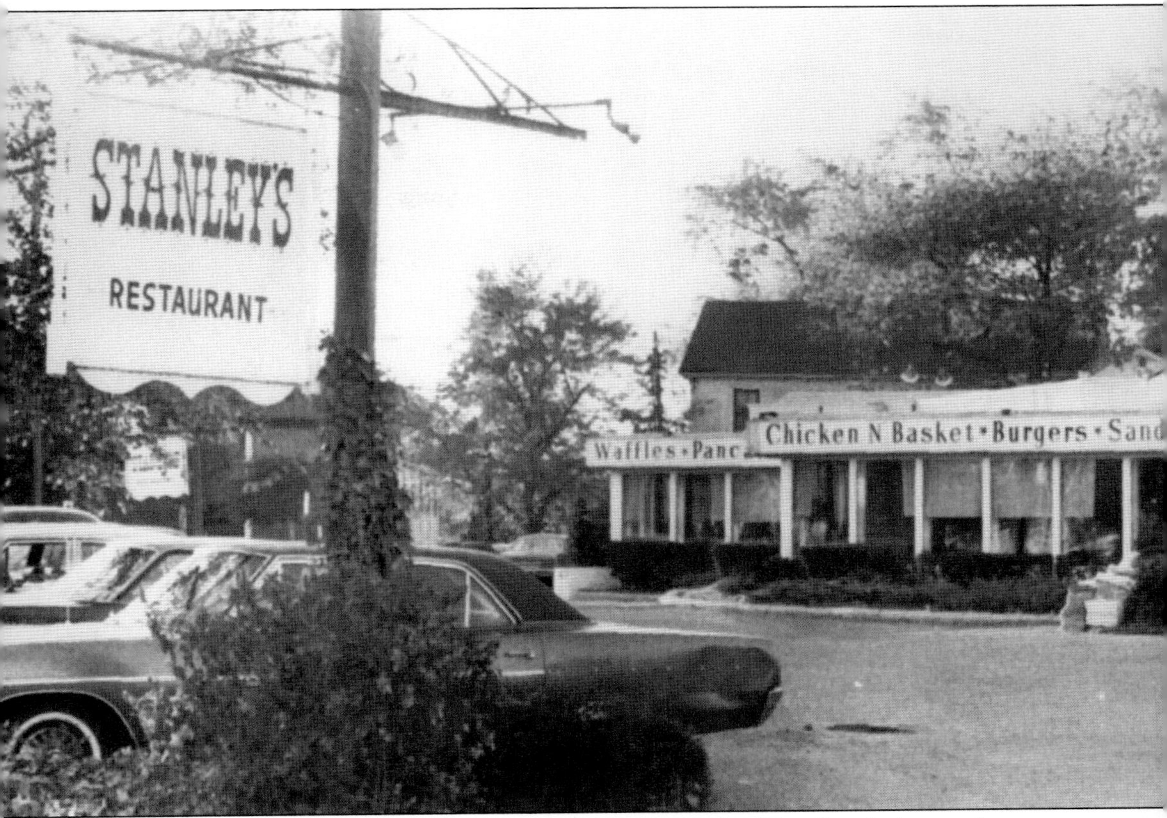

Stanley's Restaurant, on Morris Avenue, was actually in Springfield. But Stanley's was a hangout for a good many Union Township residents, since it was so close to the Union border. The cuisine was not fancy; some of Stanley's regular customers described the food as "glorified diner." But even if the food was not gourmet cuisine, the atmosphere was friendly. It was a good place to go for chicken or hamburgers and maybe a house salad. Stanley's closed its doors some years ago, along with many of its competitors just across the line in Union. (Courtesy of Howie Frisch.)

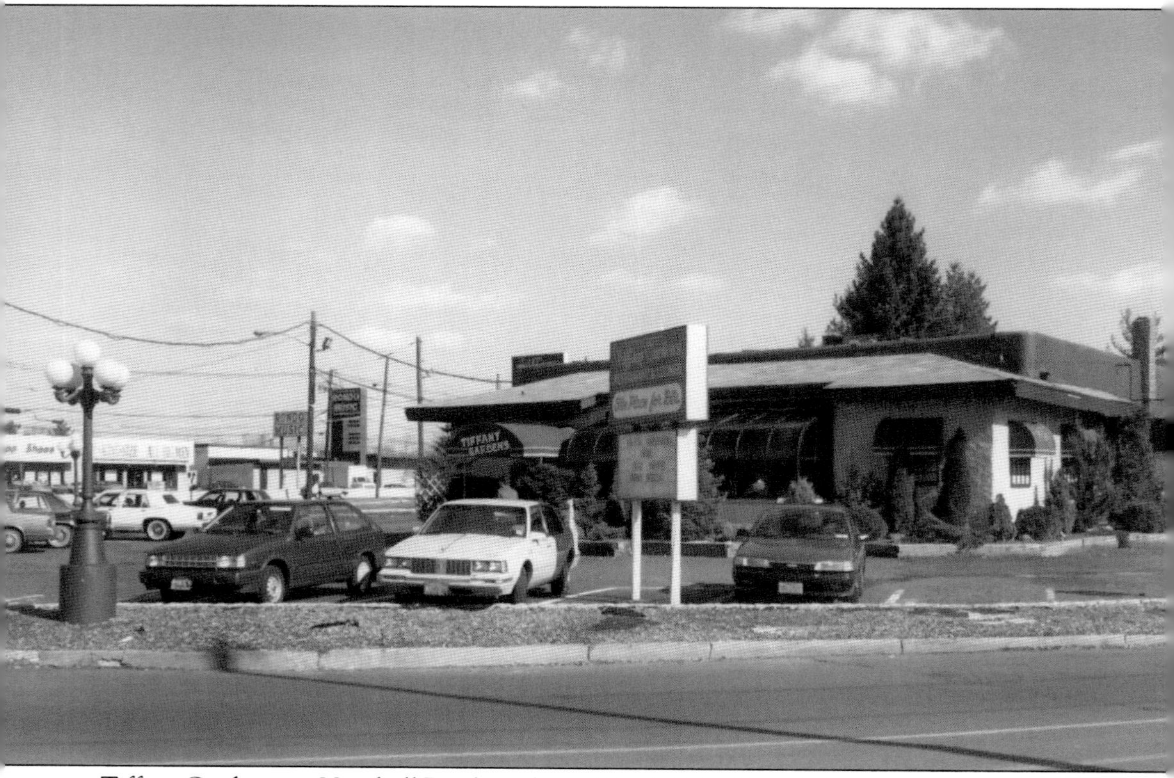

Tiffany Gardens, on Vauxhall Road, used to call itself "The Place for Ribs." It is now Tiff's Burger and Ale House. In the background, on the other side of Route 22 (eastbound lane), are Knapp Shoes and the unmistakable sign of Rondo Music—the giant keyboard on Route 22—both of which are gone. The highway is still there, however, and its traffic is as insane as ever. It is nice to know that some things, at least, never change. (Courtesy of UTHS.)

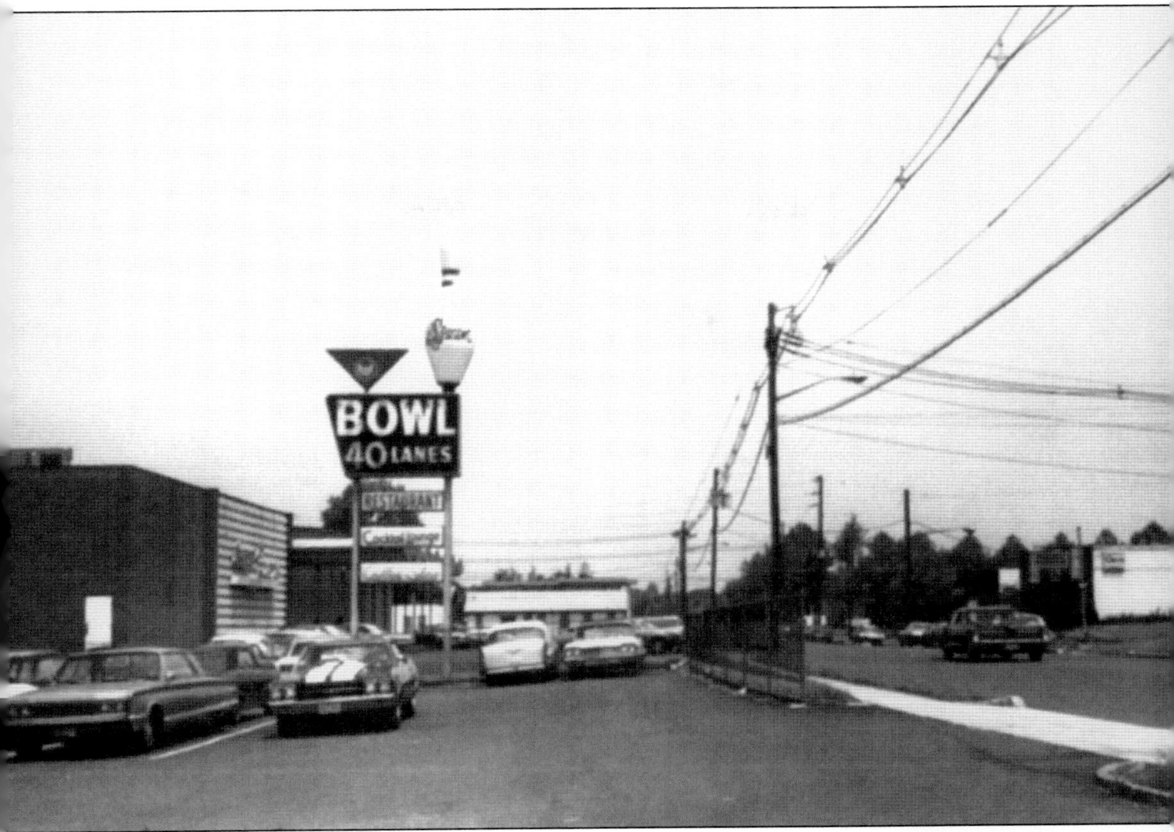

This is the Four Seasons Bowling, on West Chestnut Street, sometime during the late 1960s. Besides the advertised 40 bowling lanes, the Four Seasons also featured a cocktail lounge and restaurant. According to legend, a vocal group calling themselves the Four Lovers auditioned for an engagement in the lounge. They were turned down for the job, but liked the name of the establishment so much that the boys decided to change the name of their group. The Four Seasons had a string of hit pop tunes through the years, and the group was inducted into the Rock and Roll Hall of Fame in 1990. (Courtesy of UTHS.)

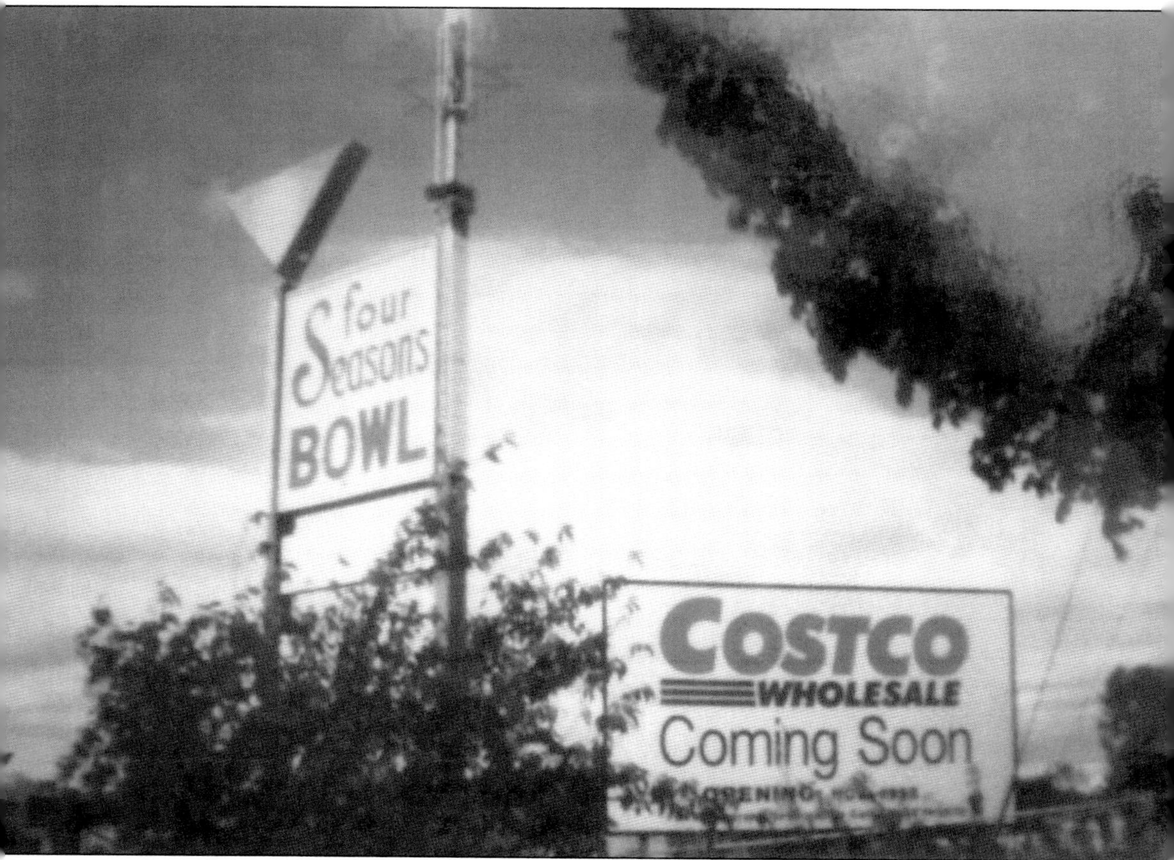

By the 1990s, bowling was not nearly as popular as it had been in the 1950s and 1960s. The site of the Four Seasons bowling lanes was sold to Costco Wholesalers, and the bowling alleys were demolished to make room for the new Costco building. In the photograph, the sign for Four Seasons Bowl temporarily coexists with the sign "Costco Wholesale Coming Soon." It is probably fortunate that no singing group showed up for an audition after the 1990s—the Four Costcos just does not have the same ring to it. (Courtesy of UTHS.)

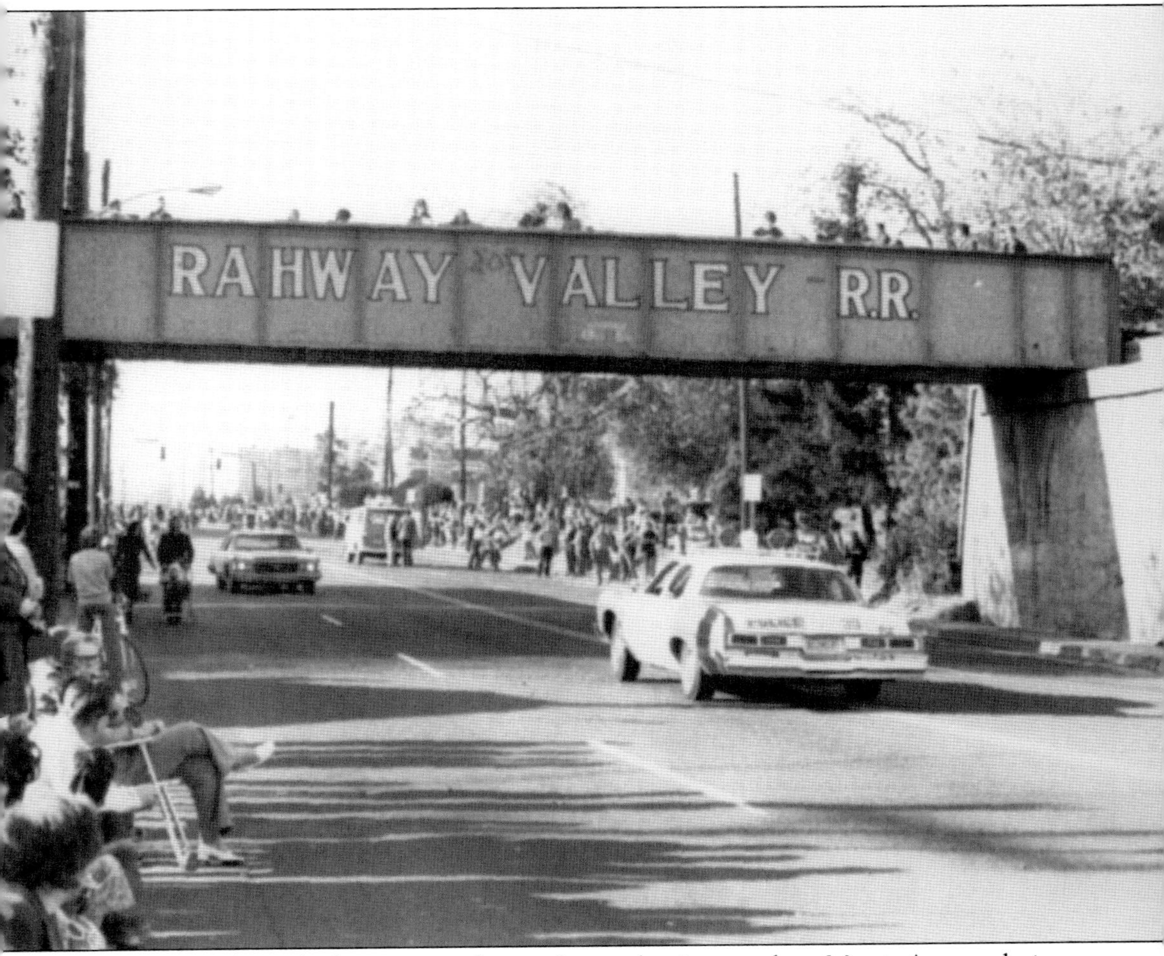

A parade—or at least the beginnings of a parade—makes its way along Morris Avenue during the mid-1970s. The Rahway Valley Railroad Bridge was one of Union Township's least attractive landmarks. Drivers of tractor-trailers used to get stuck under the bridge at regular intervals; the clearance is given as 13 feet, 6 inches, just under the "Rahway Valley R.R." sign, but the truck drivers would misjudge and jam their rigs under the trestle just the same. When the old bridge was finally pulled down, no one mourned the loss. (Courtesy of Howie Frisch.)

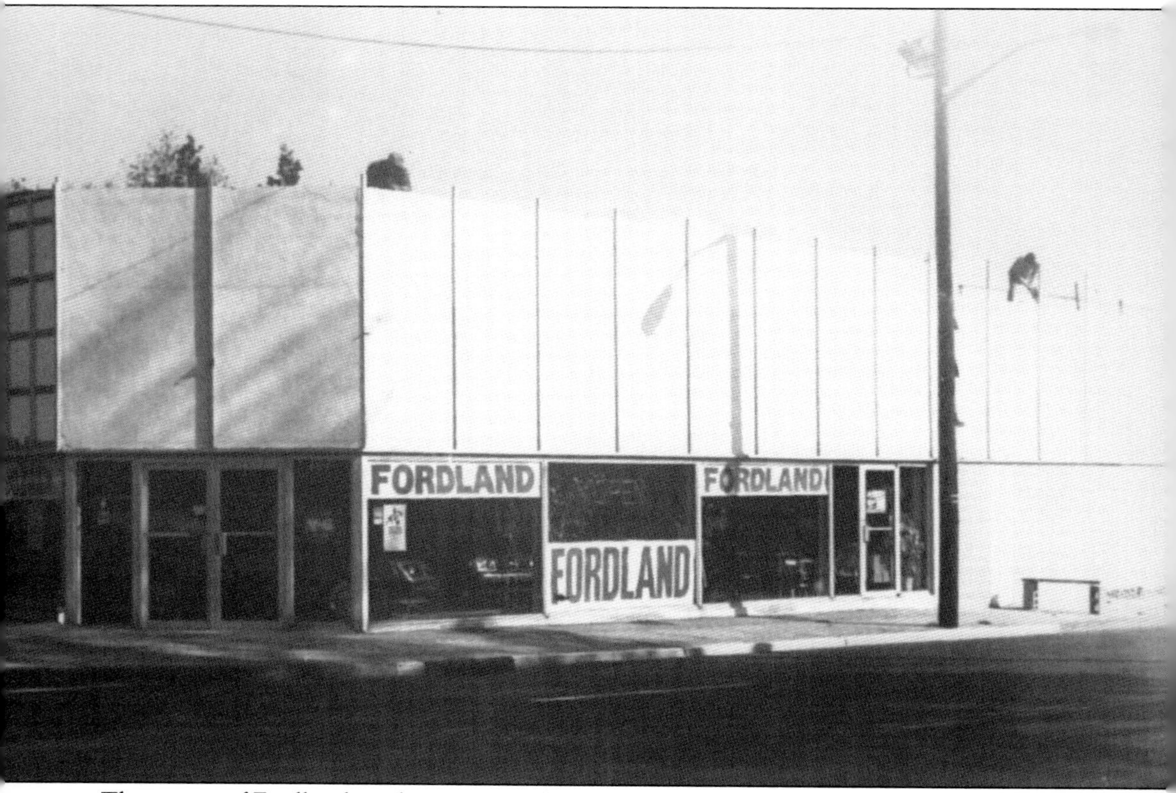

The owner of Fordland used temporary plain paper signs until the permanent signs were ready. Fordland, at the corner of Pine Avenue and Morris Avenue, has previously been Brown Ford, before Brown sold the business. Several other businesses have occupied the premises since Fordland disappeared, including a surgical supply firm. (Courtesy of Tom Haggerty)

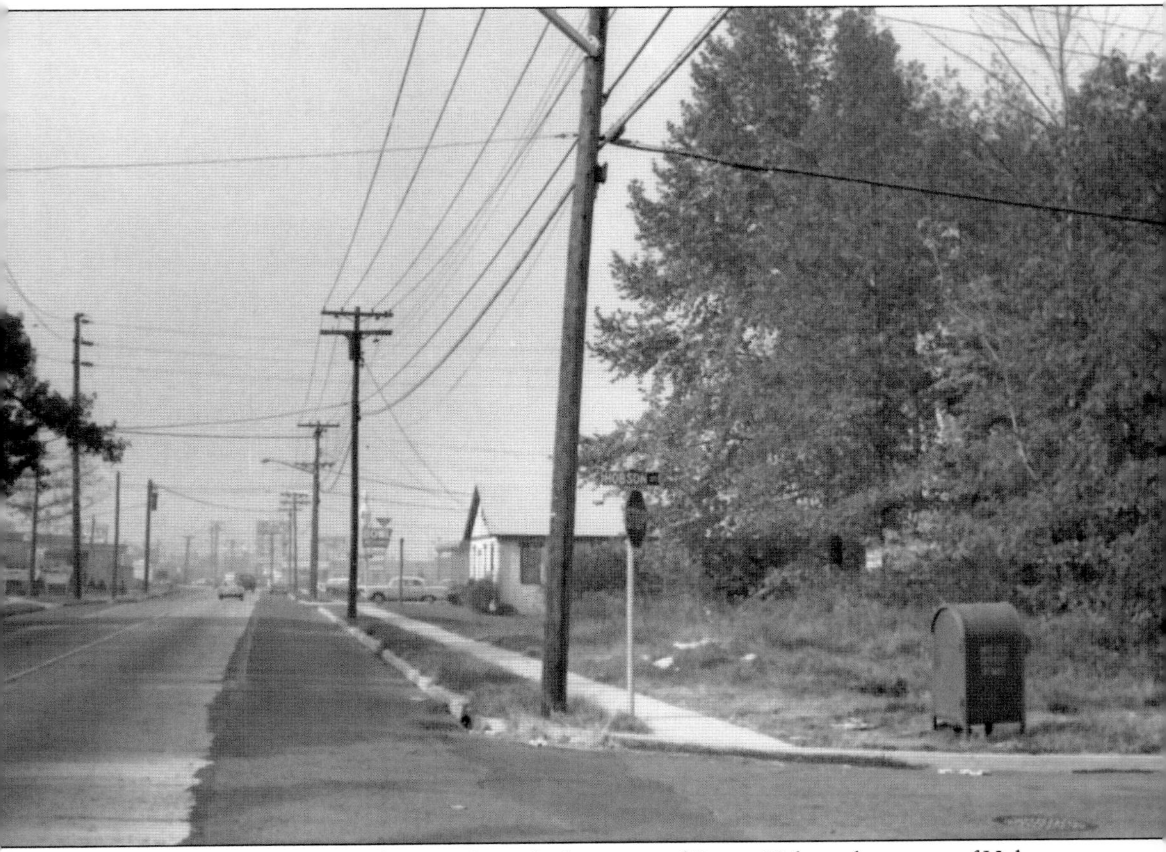

Pictured here is a view of West Chestnut Street looking toward Route 22 from the corner of Hobson Street on a summer day during the early 1960s. The sign for the Four Seasons is in the center, and R&S Stores is off in the distance. Beyond R&S, lost in the morning haze and not visible in the photograph, is the Flagship. Union's main branch of the post office, which would be on the left-hand side of the street, would not be built for several more years. (Courtesy of UTHS.)

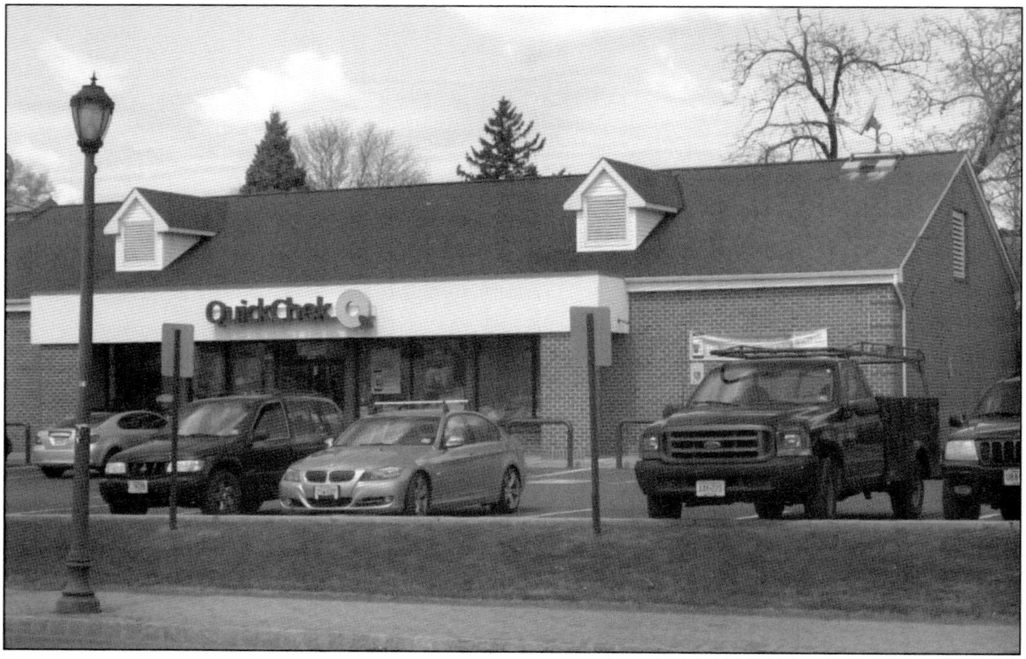

Pictured here is the corner of Stuyvesant Avenue and Vauxhall Road during the spring of 2015. A QuickChek fills the site once occupied by Corrigan's Village Inn Tavern. A local wit remarked that beer and whisky had been replaced by Coke and Pepsi. (Photograph by the author.)

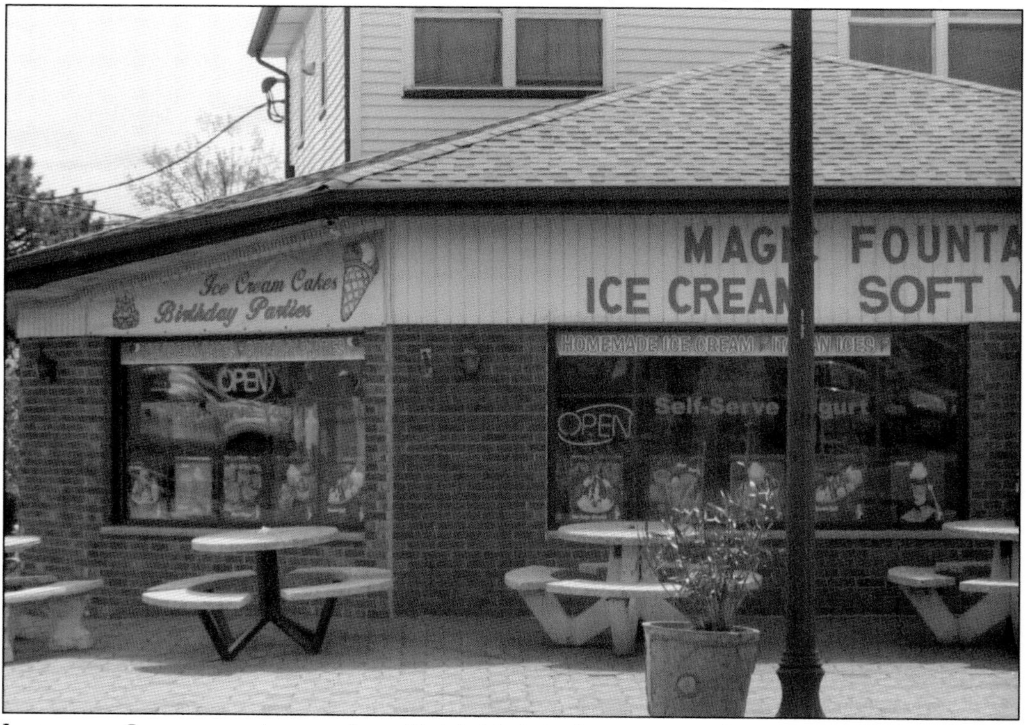

Just across Stuyvesant Avenue from QuickChek is the yogurt and ice-cream shop. The Esso service station that had stood on that particular spot has been gone for many years. (Photograph by the author.)

Two

The High School (and Other Schools)

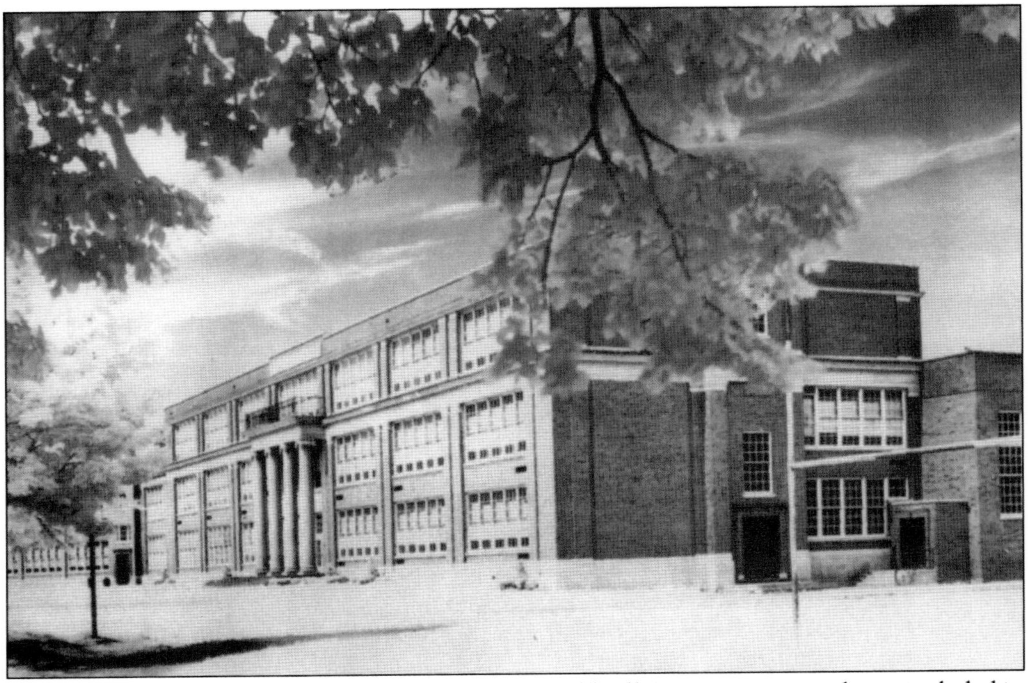

This is an artist's rendition of Union High School's Caldwell Avenue entrance that is included in the 1956 Union High yearbook. Six decades after the drawing was made, the building still looks very much the same. (Courtesy of Ralph H. Johnson.)

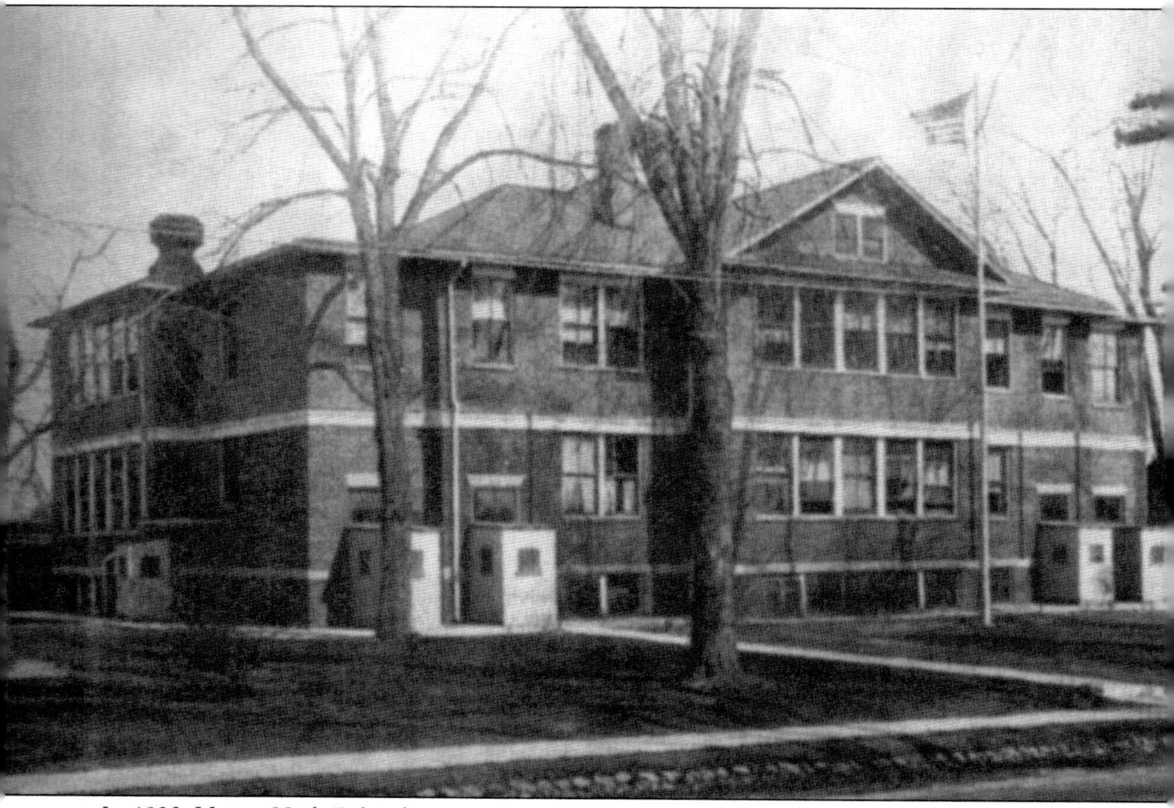

In 1923, Union High School was on Stuyvesant Avenue, across the street from the cemetery of Connecticut Farms Church and just up the hill from West Chestnut Street. Later in the decade, the school would move to its new quarters on Morris and Caldwell Avenues. The building would become the civic center, also known as the recreation center. This photograph is from the 1923 Union High School yearbook. (Courtesy Richard Pisz.)

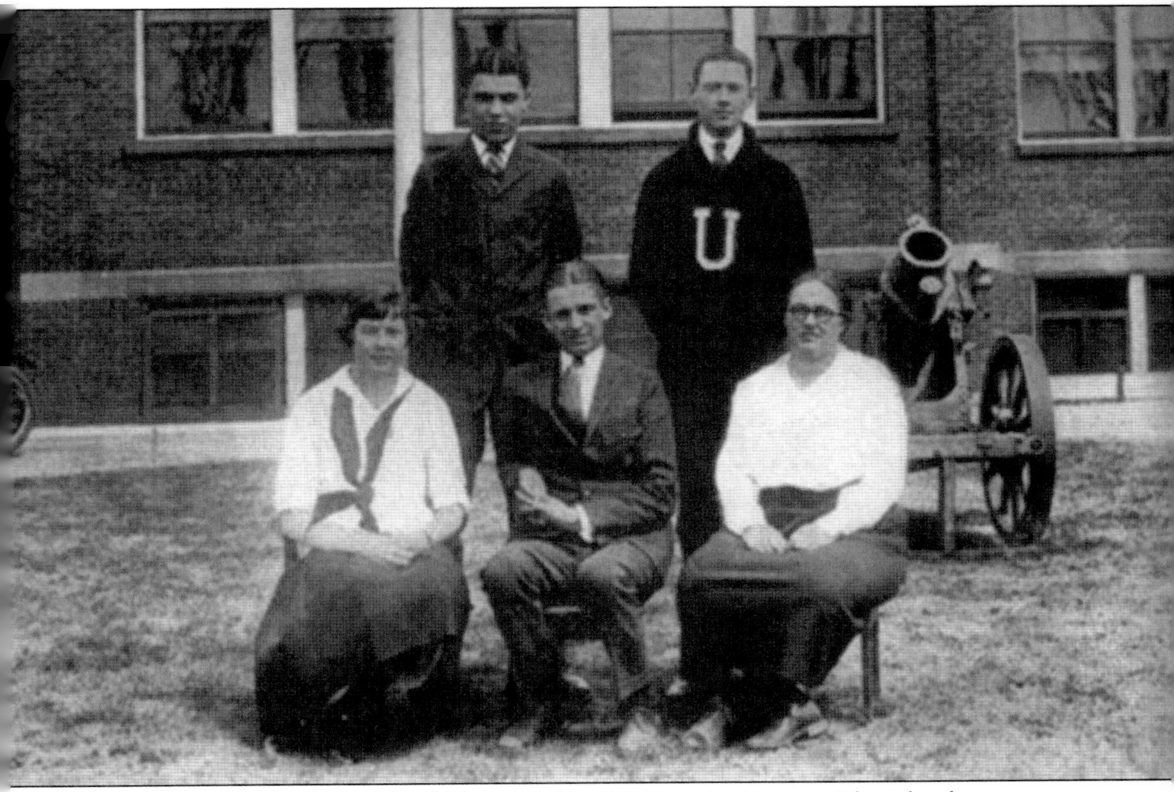

For many years, Union High School's foremost icon has been its cannon. The school newspaper was called the *Cannon*, and the high school seal also prominently features a cannon. In this photograph, which dates from the early 1920s, the debating team poses with an artillery piece of unknown origin. Nobody seems to know exactly what it is, where it came from, or what happened to it. (Courtesy of Richard Pisz.)

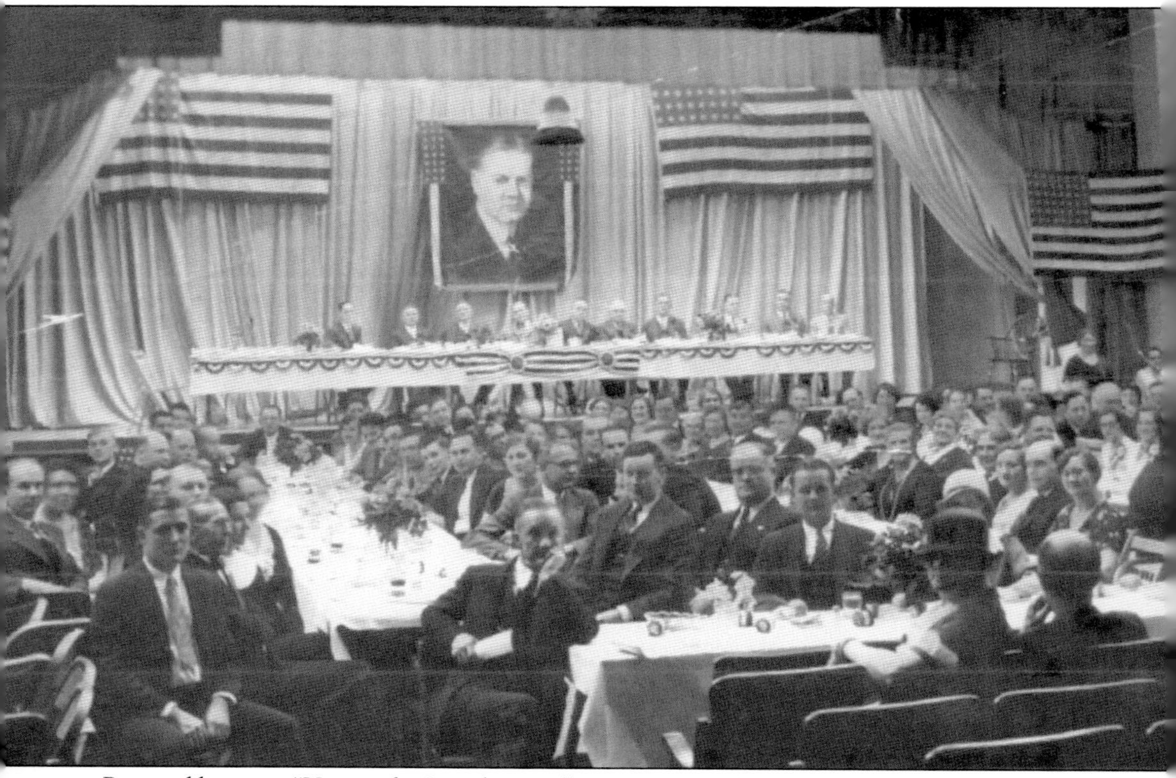

Pictured here is a "Hoover for President" rally at Union High School, likely in 1928. Republican candidate Herbert Hoover defeated Democrat Al Smith in a landslide that year. But four years later, Democrat Franklin D. Roosevelt reversed this result; in the depths of the Great Depression, Roosevelt offered Americans the New Deal and won an overwhelming victory over President Hoover. But the Republicans of Union Township backed Hoover in both elections, win or lose. No Republican would occupy the White House again until Dwight D. Eisenhower in 1953, two decades later. (Courtesy of UTHS.)

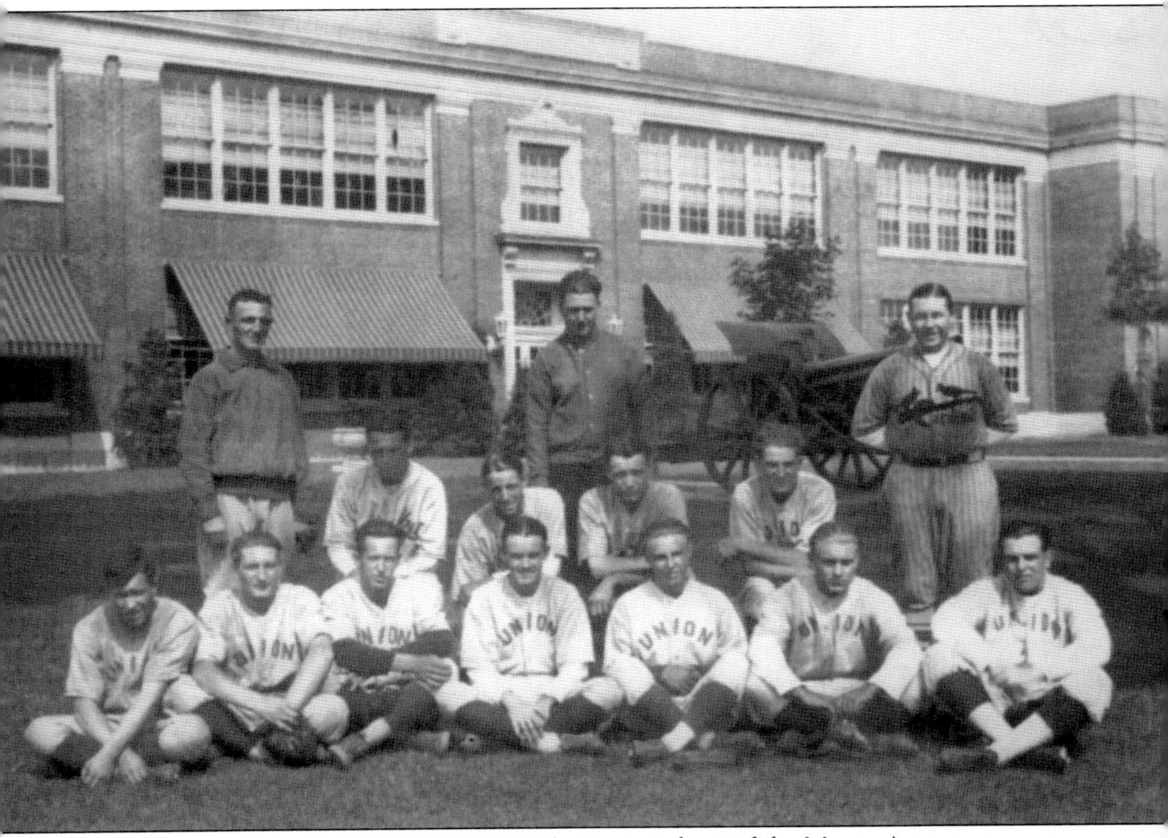

The Union Cardinals baseball team poses on the grass in front of the Morris Avenue entrance of Union High School. The unidentified man standing on the right is wearing a uniform that is obviously based on the uniform worn by the St. Louis Cardinals. One of the main points of interest is the front of the building, namely the striped awnings over the windows on the ground floor. Also, the high school cannon has acquired a coating of either black or dark gray paint. (Courtesy of UTHS.)

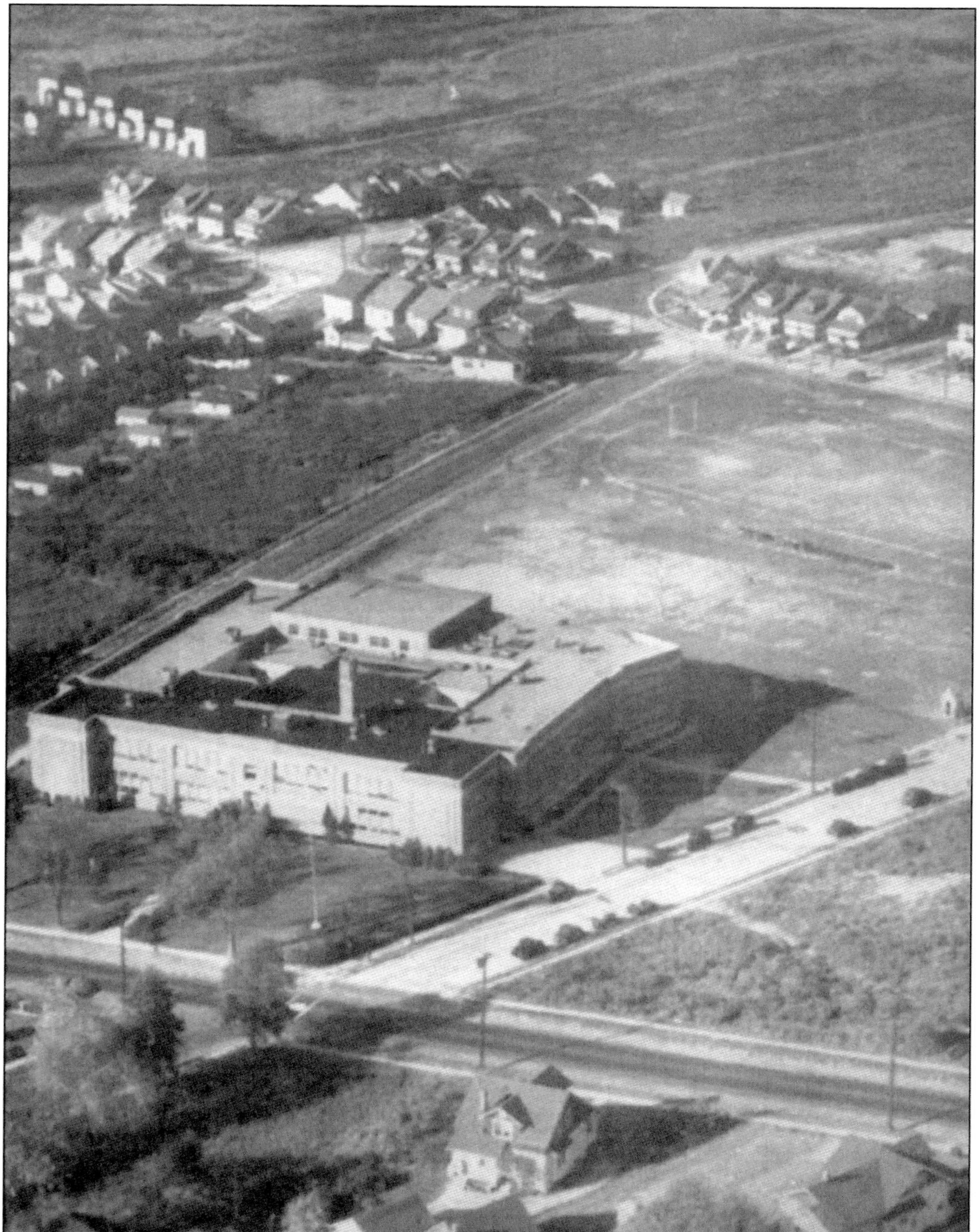

Union High School is pictured here from the air about 1930. The photograph was taken before the new addition to the school was built. This view gives some idea of how rural Union Township really was in those days, when there were more open fields than houses. Many streets were unpaved in the early 1930s, including Stuyvesant Avenue and stretches of Morris Avenue. (Courtesy of UTHS.)

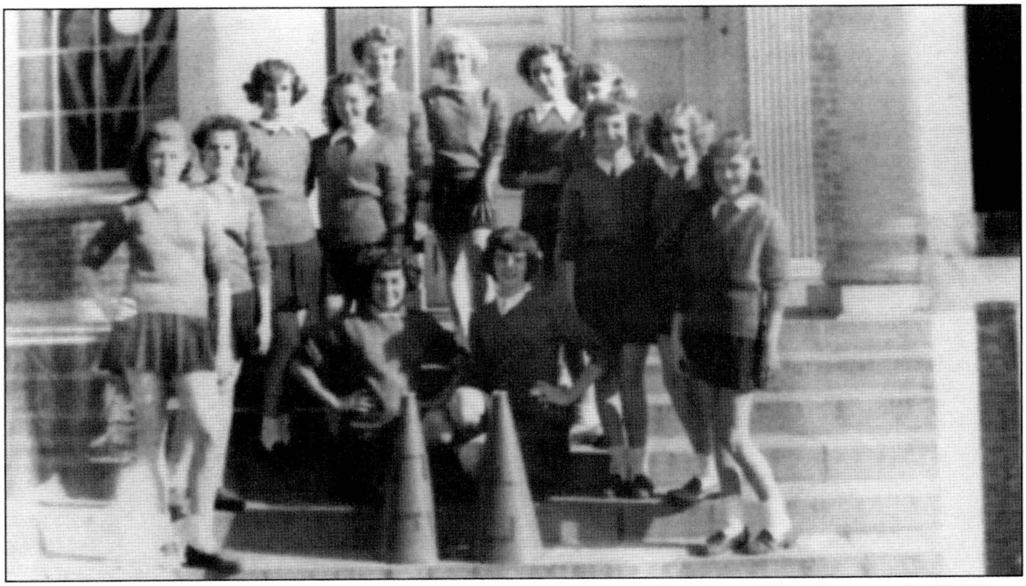

Pictured here is the cheerleading squad of Connecticut Farms School in 1950. The initials "C.F." are faintly visible on the megaphones. Cheerleaders made football games livelier and more animated, especially if the home team was losing. Sometimes, the cheerleading squads were better than the football teams. (Courtesy of UTHS.)

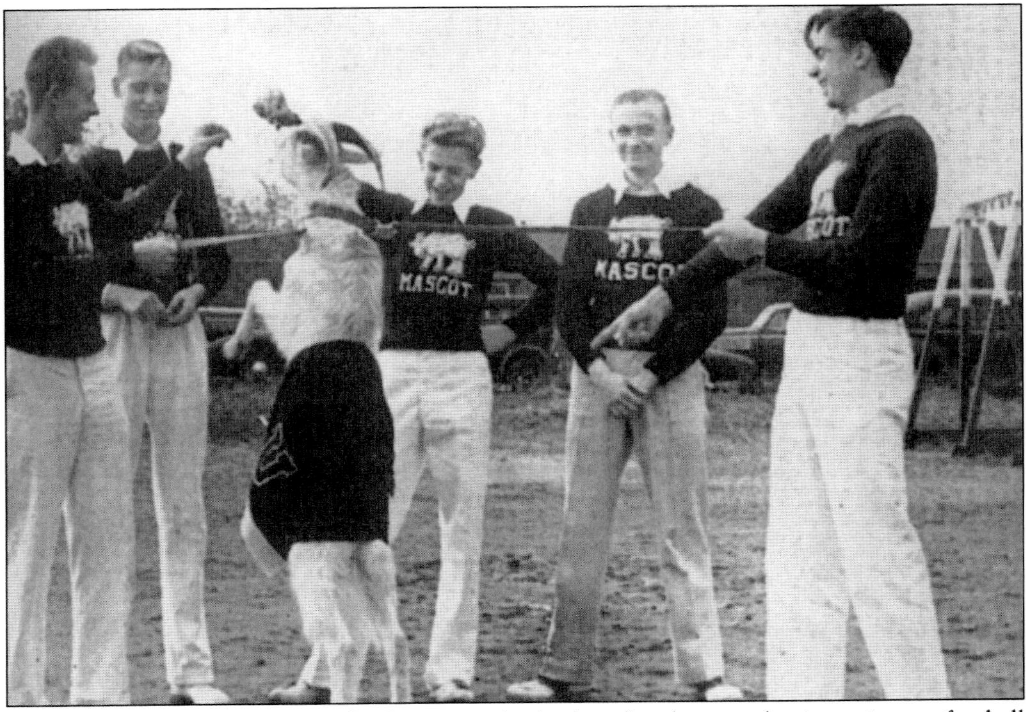

Union High School's mascot, Willie Butt, turns his back to the photographer just prior to a football game in 1942. According to a member of the Union High School football squad, Willie Butt was the mascot from the 1940s until the early 1960s. He lived in a barn on the Ideal Dairy Farm grounds, just a short distance away. The same source recalls that the school still had a mascot during the late 1960s, but he did not appear at every football game. (Courtesy of UTHS.)

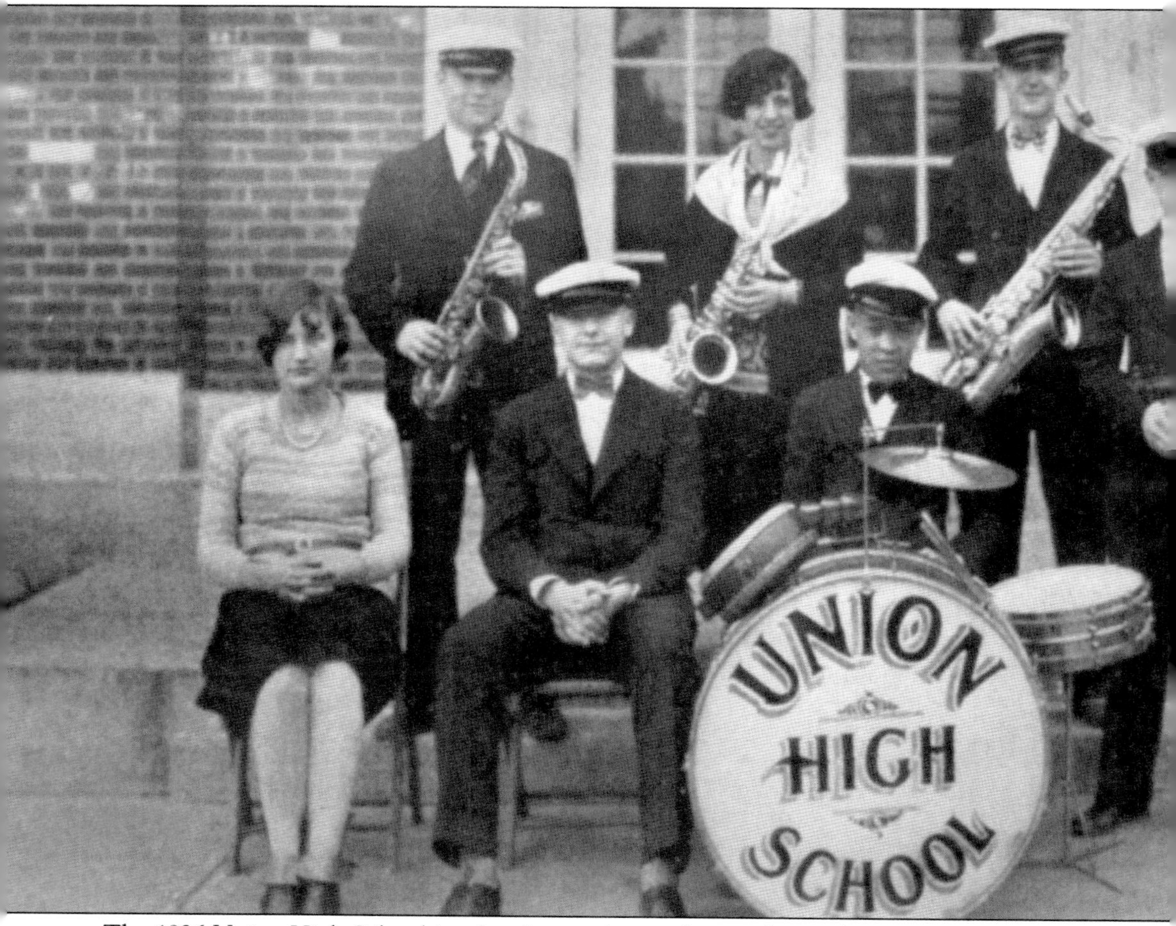

The 1926 Union High School jazz band, complete with saxophone players and a violinist, look very jazzy in their peaked caps and bow ties. Among the top songs of 1926 were "I'm Sittin' On Top of the World," performed by Al Jolson, "Birth of the Blues," by Paul Whiteman, and Fred Astaire's "Fascinating Rhythm." No record exists of what the Union High School jazz band was playing that year. Presumably, the group would have played all of the above new and controversial songs. (Courtesy of UTHS.)

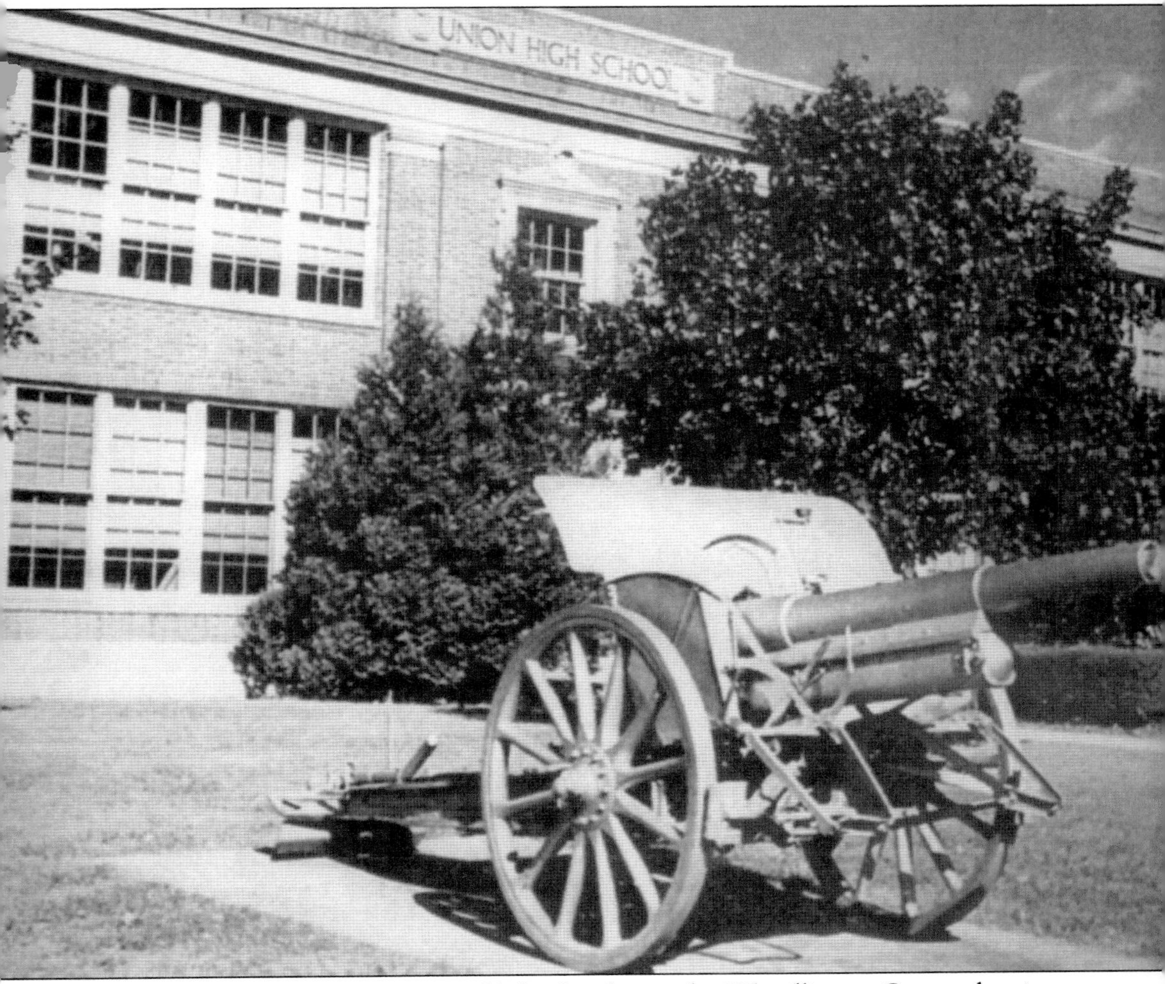

One of Union Township's most recognizable landmarks was the 105-millimeter German howitzer that graced the Morris Avenue entrance of Union High School. The big gun was captured from the Germans during World War I, and it was donated to a scrap dealer during World War II. According to an account in an August 1969 edition of the *Union Leader*, the junk dealer "thought it would look nice in his front yard" and decided to keep it as a sort of outsized lawn ornament instead of breaking it up as part of the war effort. "The senior boys didn't like that very much" and decided to take the cannon back. About 50 or 60 boys attached the gun to the rear end of a truck and towed it back to its ancestral home on Morris Avenue. The junk dealer threatened to press charges against the boys for making off with his property, but nothing ever came of his threat. (Courtesy of UTHS.)

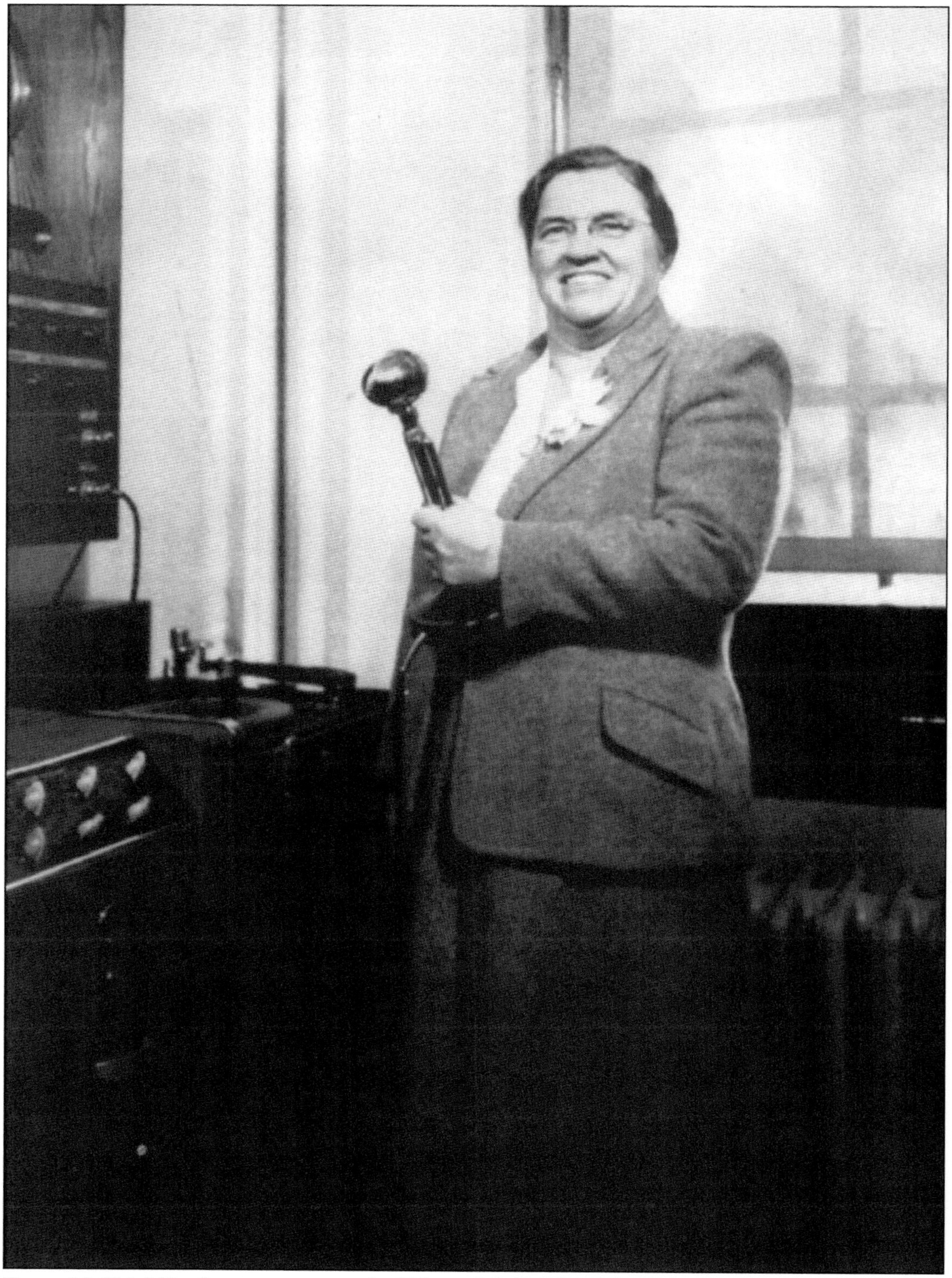

Grace M. "Ma" Durling was principal of Union High School from the 1920s to the early 1950s. She was also, at various times during her tenure, coach for the boys' basketball, football, and baseball teams and the girls' basketball team. Durling had a no-nonsense approach when it came to discipline and could make life extremely unpleasant for anyone who broke the rules. In this undated photograph, she is smiling—something she rarely did while on the job, at least according to those who remember her well. (Courtesy of UTHS.)

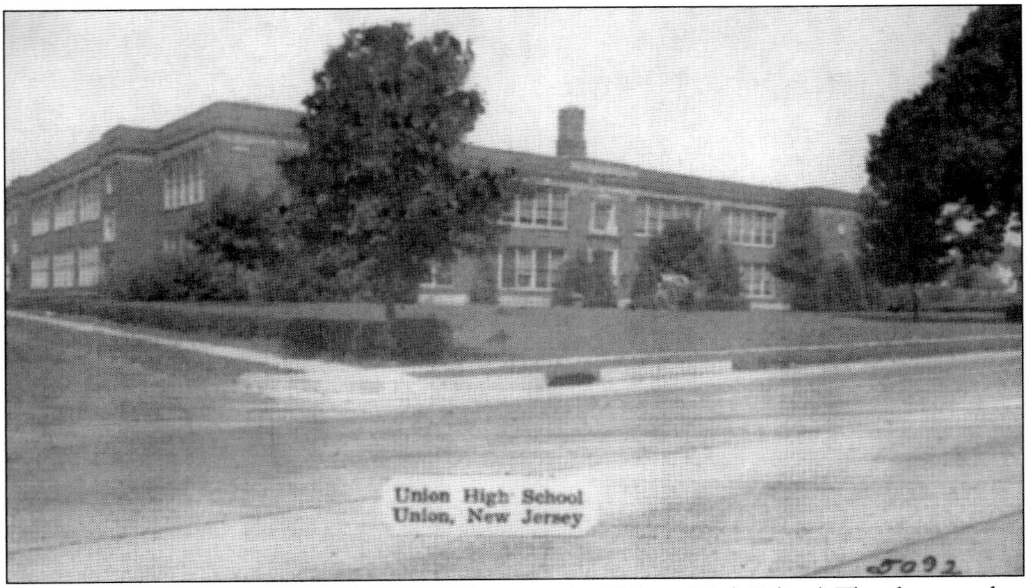

Pictured here in the late 1940s is the Morris Avenue side of Union High School. The photographer used a wide-angle lens for this shot; even though he was standing just on the other side of Morris Avenue, the building seems a mile away. Barely visible in the center of the photograph is the school's famous cannon. (Courtesy of UTHS.)

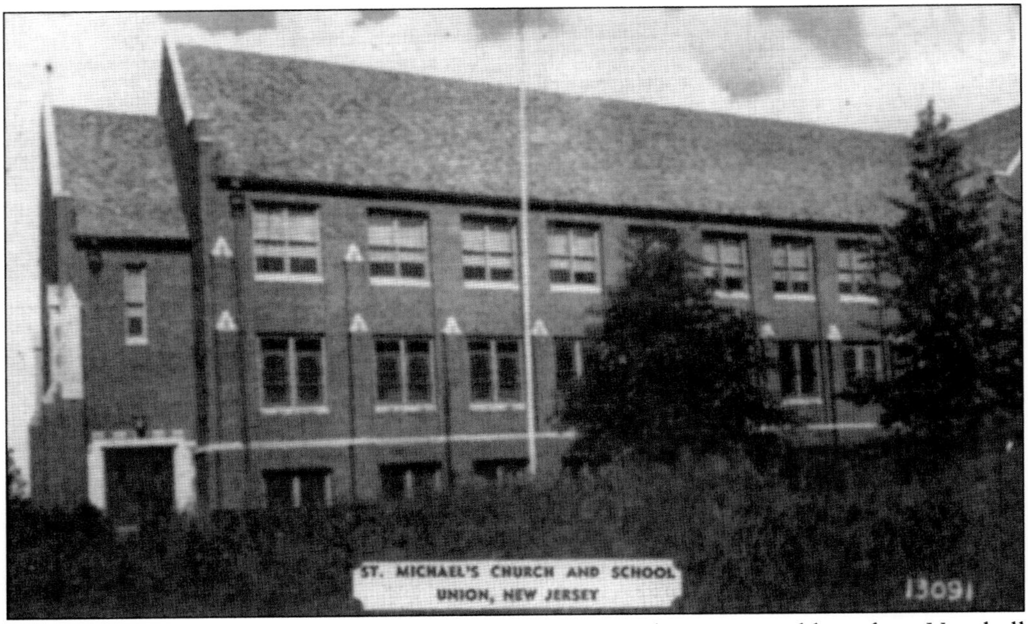

St. Michael's School, with the church just visible to the right, is pictured here from Vauxhall Road. The photograph probably dates from the 1940s, but the view has not changed very much over the years. The students of St. Michaels still wear their distinctive uniforms, another item that has stayed the same. (Courtesy of UTHS.)

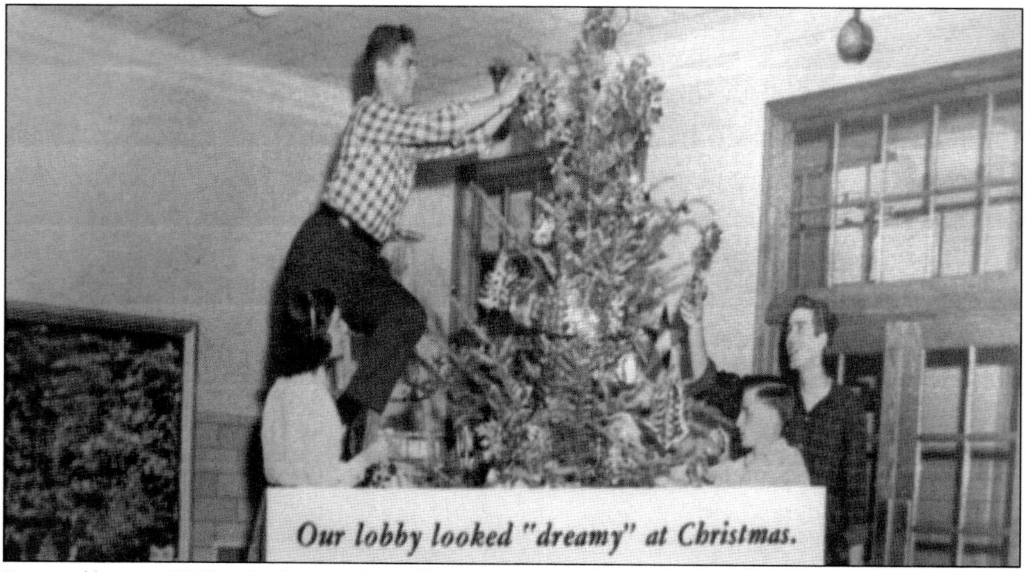

Pictured here in 1955 is the "dreamy" Caldwell Avenue lobby of Union High School at Christmastime. Trying not to fall off the ladder when placing the star, Ralph H. Johnson (class of 1956) helps friends decorate the Christmas tree for the benefit of the photographer. This lobby is now the main entrance of Burnet Middle School. (Courtesy of UTHS.)

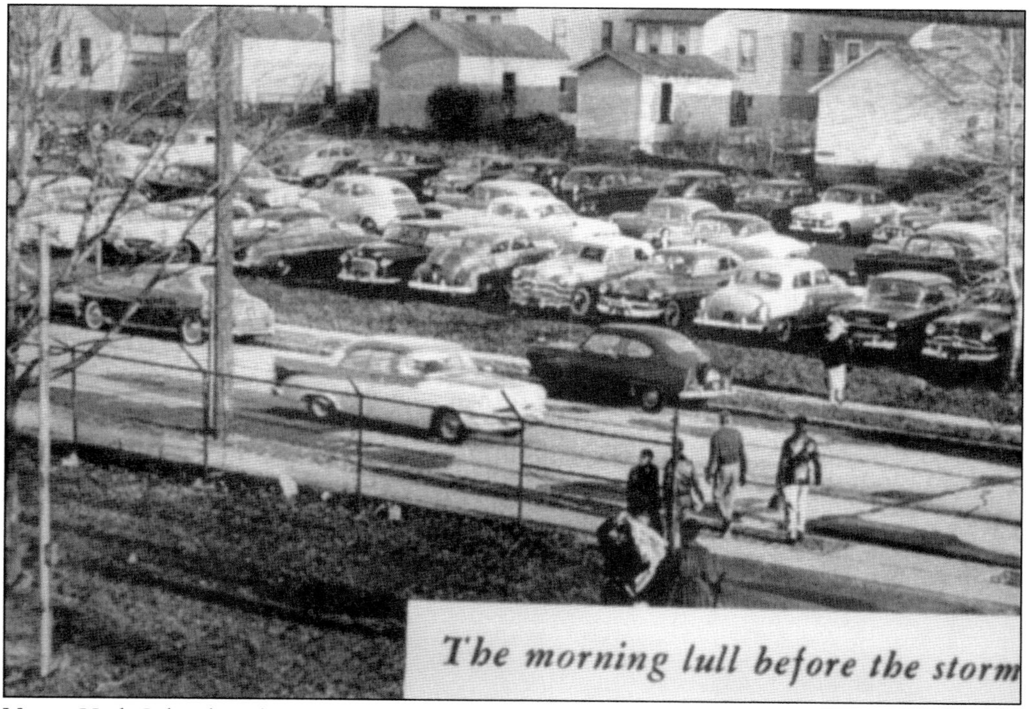

Union High School students park their cars in the lot on Jeanette Avenue before trudging off to their morning classes in 1956. The houses in the background are on Woolley Avenue. The high school's Caldwell Avenue entrance was three streets away. Even though the price of gasoline was only about 19¢ per gallon, it still would have been cheaper and easier for most of the students to walk from home. (Courtesy of UTHS.)

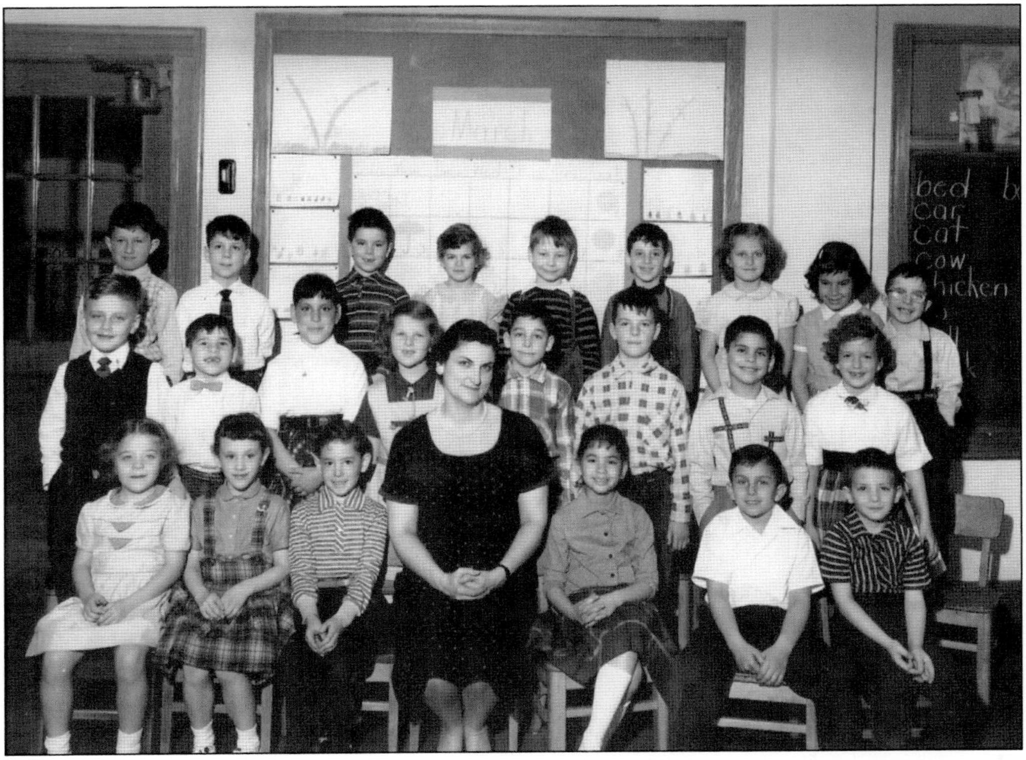

Mrs. Fadden's first grade class from the Franklin School is pictured here in March 1958. This is a fairly typical-looking grammar school class from that era—well-scrubbed, well-fed, and cheerful. In the nation's collective mind's eye, everybody was cheerful and prosperous back in the Eisenhower era. The chubby kid standing on the far left of the middle row is the author. (Author's collection.)

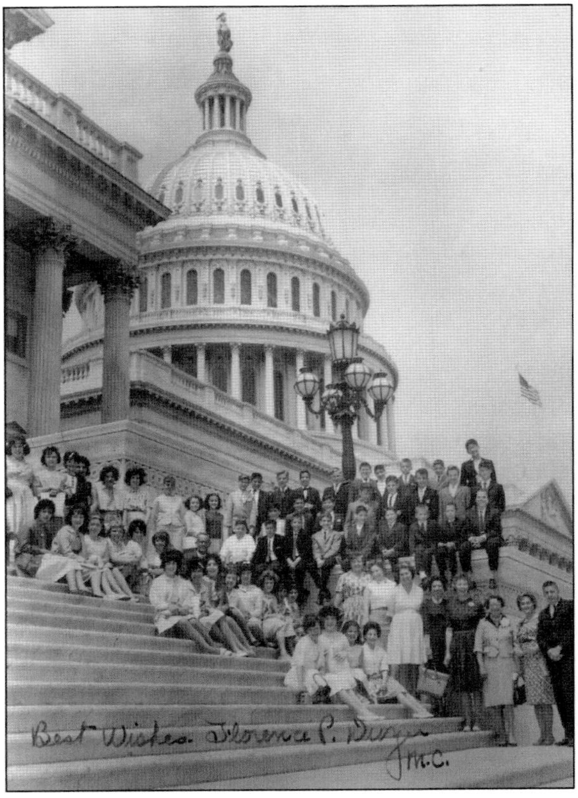

Franklin School's sixth-grade class visits Washington, DC, in May 1963, when John F. Kennedy was president. Congresswoman Florence P. Dwyer is the third person from the left. Four months after this photograph was taken, these kids would go on to junior high—half to Kawameeh Junior High School, the other half to Burnet Junior High School. Many Franklin School graduates regretted having their class broken up, which meant losing contact with classmates they had known since kindergarten. (Author's collection.)

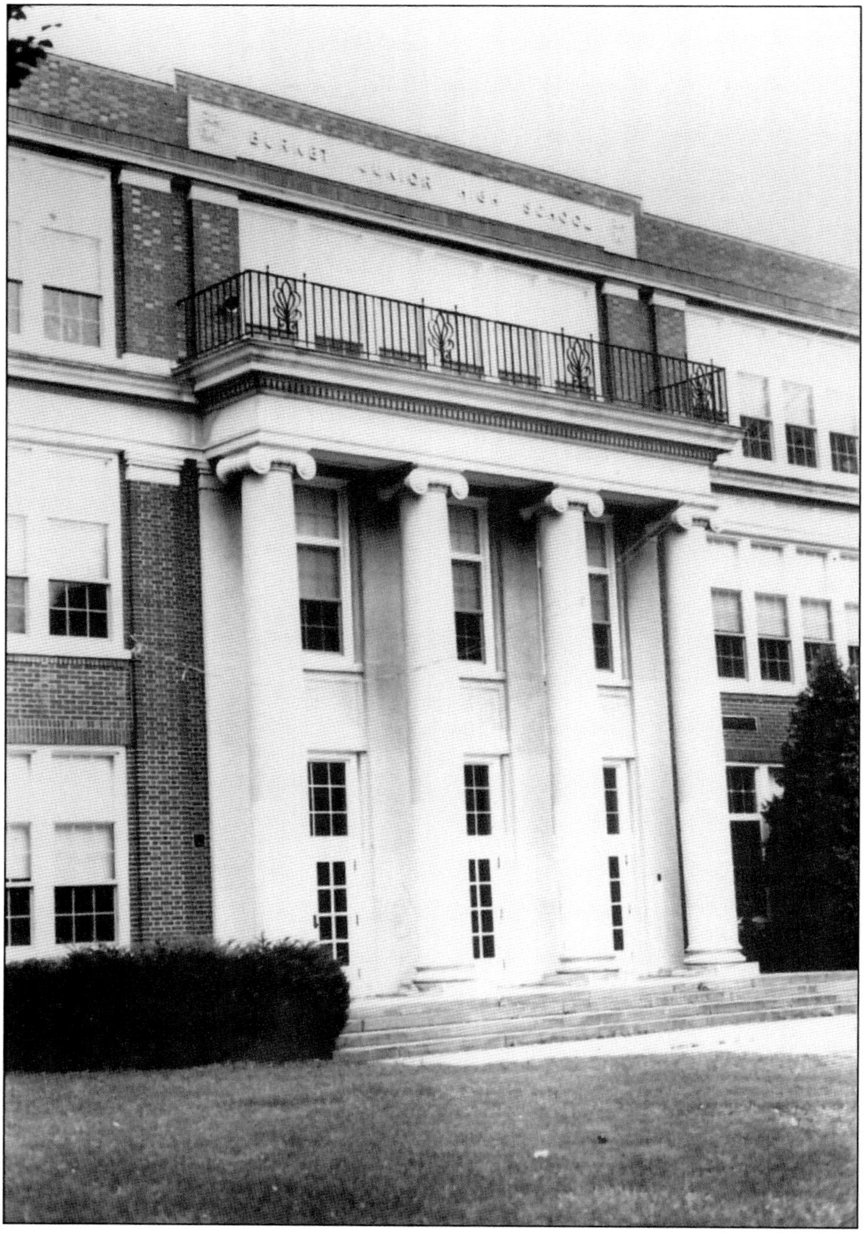

This photograph, taken around 1970, is of Burnet Junior High School, which had only just relocated from North Third Street. The staid Ionic columns that once graced the main entrance of Union High School and, later on, Burnet Junior High School now perform the same function for Burnet Middle School. The columns are actually two-tone; about one-third of the way up, they suddenly become a bit darker. They have been that way since the fall of 1966. Just as the 1966–1967 school year was about to begin, members of the Union High School class of 1967 painted 1967 on the columns in white paint, with one number per column. ("Class of '67" was also painted all over the outside of the building, also in white paint.) School authorities had the numbers sandblasted off the columns, but only about one-third of the way up. The rest of the columns were left as is, probably to save on sandblasting fees. The lines of demarcation become a bit less visible with each passing year, but they are still there. (Courtesy of UTHS.)

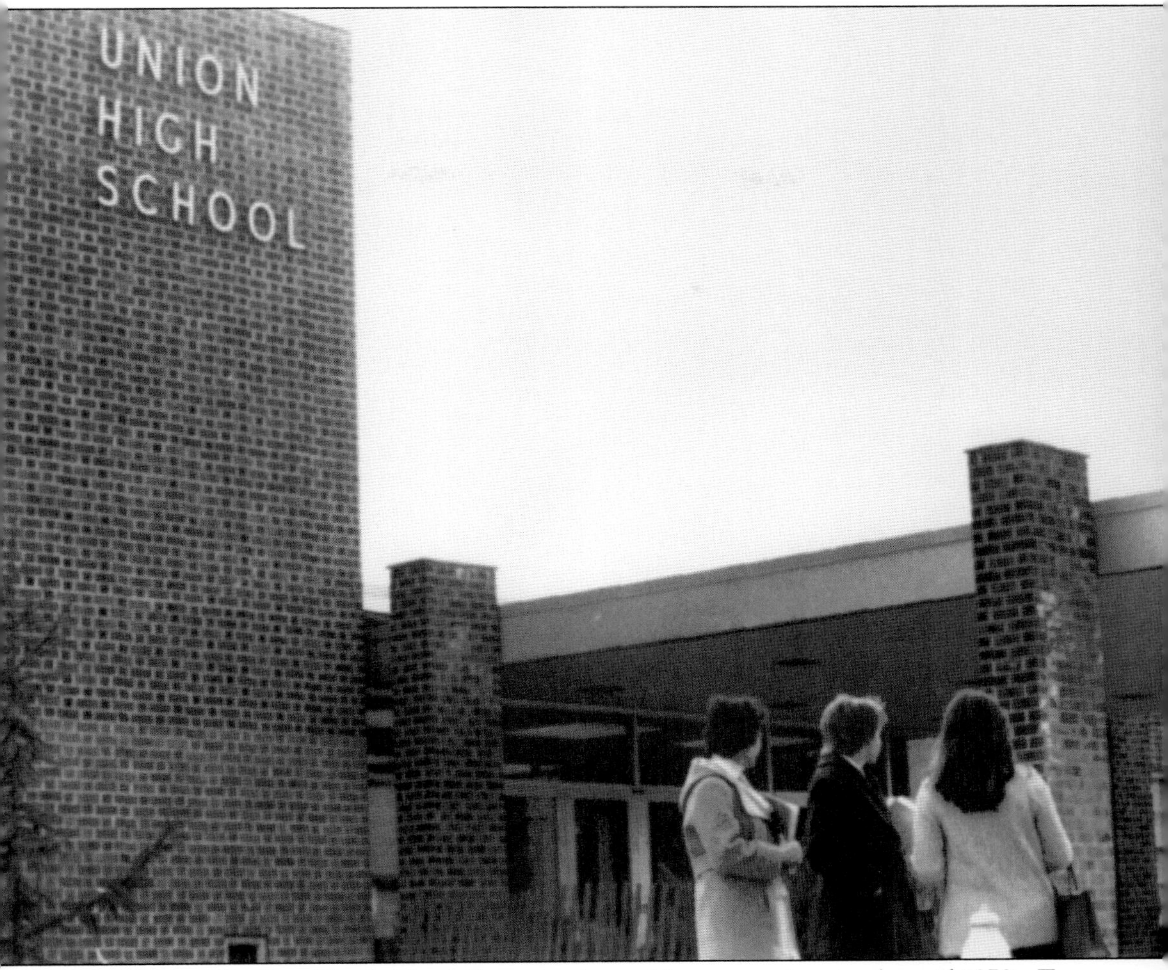

Union High School on North Third Street is pictured here sometime in the mid-1970s. To people of a certain age, this is the new high school. The first group of students to graduate from this building was the class of 1970. Prior to the 1969–1970 academic year, the building had been Burnet Junior High School. Burnet moved into the old high school building, on the corner of Morris and Caldwell Avenues, in September 1969. (Courtesy of Howie Frisch.)

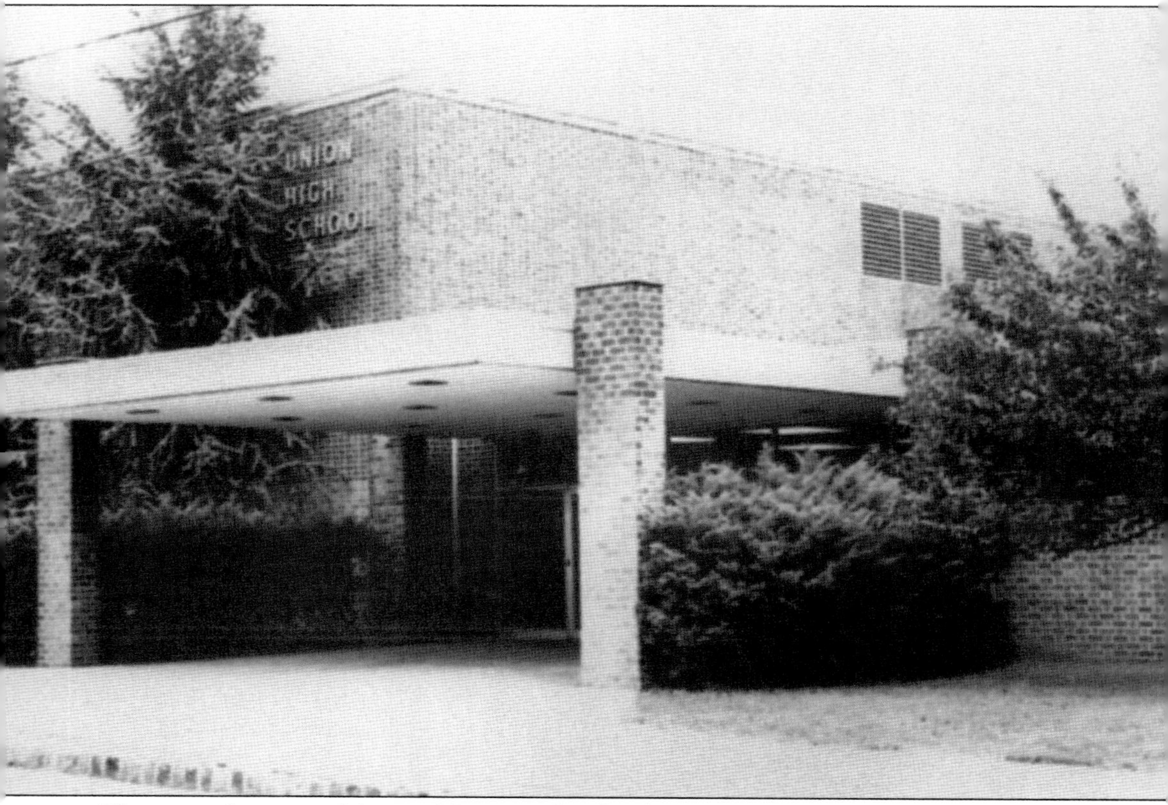

This is another view of the new Union High School on North Third Street. The photograph has no date, but it was probably taken in the early 1970s, shortly after the move from Morris Avenue. (Courtesy of UTHS.)

Three

MAYOR ED

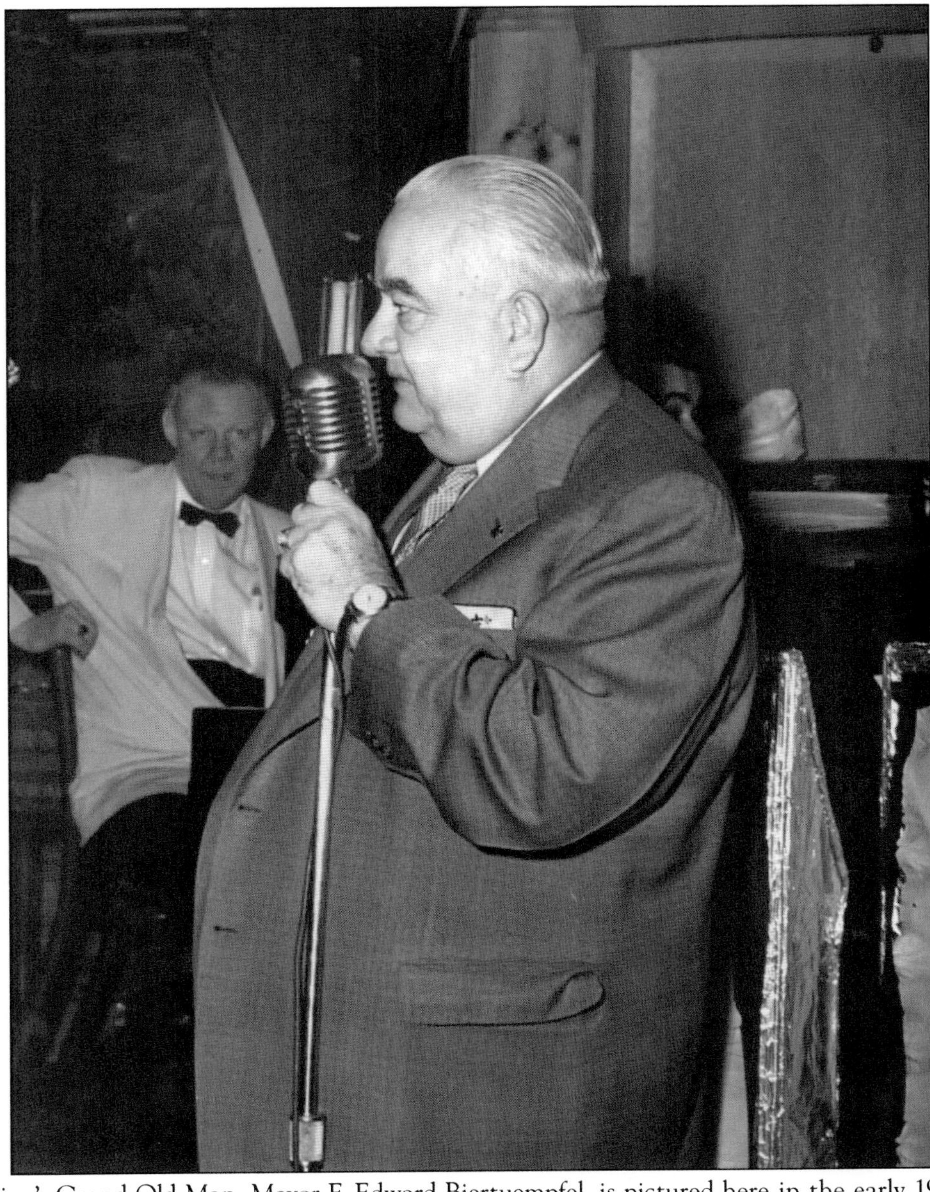

Union's Grand Old Man, Mayor F. Edward Biertuempfel, is pictured here in the early 1960s. Mayor Biertuempfel was regarded as "Mr. Union" from 1939, when he first became mayor, until his death in 1973. There are very many who consider the Biertuempfel years to be Union's golden era. (Courtesy of UTHS.)

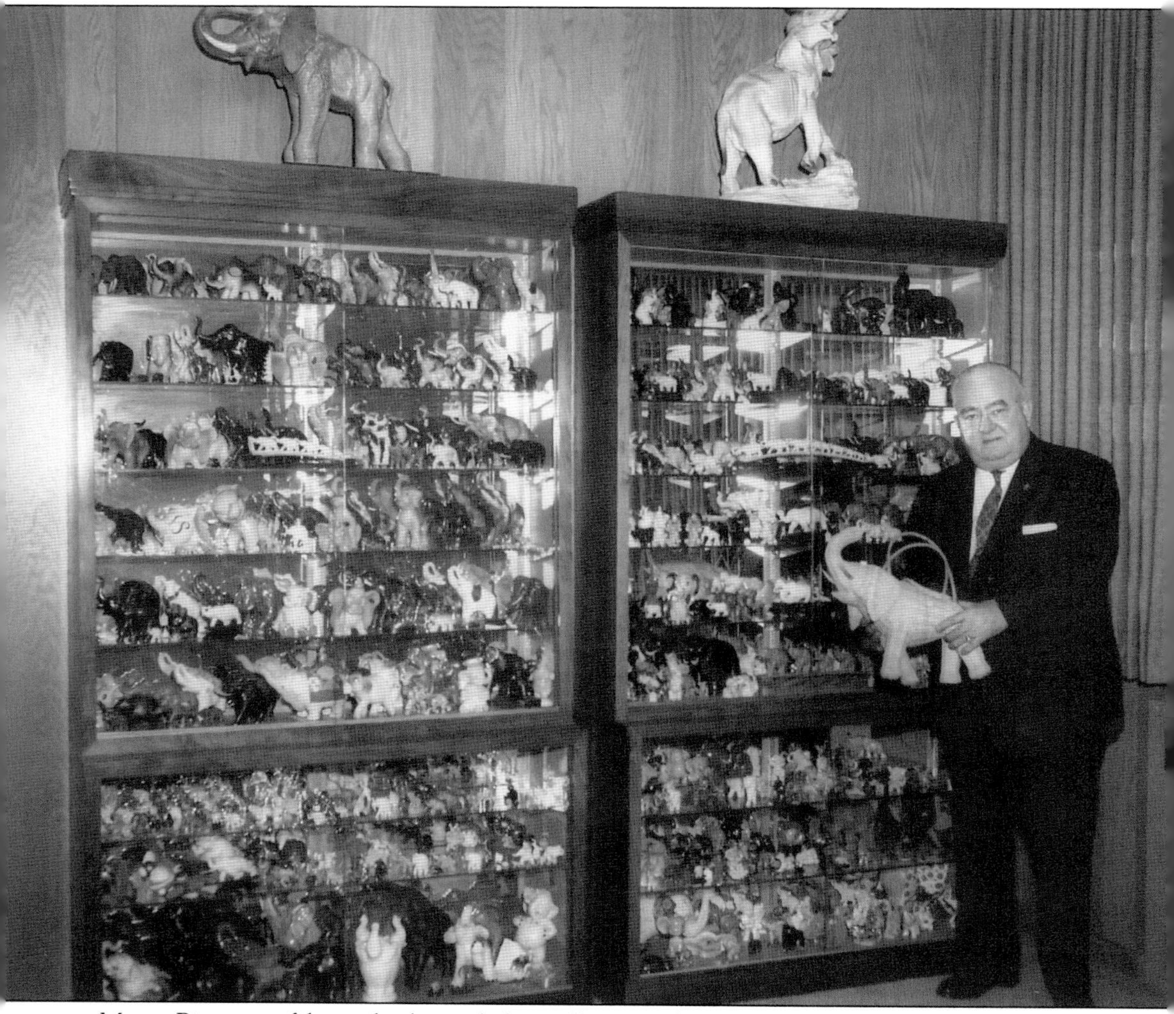

Mayor Biertuempfel stands alongside his collection of ceramic elephants in the 1960s. Friends and acquaintances had given him many elephant statuettes over the years. He acquired so many that he had to keep them in a glass case. Because the elephant is the symbol of the Republican party, and Biertuempfel was the leader of the Republicans since the 1930s, the mayor's collection certainly was appropriate. (Courtesy of UTHS.)

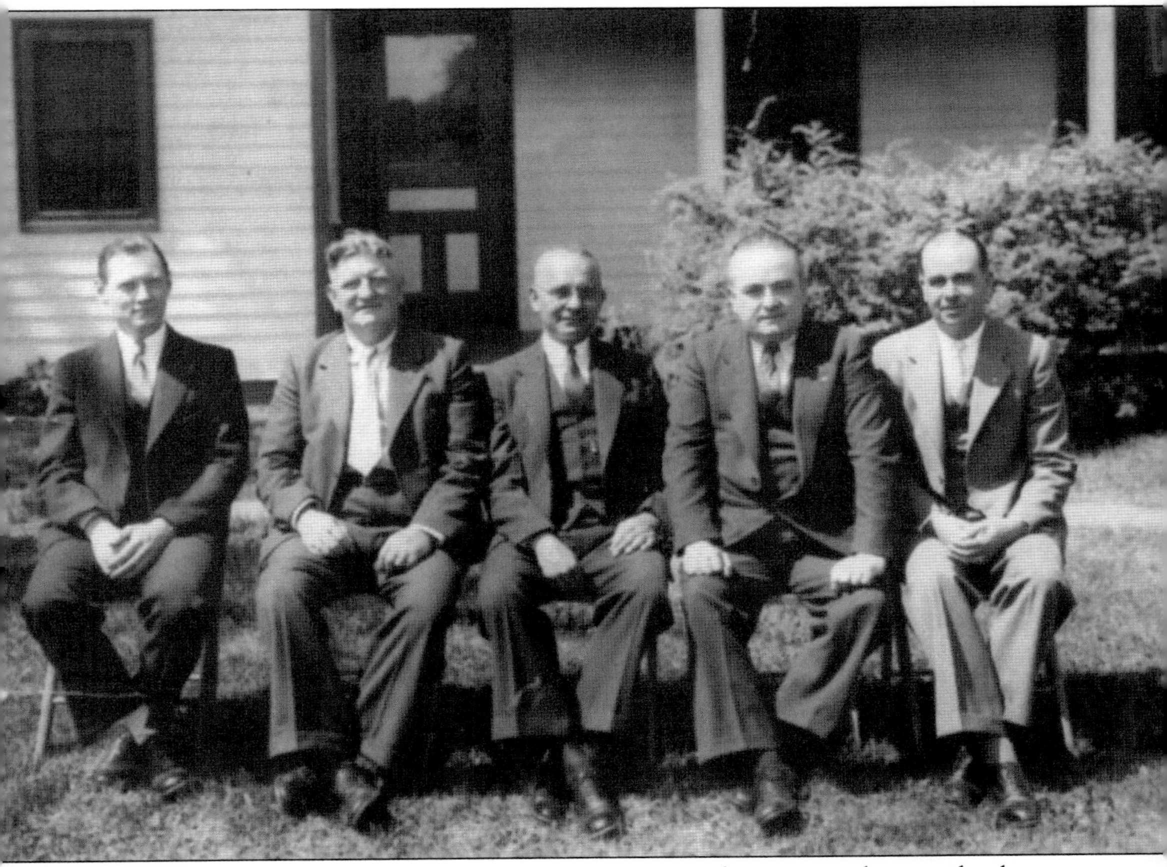

These are the Union Township's committee members in the mid-1930s, in a photograph taken at police headquarters on Caldwell Avenue. Mayor Charles Schramm (center) is flanked by, from left to right, committeemen Nelson Kieb, William Northnagel, F. Edward Biertuempfel, and Benjamin Romano. Biertuempfel had been on the township committee since 1930 but would not become mayor for several more years. At the time, Union was still very rural and undeveloped—the police headquarters was little more than a glorified two-story house. During the coming decade, the town would become much more suburban and developed. (Courtesy of UTHS.)

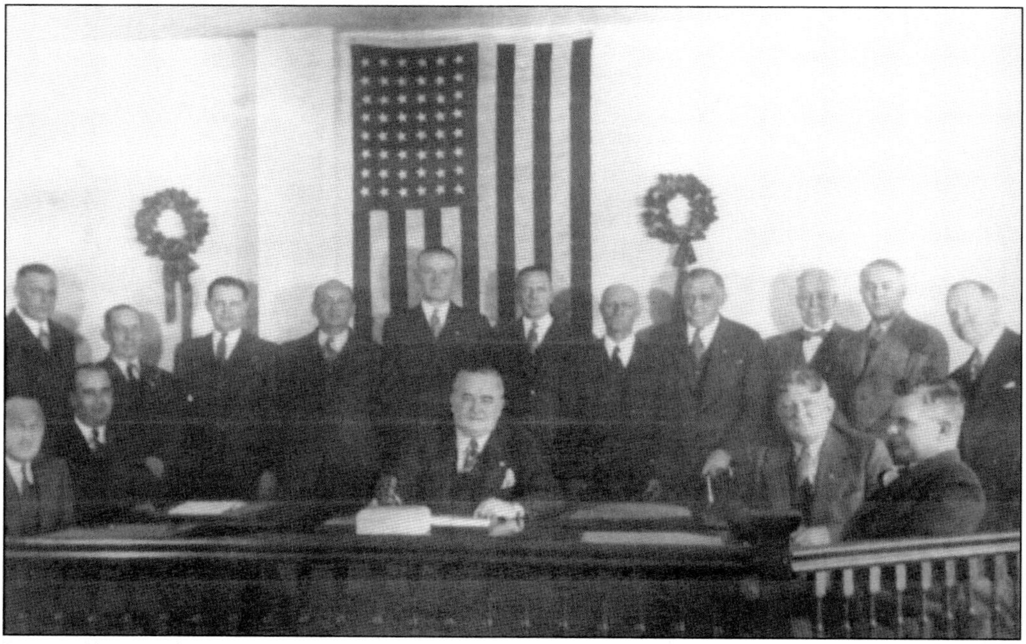

Pictured here is the Union Township's organization meeting in January 1939, shortly after F. Edward Biertuempfel was appointed mayor for the first time. He would go on to be appointed mayor for the next 34 consecutive years. This meeting was held at Union's municipal offices and meeting hall at 2004 Morris Avenue, across the street from Union Center National Bank and just down the street from Walgreens Drugs. Note the 48-star American flag in the background; Alaska and Hawaii would not become states for another 20 years, in 1959. (Courtesy of UTHS.)

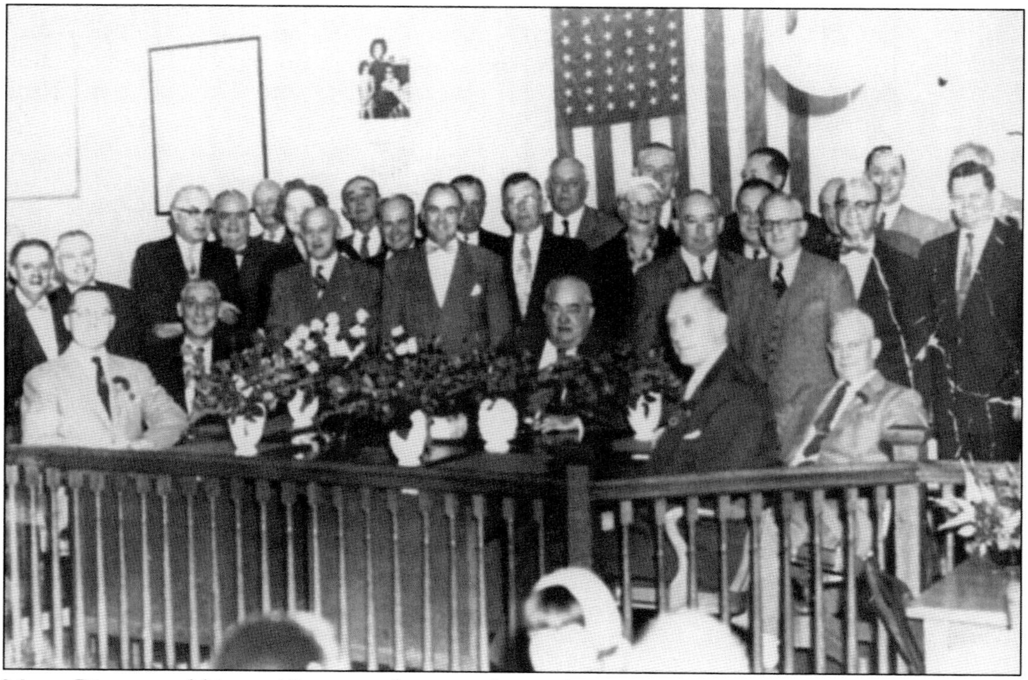

Mayor Biertuempfel is presiding over the annual township organization meeting on New Year's Day 1955. At this point in time, he had been mayor of Union for 16 years. (Courtesy of UTHS.)

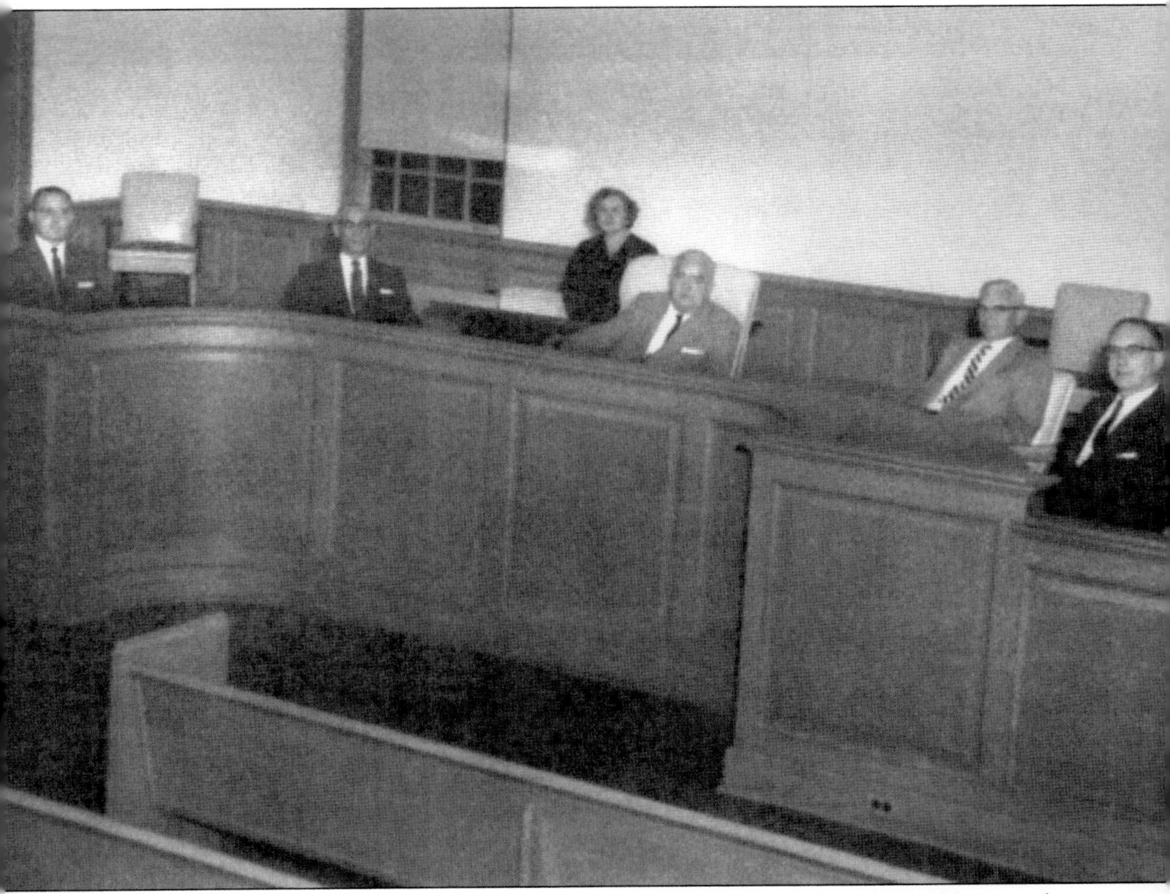

In 1957, the township committee moved from 2004 Morris Avenue, in the Falls Building, to the brand-new municipal building in Freiburger Park. In the photograph, the committee meets at its new home for the first time. The members are, from left to right, Robert Ostertag, Koloman G. Kiss, Mary E. Miller (township clerk), F. Edward Biertuempfel (mayor), Robert R. Lackey, and Roy E. Kitchell. (Courtesy of UTHS.)

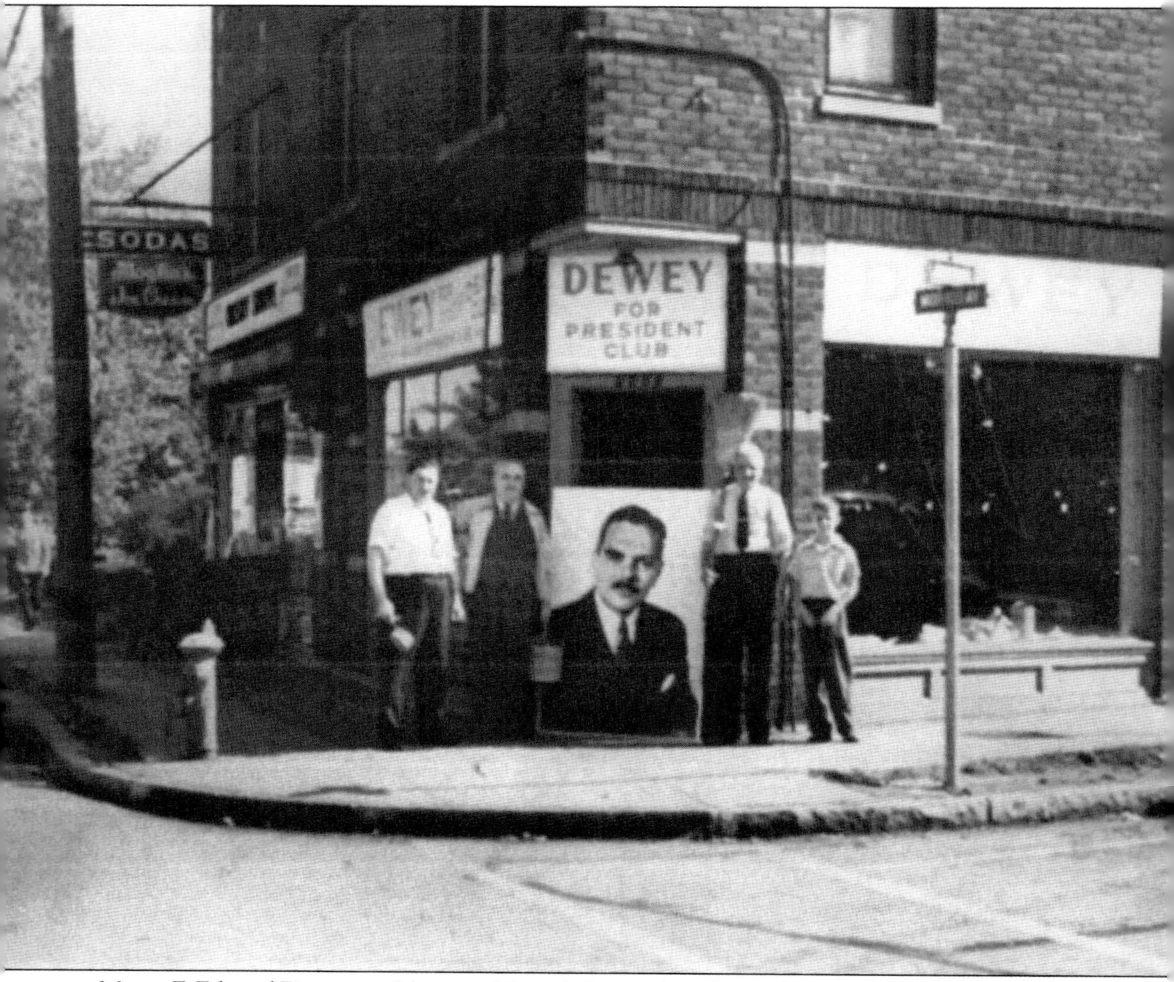

Mayor F. Edward Biertuempfel, second from left, stands in front of the "Dewey for President Club" headquarters on the corner of Johnson Place and Morris Avenue in 1948. Thomas E. Dewey was predicted to win the election that year, but incumbent president Harry S. Truman fooled all the experts and won another four-year term that November. The site, including the ice-cream shop next door, is now the car park for the doctors' offices just up the street on Morris Avenue. (Courtesy of UTHS.)

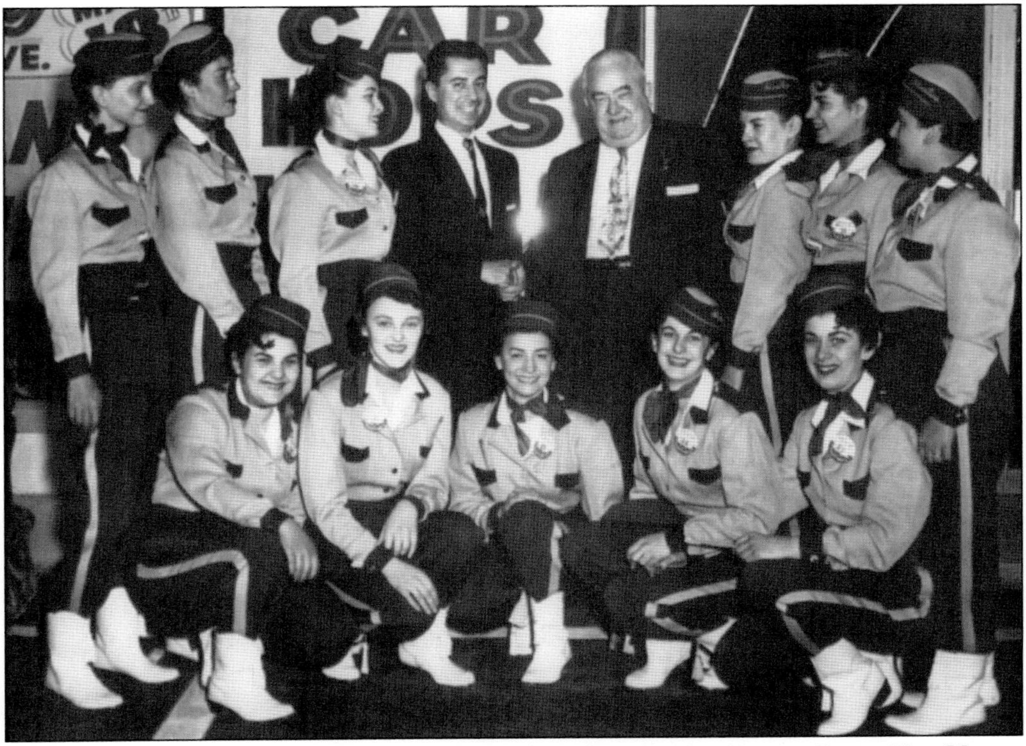

Mayor Biertuempfel poses with the waitresses at the Adventure Car Hop, on Route 22 in Union, along with one of the car hop's owners, John Skugaras, in the late 1950s. There were other car hops in the area, as well; the Big Top Car Hop and the Garden of Eatin' were two others. These car hops, or at least the Adventure, had reputations for being safe havens for drag racers who regularly disrupted traffic on Route 22. The police hated the Adventure Car Hop, while teenagers—or at least those who had fast cars—loved the place. It went out of business either in 1959 or 1960. (Courtesy of UTHS.)

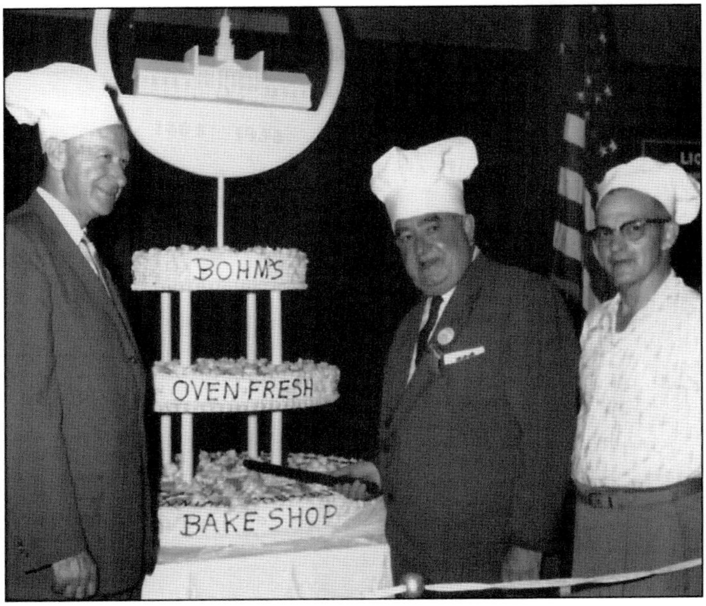

Mayor Biertuempfel and township committeeman Samuel Rabkin pose with Rudolph Bohm, the owner of Bohm's Oven Fresh Bake Shop. Biertuempfel and Rabkin are each wearing a white toque—the traditional chef's or, in this case, baker's hat. This photograph dates from 1958; the cake commemorates the 150th anniversary of Union Township. (Courtesy of UTHS.)

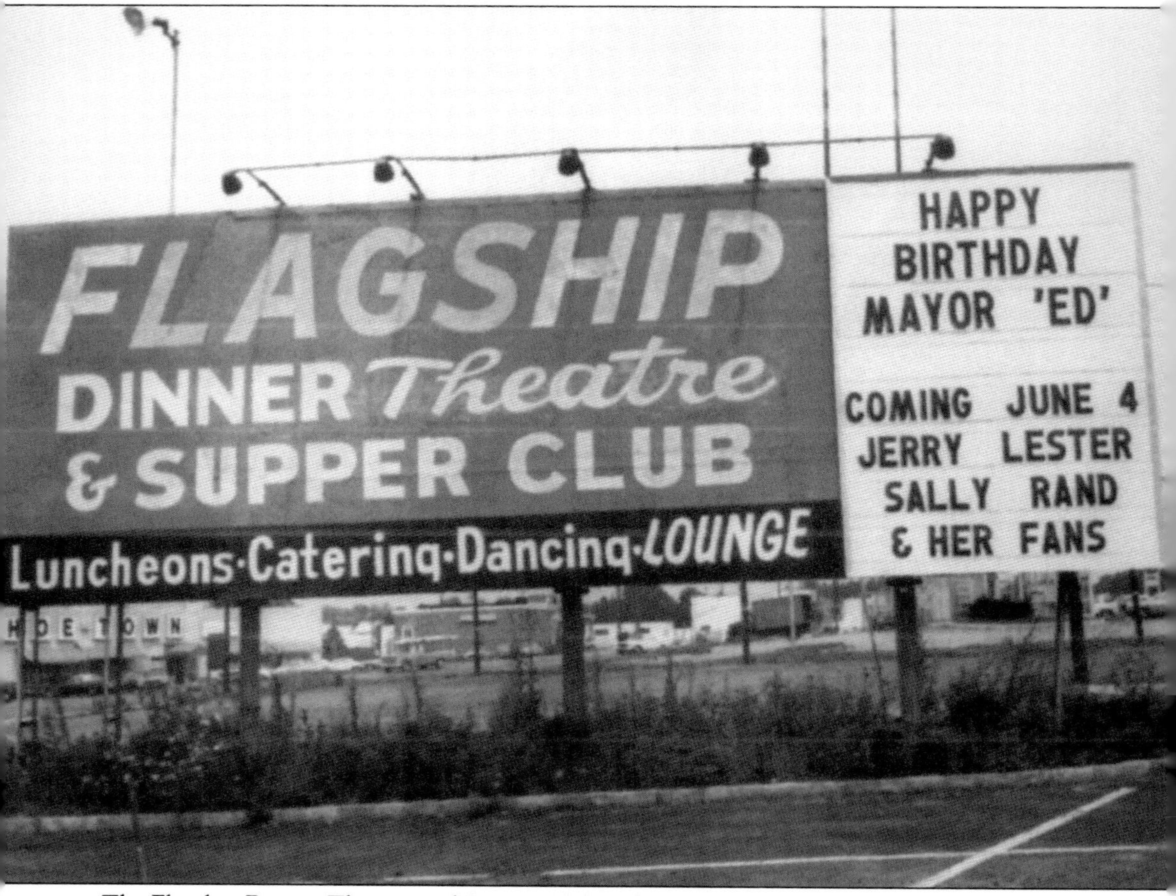

The Flagship Dinner Theatre and Supper Club wishes Mayor Ed a happy birthday; unfortunately, the year of the birthday celebration is not indicated. But Jerry Lester, who is coming to the Flagship on June 4, hosted a late-night television talk show called *Broadway Open House* in the early 1950s, long before either Johnny Carson or Jay Leno made their debuts. Sally Rand was a burlesque fan dancer with a risqué-looking but actually modest dance routine, who kept performing from the 1930s until the 1970s. (Courtesy of UTHS.)

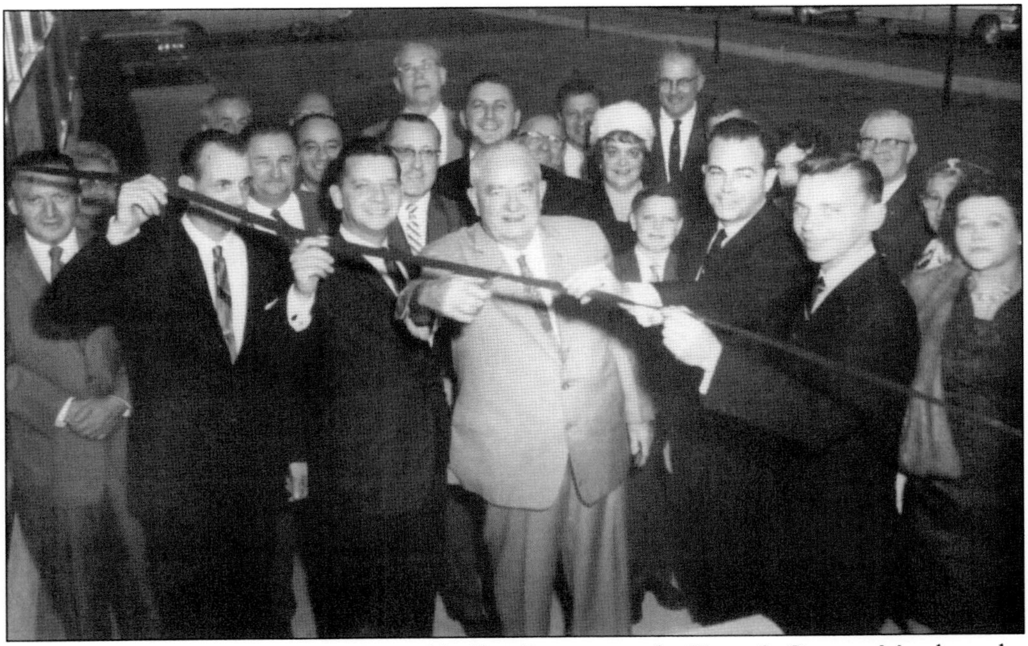

In this photograph is Mayor Biertuempfel officially opening the Town & Campus Motel, on the corner of Green Lane and Morris Avenue. Newark State College was just on the other side of Green Lane; part of Schering Pharmaceuticals can be seen in the background, just across Morris Avenue. (Most of the cars parked on Morris Avenue have tailfins.) Newark State College had not yet expanded into Kean University. Schering would become Schering-Plough and then Merck Pharmaceuticals, and this site is now vacant. (Courtesy of UTHS.)

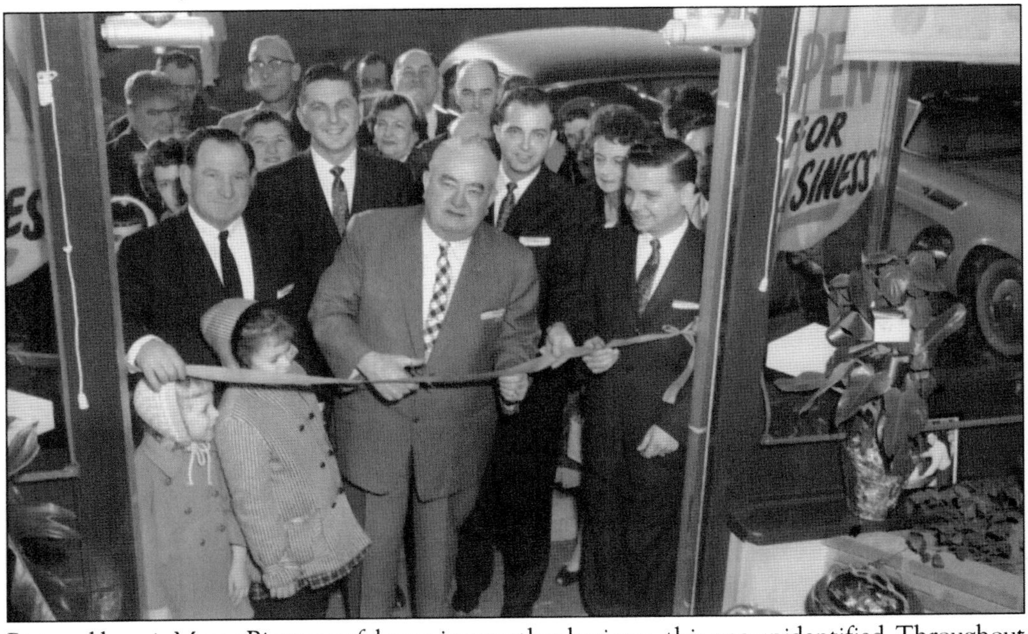

Pictured here is Mayor Biertuempfel opening another business, this one unidentified. Throughout his years as mayor, Biertuempfel's photograph was always in the local newspaper—giving speeches, opening new businesses, kissing babies. He was an old-time politician and knew how to campaign for himself and for his party. (Courtesy of UTHS.)

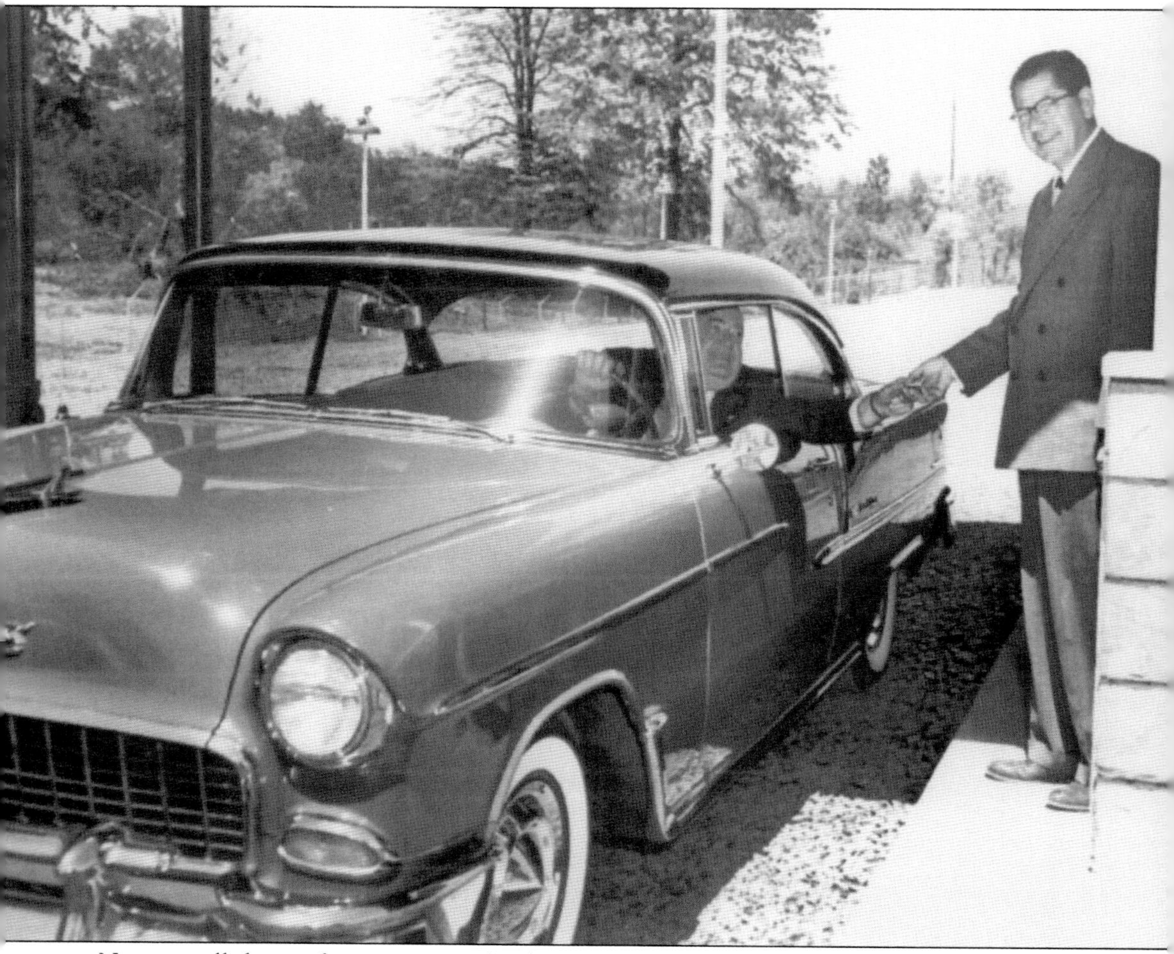

No one really knows for certain exactly what Mayor Biertuempfel was doing when this photograph was taken. It has been suggested that he is paying admission to the Union Drive-In Theatre on Route 22, but this is only an opinion. One thing is certain: the mayor is driving a 1955 Chevrolet. He always drove a Chevy, usually red and always from L&S Chevrolet on Morris Avenue in Union. Every day, he would drive his daughter to work in Newark. On the way back, he would sometimes stop and give a lift to one of Union's students on the way to school. (Courtesy of UTHS.)

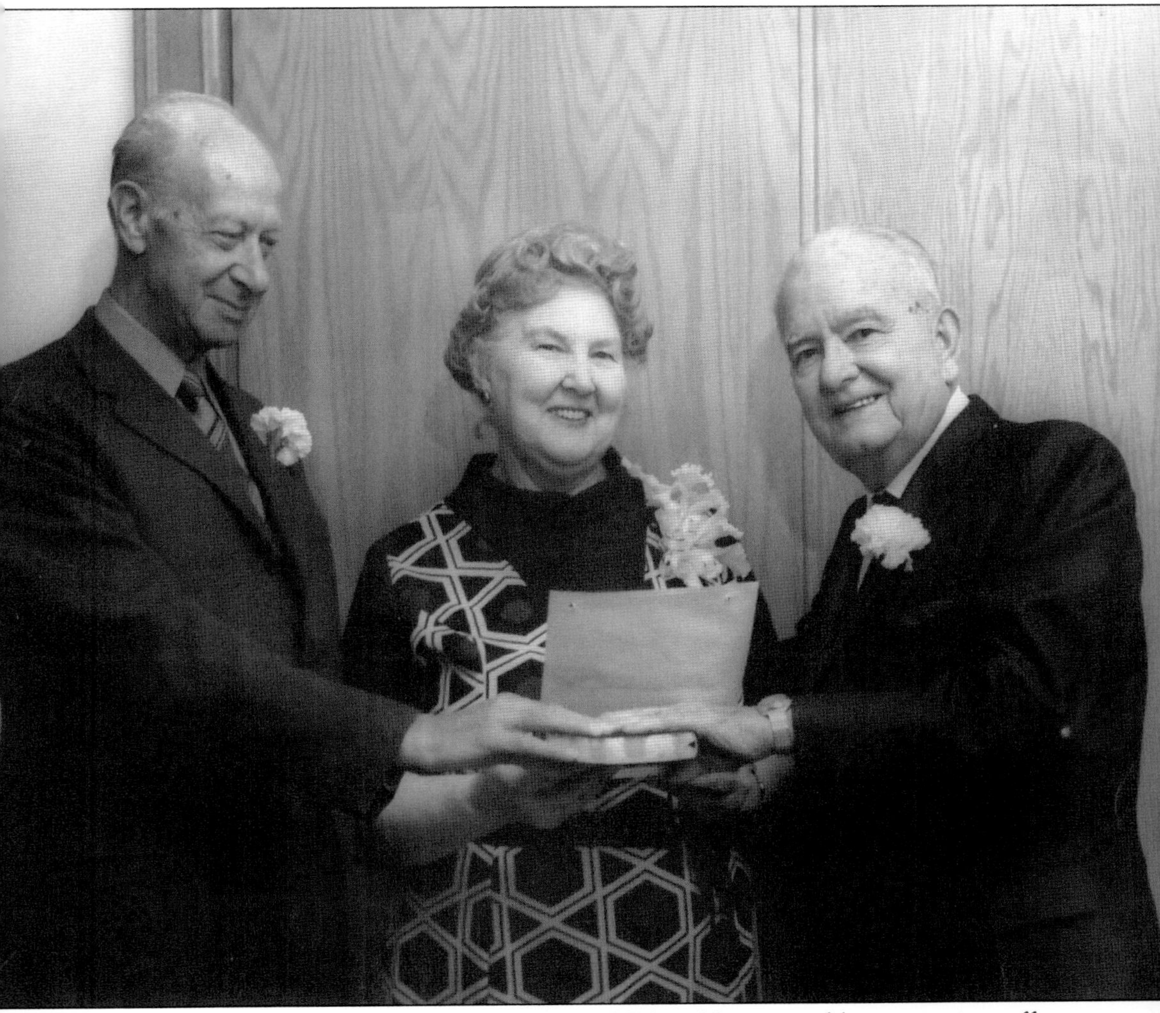

Township committeeman Samuel Rabkin and Mayor F. Edward Biertuempfel are sworn into office on New Year's Day 1972 by township clerk Mary E. Miller. Mayor Biertuempfel had attempted to resign on at least one occasion during his long tenure as mayor, but his fellow Republicans just would not let him. He was too well liked, and his coattails were too broad for his party to let him go. By the 1970s, Biertuempfel had become an icon—an entire generation of Unionites had not known any other mayor. (Courtesy of UTHS.)

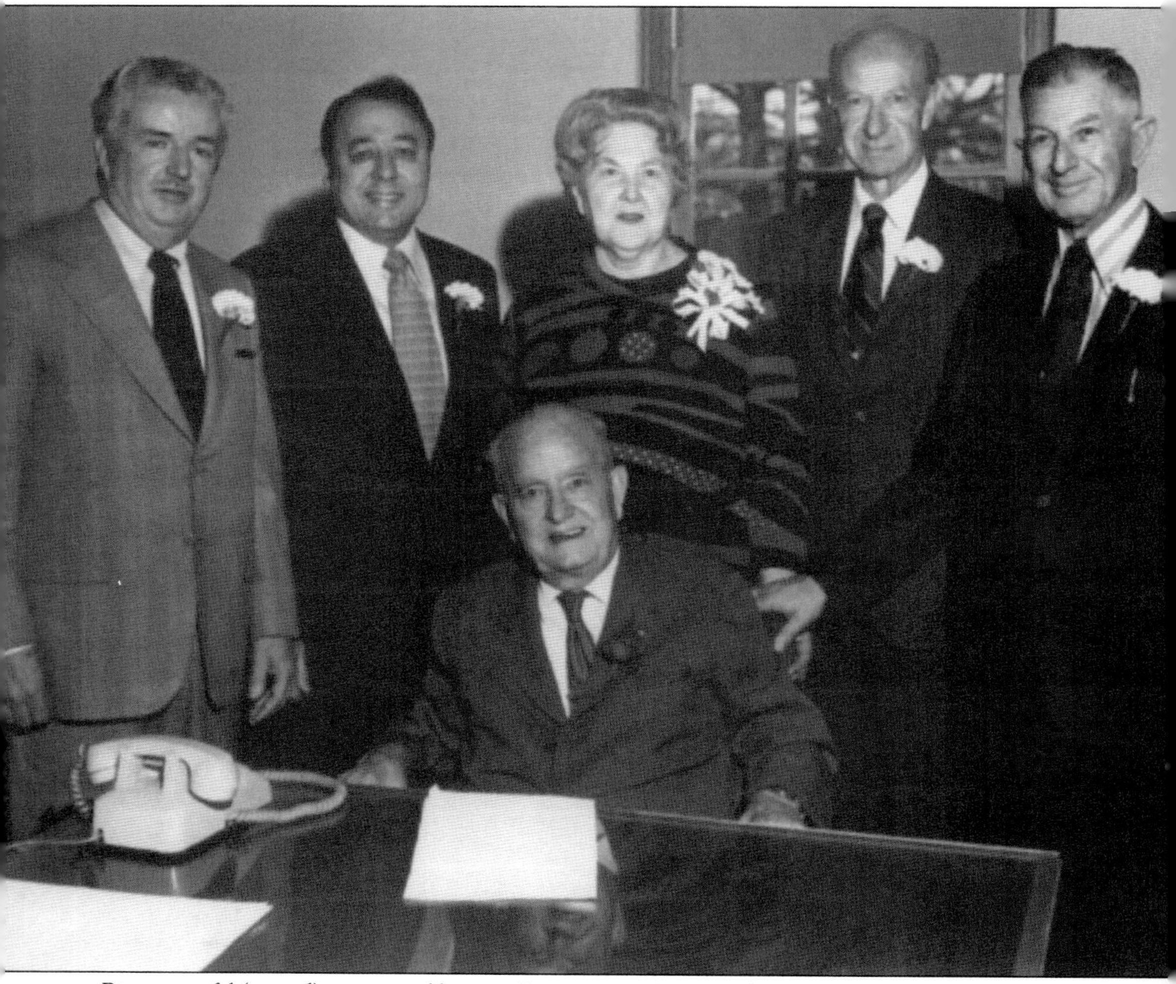

Biertuempfel (seated) is pictured here on January 1, 1973, attending what would be his last township organization meeting. Biertuempfel died just over three months after this photograph was taken, on April 19, 1973. He had been mayor of Union since 1939—34 straight years—and probably made more of an impact on Union Township than any other individual. Even the venerable *New York Times* ran a short obituary, noting that the mayor "was 78 years old, and had been in poor health for several years." Standing are, from left to right, township committeemen James Conlon and Anthony Russo, clerk Mary E. Miller, and committeemen Samuel Rabkin and John Yacovelle. (Courtesy of UTHS.)

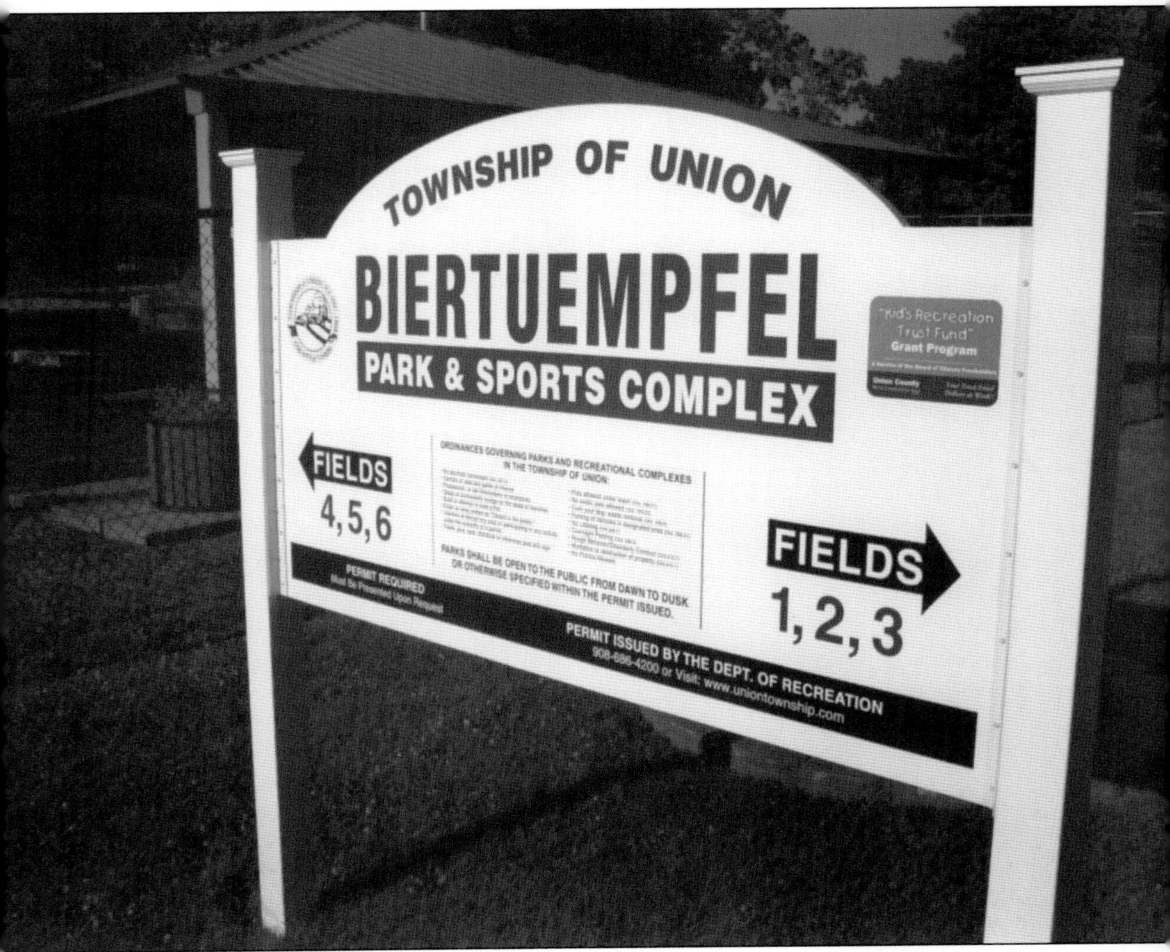

Biertuempfel Park has been the site of the township's annual Fourth of July festivities and fireworks for decades, as well as the site for numerous baseball and football games over the years. Biertuempfel Park and Sports Complex is made up of six playing fields, including tennis courts, and spreads out on both sides of Winslow Avenue. Biertuempfel Park itself is still home of Union's famous fireworks display, which still creates a colossal traffic jam on all the streets in the vicinity. (Photograph by the author.)

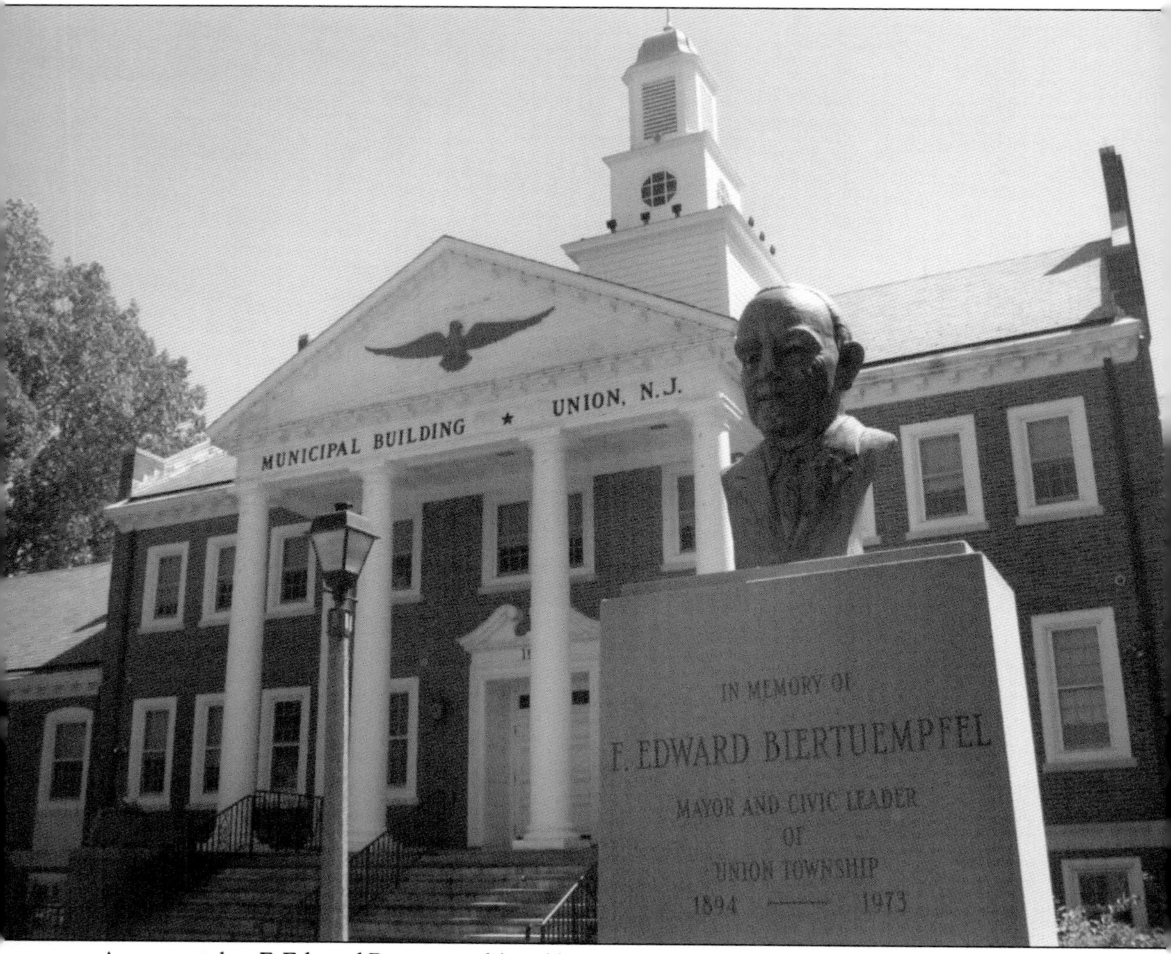

A memorial to F. Edward Biertuempfel and his many years of public service was installed in front of Union Township's municipal building in June 1976. The full inscription reads: "In Memory of F. Edward Biertuempfel Mayor and Civic Leader of Union Township 1884 – 1973." (Photograph by the author.)

Four

Union Center through the Years

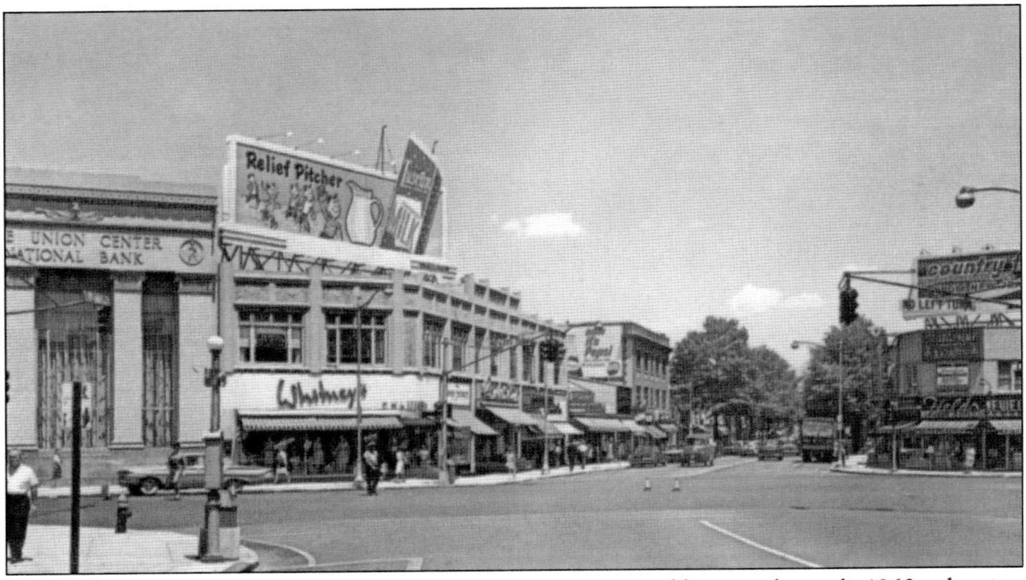

The intersection of Morris and Stuyvesant Avenues is pictured here in the early 1960s; that is a 1961 Chevrolet passing in front of Union Center National Bank. Field's Jewelers and Whitney's fashions were still doing a brisk business, along with Thom McAn shoes and McCrory's five-and-ten. The "Relief Pitcher" billboard high above Whitney's advertises Tuscan Milk, which is another local industry that has disappeared. (Courtesy of UTHS.)

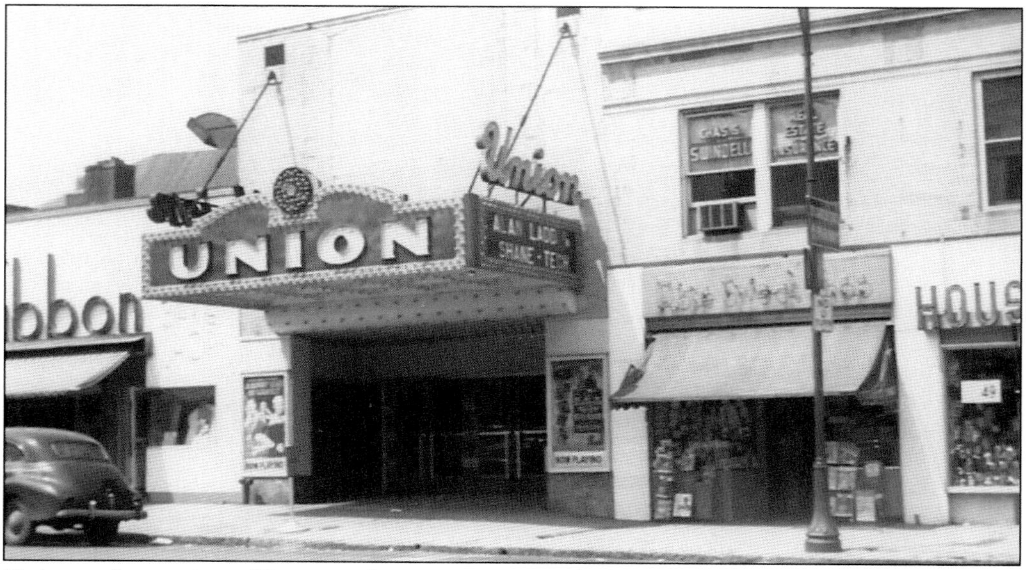

Going to the movies in Union used to mean going to the Union Theatre on Stuyvesant Avenue. The marquee has changed since the 1950s, but the theater is still there, next door to the Blue Ribbon. The Union Cinema, or Union Theatre (or Union Movies), is one of Union Township's most recognizable landmarks—anyone driving on Stuyvesant Avenue past knows exactly where he or she is. At the time of the photograph, the featured film was *Shane*, from 1953, starring Alan Ladd. (Courtesy of UTHS.)

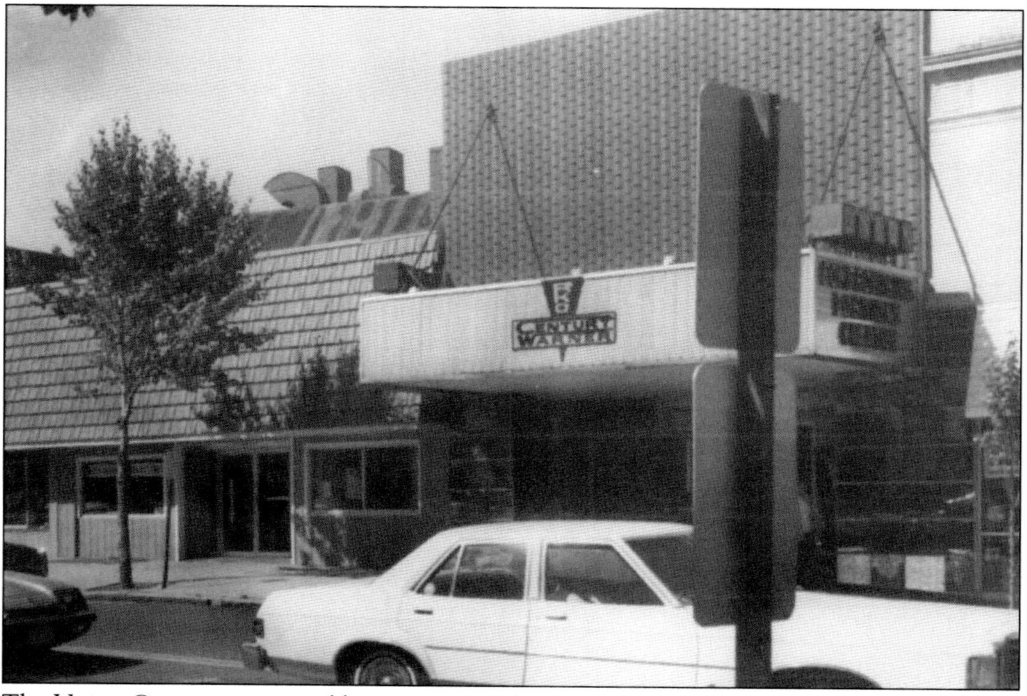

The Union Cinema is pictured here sometime during the 1980s. After it was acquired by RKO Century Warner, some complained that the familiar marquee had been turned into something ugly and horrible. It certainly had changed, for better or worse. But the old movie house still showed the latest films, just as it had done for over 50 years. (Courtesy of UTHS.)

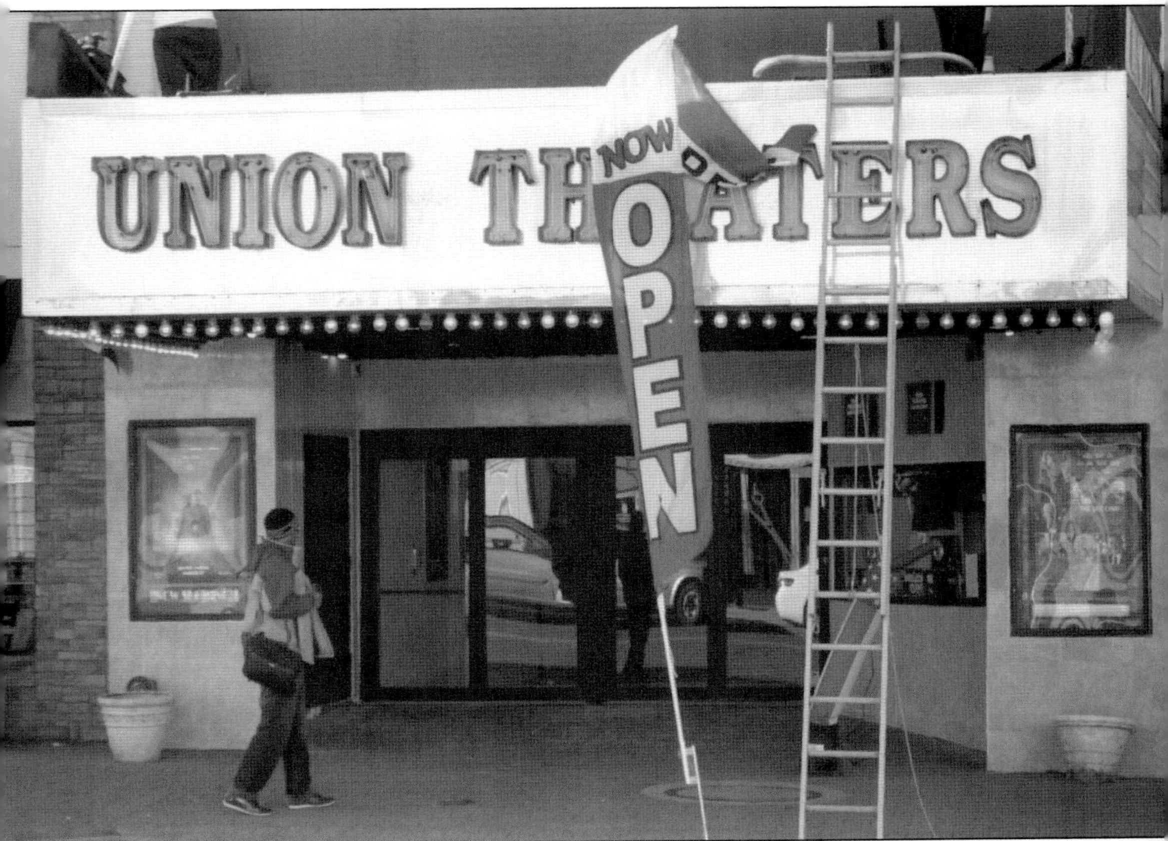

Union Township nearly lost one of its landmarks and institutions when the Union Cinema closed its doors in 2013. At that point in time, the inside of the cinema was in deplorable condition; among other things, the seats were broken and, according to one source, the roof was falling down. But in the early part of 2015, a new owner bought the cinema and completely renovated it. At the end of March 2015, Union Theaters finally reopened after being dark for two years. Pictured here is the cinema's grand opening. They just do not make films like *Shane* and *Casablanca* anymore, but the Union Movies will feature a full selection of what Hollywood is turning out these days. (Photograph by the author.)

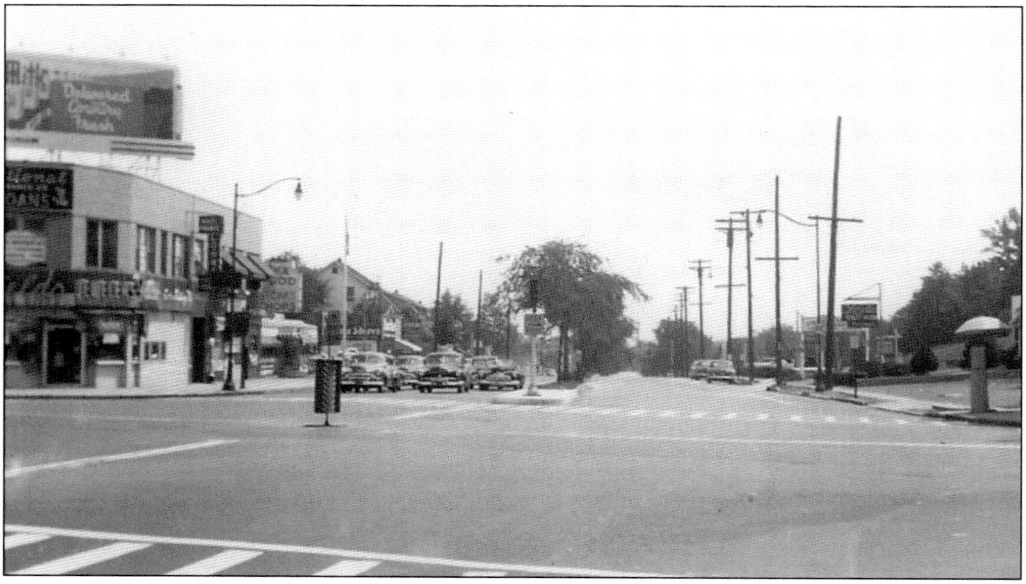

Pictured here is Morris Avenue, at the intersection of Stuyvesant Avenue, in the early 1950s. Field's Jewelers, on the left, was a fixture in Union Center for many years. Traffic was lighter then, and the pace of life was much slower. Automobiles were also larger and heavier in those days, but the price of gasoline was about 20¢ per gallon. Nobody was all that concerned about gasoline mileage. The municipal building and the public library had not yet moved into Friberger Park, off to the left of the photograph, which was still a park, with grass and picnic benches, in those days. (Courtesy of UTHS.)

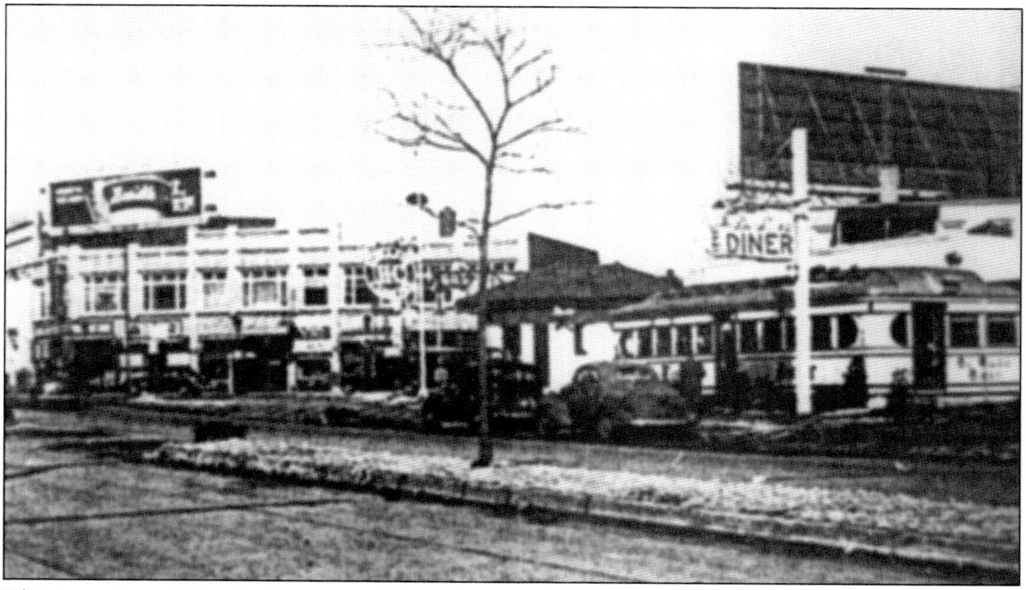

This is a view of Morris Avenue at Union Center during World War II, looking toward Lerner's Department Store. Morris Avenue itself is still paved with concrete and has not yet been covered with asphalt. The single-pump Sinclair service station and the DeLuxe Diner—home of the famous DeLuxe hamburger—were still prominent features of the center. Union Center would undergo a great many changes after the war, along with the rest of Union Township. (Courtesy of UTHS.)

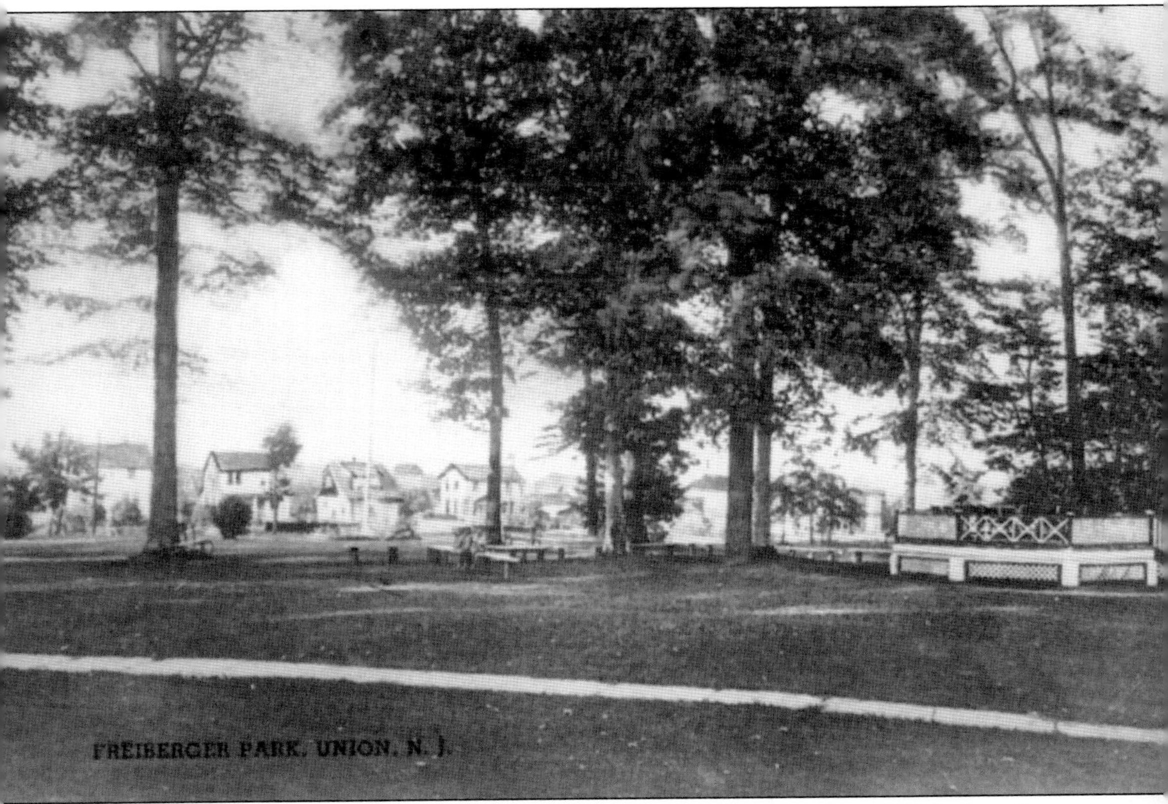

This is Friberger Park, in an undated (and misspelled) photograph. The scene probably dates from the 1940s. The public library and town hall would not be built for years to come. As evidenced by the picnic benches in the center and the bandstand on the right, the site was still very much a park in the literal sense. At the time this photograph was taken, Friberger Park was still a long way from being the hub of the township's municipal government, which it would become in the 1950s. (Courtesy of UTHS.)

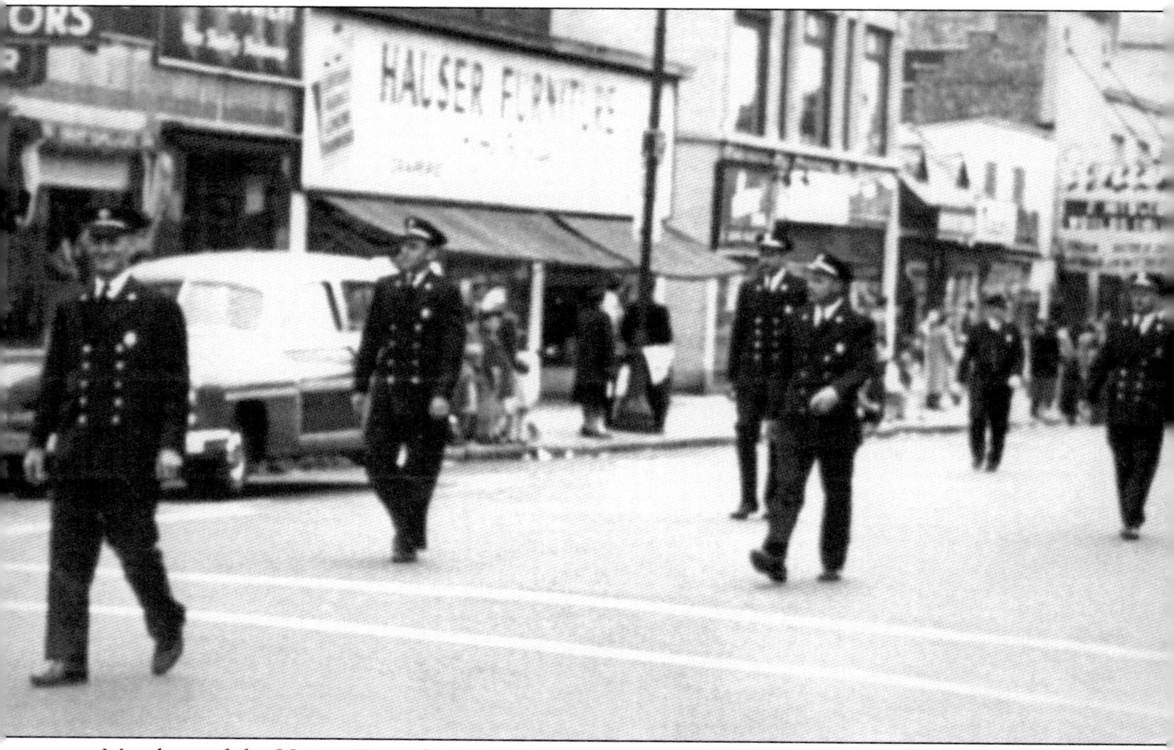

Members of the Union Township Fire Department parade along Stuyvesant Avenue during the early 1950s. The Union Cinema was featuring the film *When Worlds Collide*, a science-fiction epic released in 1951 starring Richard Derr and Barbara Rush. Hauser Furniture occupies the site that had been Acme Markets a few years earlier. The station wagon parked in front of Union Wines and Liquors is a genuine woody, with real wood paneling running along both sides of the car. (Courtesy of UTHS.)

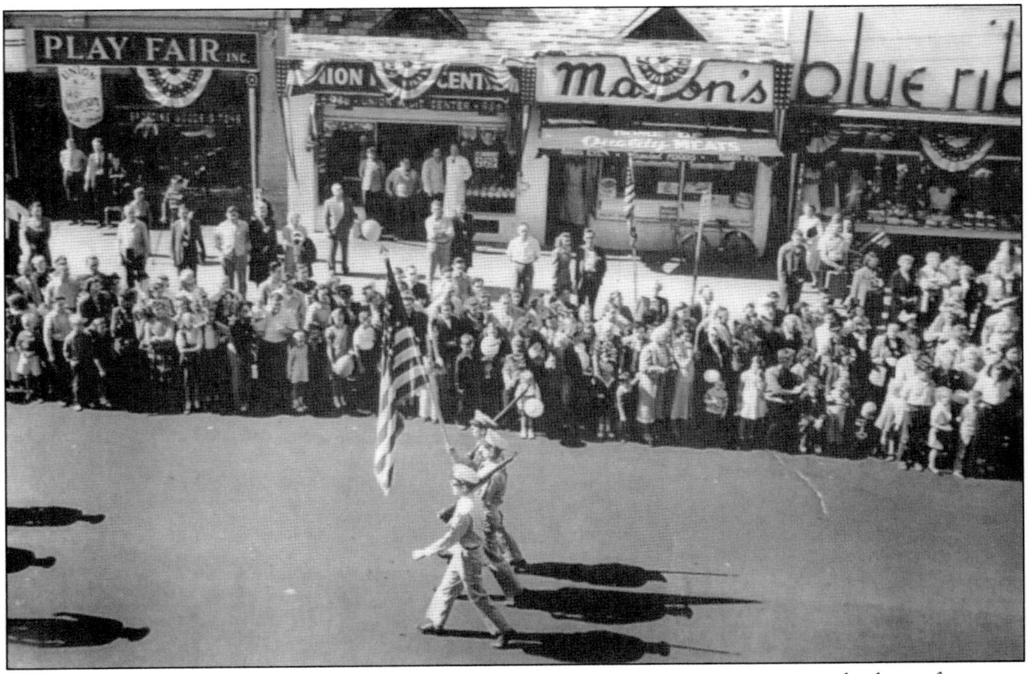

A color bearer and his honor guard march up Stuyvesant Avenue, stepping into the late-afternoon sun. The parade is probably part of Union's 140th anniversary celebration, which took place in 1948. The small banner below the "Play Fair" sign next to the red, white, and blue bunting reads, "Union, NJ – 140th Anniversary – 1808–1948." Play Fair, Union Fruit Center, and Mason's, "The Home of Quality Meats," are all long gone. Only the Blue Ribbon has stayed on through the years. (Courtesy of Union Township.)

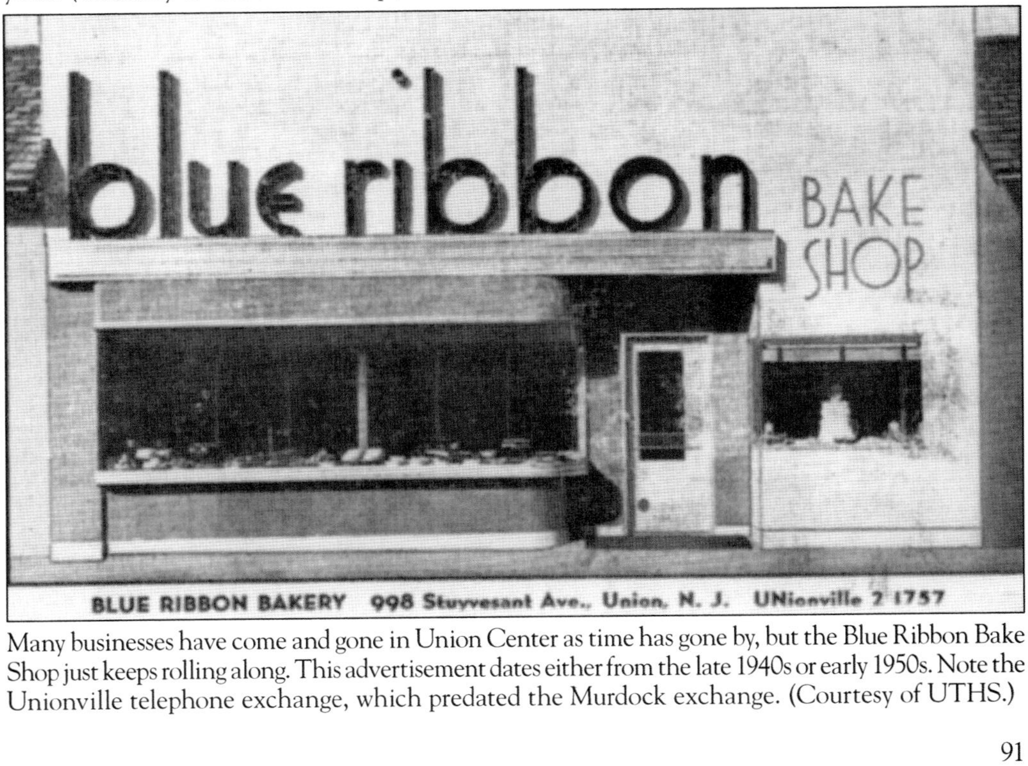

Many businesses have come and gone in Union Center as time has gone by, but the Blue Ribbon Bake Shop just keeps rolling along. This advertisement dates either from the late 1940s or early 1950s. Note the Unionville telephone exchange, which predated the Murdock exchange. (Courtesy of UTHS.)

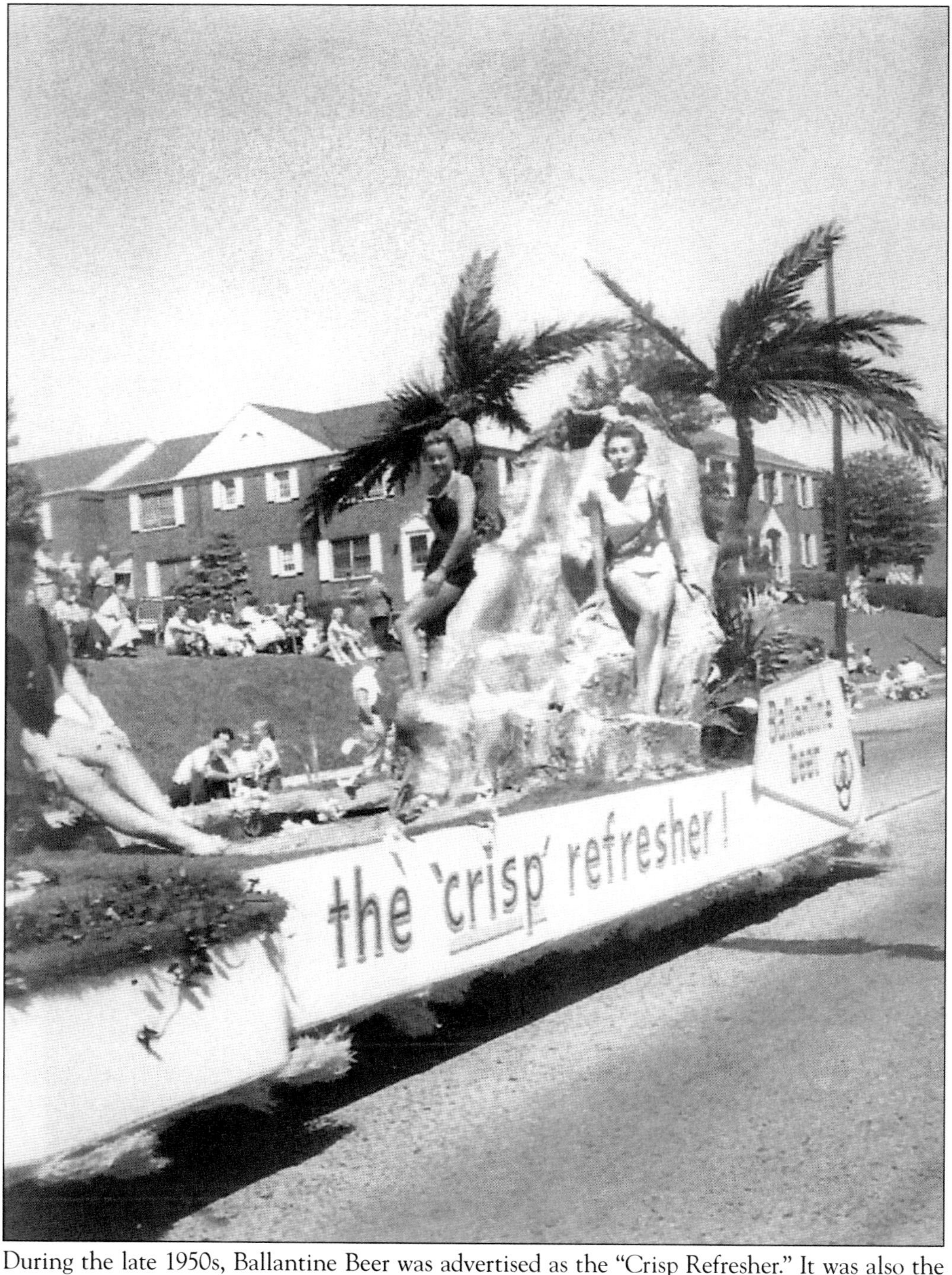

During the late 1950s, Ballantine Beer was advertised as the "Crisp Refresher." It was also the sponsor of the New York Yankees back in their glory days, when they appeared in the World Series nearly every year. Whenever Mickey Mantle hit a home run, Mel Allen would call it a "Ballantine Blast." This is the same 1958 parade in which Miss New Jersey took part. The buildings in the background are on Morris Avenue in Union Center. The Ballantine float has not yet reached the traffic light at Johnson Place. (Courtesy of Tom Haggerty)

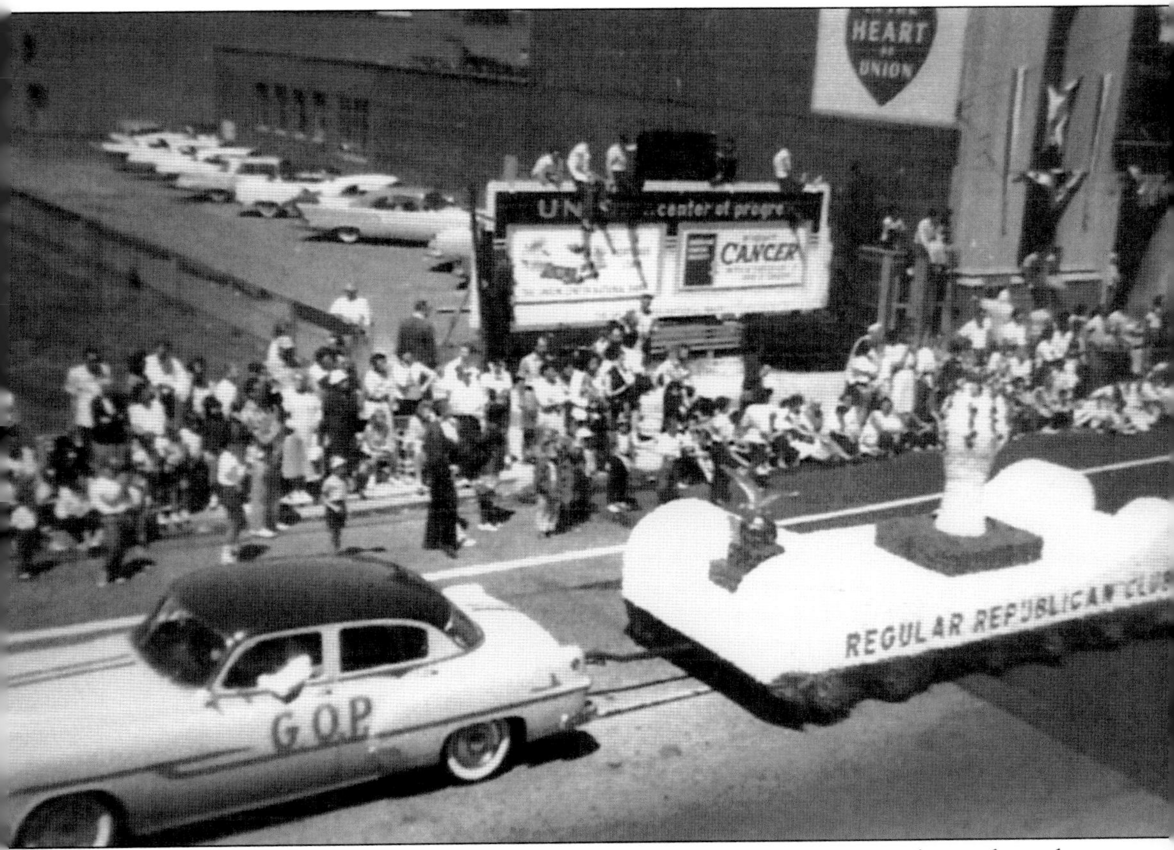

A parade, possibly for Memorial Day, makes its way along Morris Avenue sometime during the early 1950s. The building in the background is the Union Center National Bank, in the days before the bank's well-known clock and thermometer were installed. A vacant lot occupies the space next to the bank; Union was not as heavily populated or as heavily built-up is it would become in the near future. A Pontiac is towing the Regular Republican Club's float past the crowd. These were the Biertuempfel years, and Union was still a strongly Republican town. (Courtesy of UTHS.)

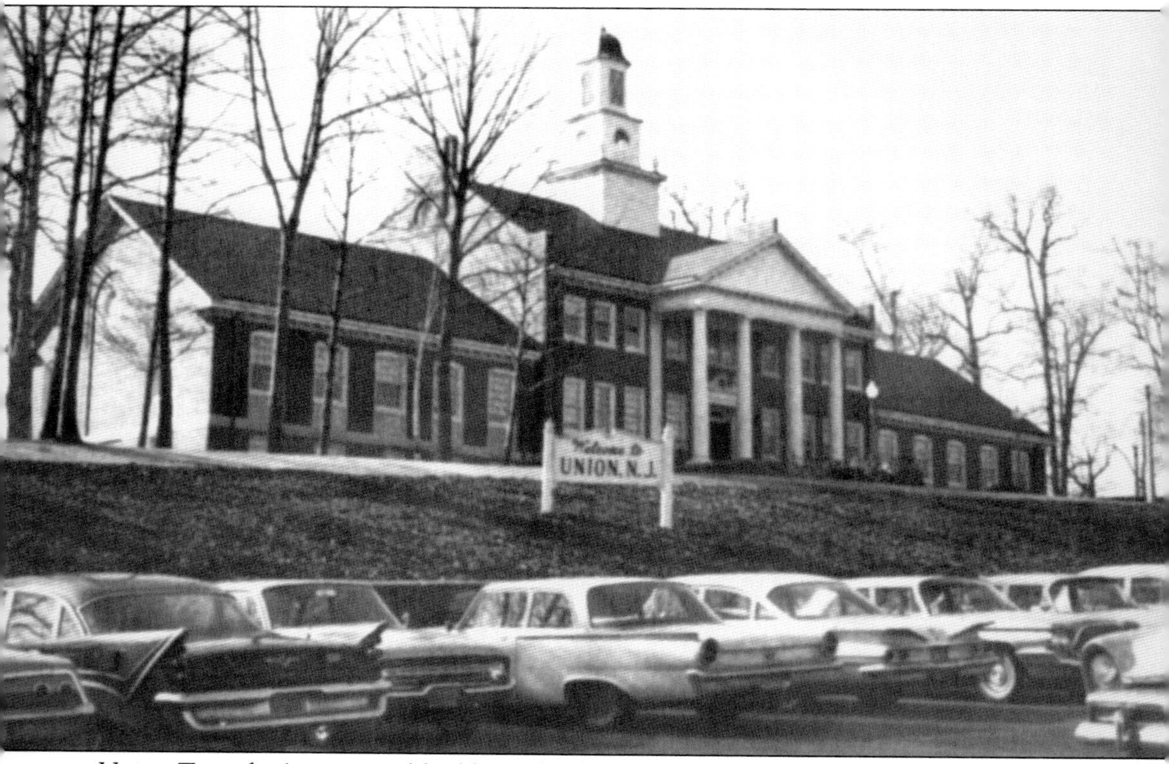

Union Township's municipal building, also known as town hall, is pictured here in the early 1960s, when property taxes were about $200 per year. (And salaries were about $100 per week.) The building had only opened a few years before, in 1957. The view looks pretty much the same over 50 years later, except that cars do not have tailfins anymore. And the parking lot is as jam-packed as ever, except these days the cars tend to be Toyotas and Mitsubishis instead of Dodges and Chevrolets. Among the cares in the photograph are a 1962 Chevrolet, a 1960 Chevrolet, and 1955 Plymouth. (Courtesy of UTHS.)

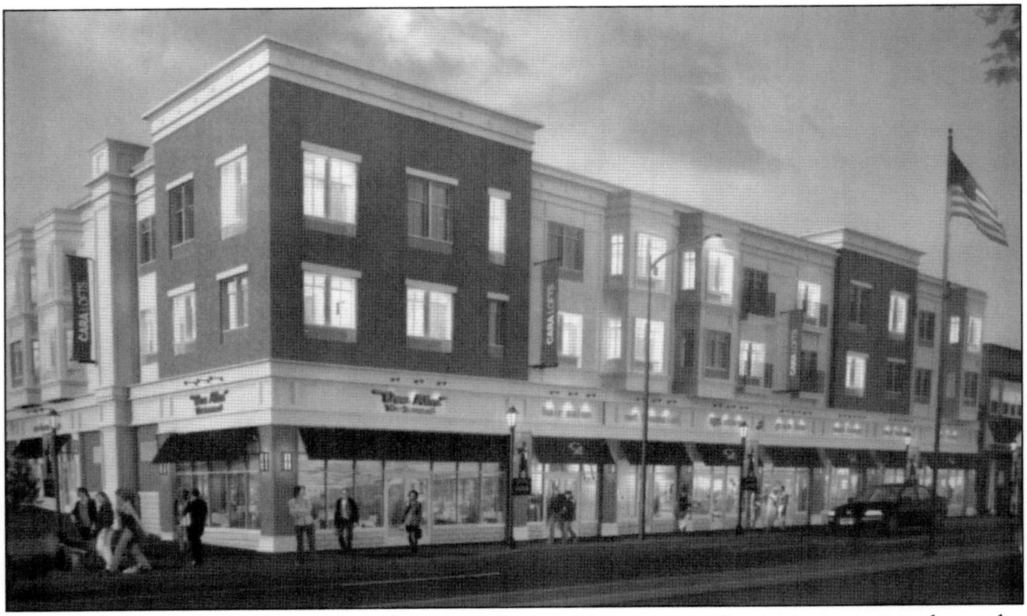

This is an artist's (or architect's) rendering of the construction on Morris Avenue, just down the hill from the Union Public Library. Don Alex's restaurant, on the corner, has taken the place of the old Lloyd Exchange travel agency, and the site of the Café Mozart, on the other end of the row, is unoccupied. "Luxury apartments," according to the advertisements, are situated above the shops and restaurants. This new construction certainly gives a different look to the center. (Courtesy of UTHS.)

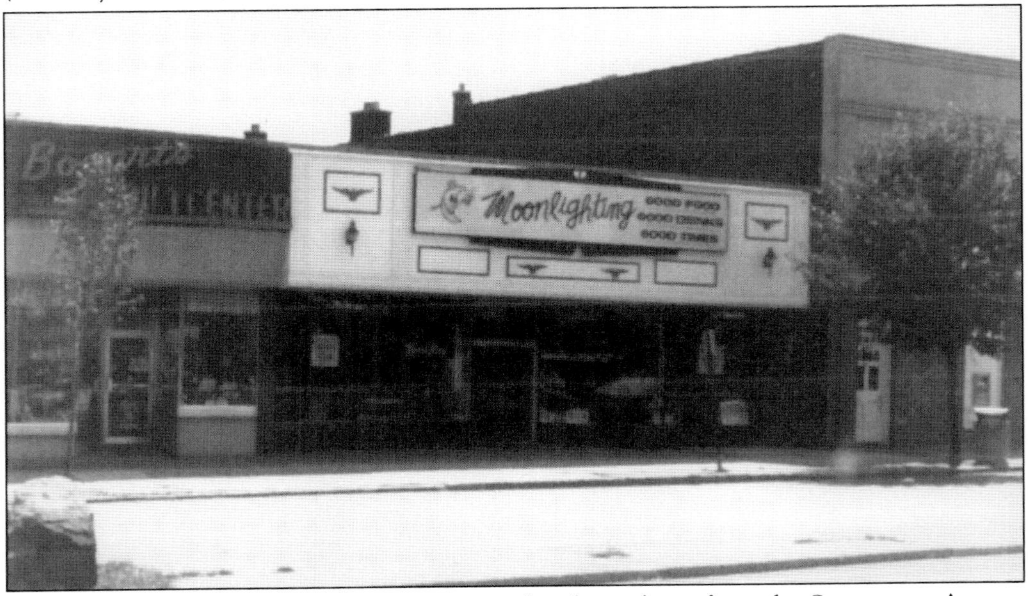

Moonlighting was a bar and restaurant just a few doors down from the Stuyvesant Avenue intersection, with Bogart's Gift Center right next door. The Café Mozart occupied the site before Moonlighting; it is now occupied by KaVa Restaurant. The Café Mozart was more continental than Moonlighting and a bit classier—coffee and imported pastries instead of beer and hamburgers. This photograph was taken before the flagpoles were installed all along the center island on Morris Avenue. (Courtesy of UTHS.)

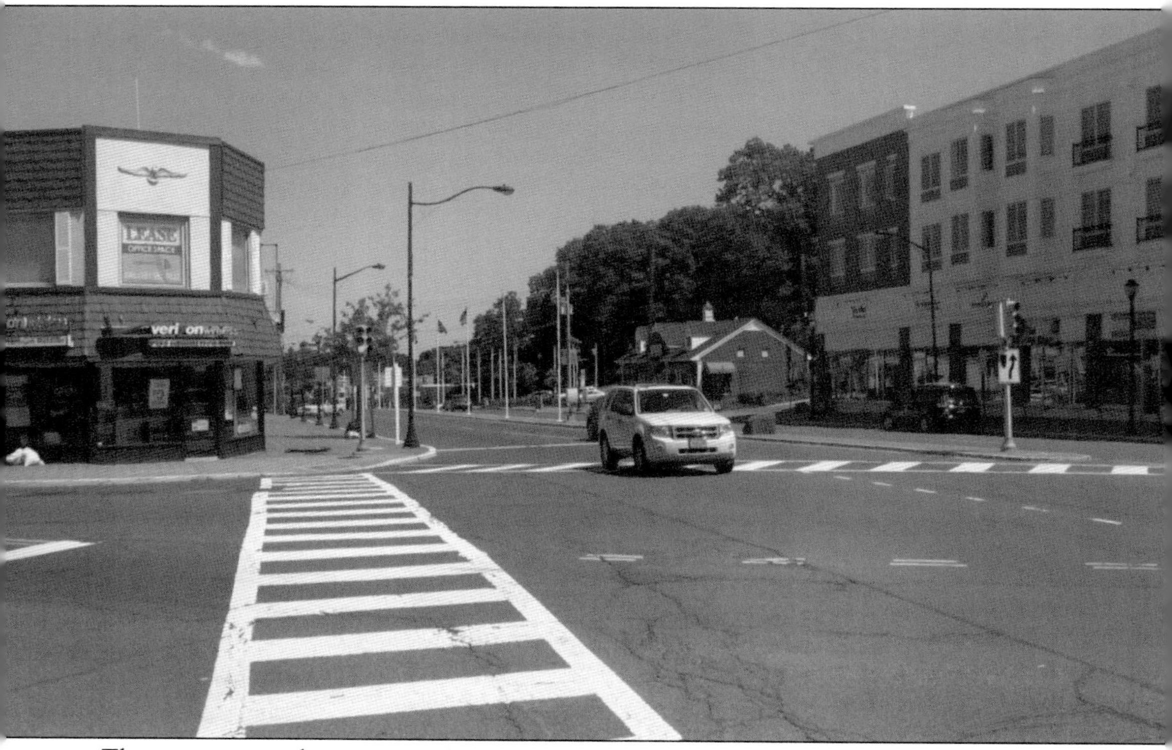

This image was taken crossing Stuyvesant Avenue, with a view looking down Morris Avenue toward Kean University (formerly Newark State College). On the opposite side of Morris Avenue, the Café Mozart, Bogart's Gifts, and the Lloyd Exchange travel agency have all been replaced by other businesses. The most significant, or at least the most noticeable, addition to the row of shops is the apartments that have been built above them. This prompts a very pertinent question from township residents—where are the tenants of these new apartments going to park? (Photograph by the author.)

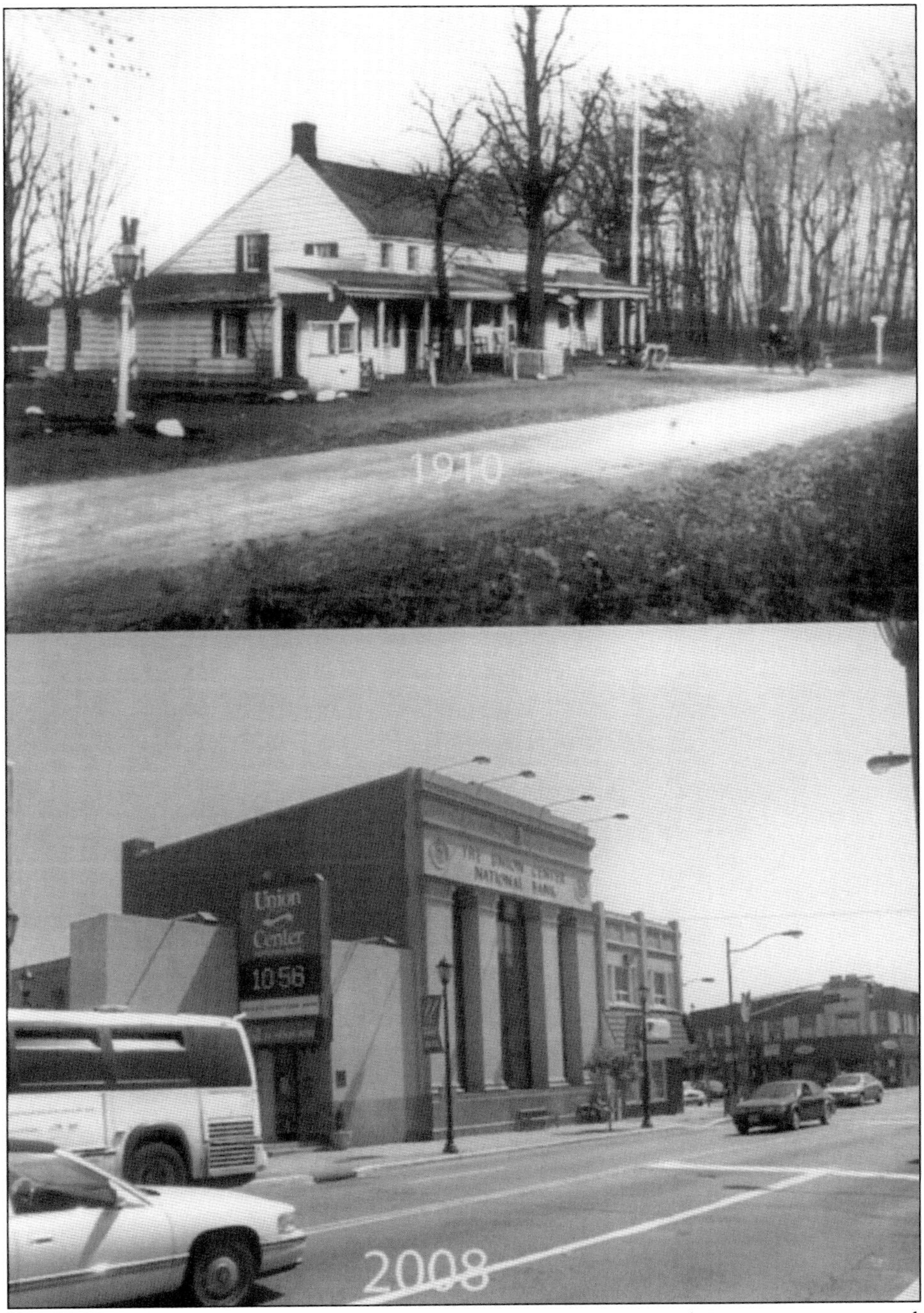

This then-and-now image created by the Union Township Historical Society gives a good idea of how much Union has changed during the 100 years between 1908 and 2008. The top black-and-white photograph shows Ye Olde Meeker Inn, which had been in business as a tavern and a roadside inn since the days of the Revolutionary War. Morris Avenue was still a narrow dirt road in those days. The other side of the intersection of Morris and Stuyvesant Avenues is still woodland. The scene probably looked the same 100 years earlier. In 2008, the Union Center National Bank had taken over the site of the Meeker Inn, Morris Avenue had been paved for decades, and the internal combustion engine had overrun the entire area. (Courtesy of UTHS.)

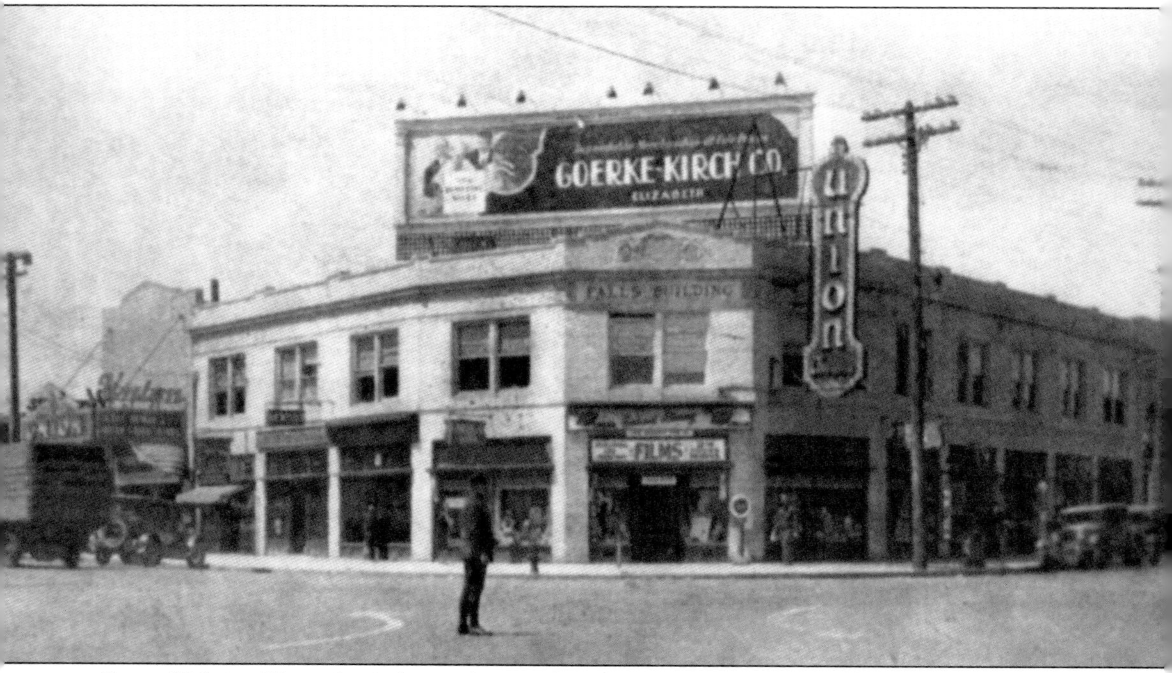

One of Union Township's finest directs the almost nonexistent traffic at the intersection of Morris and Stuyvesant Avenues during the late 1920s. The year is 1929, to be exact. The Union Cinema is featuring a Texas Guinan film, *Queen of the Nightclubs*, which was released in March of that year. (Courtesy of UTHS.)

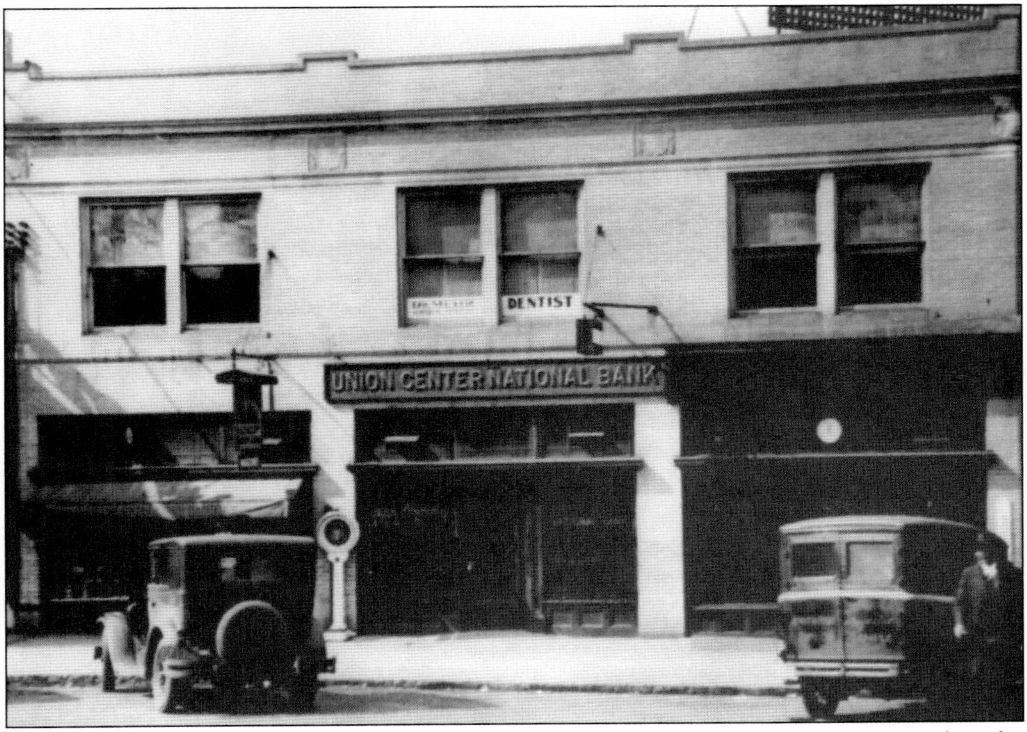

Pictured here is Union Center National Bank, on Stuyvesant Avenue, before it moved to the former site of the Meeker Inn on Morris Avenue (and long before it ever became ConnectOne Bank). The photograph dates from the 1920s. (Courtesy of UTHS.)

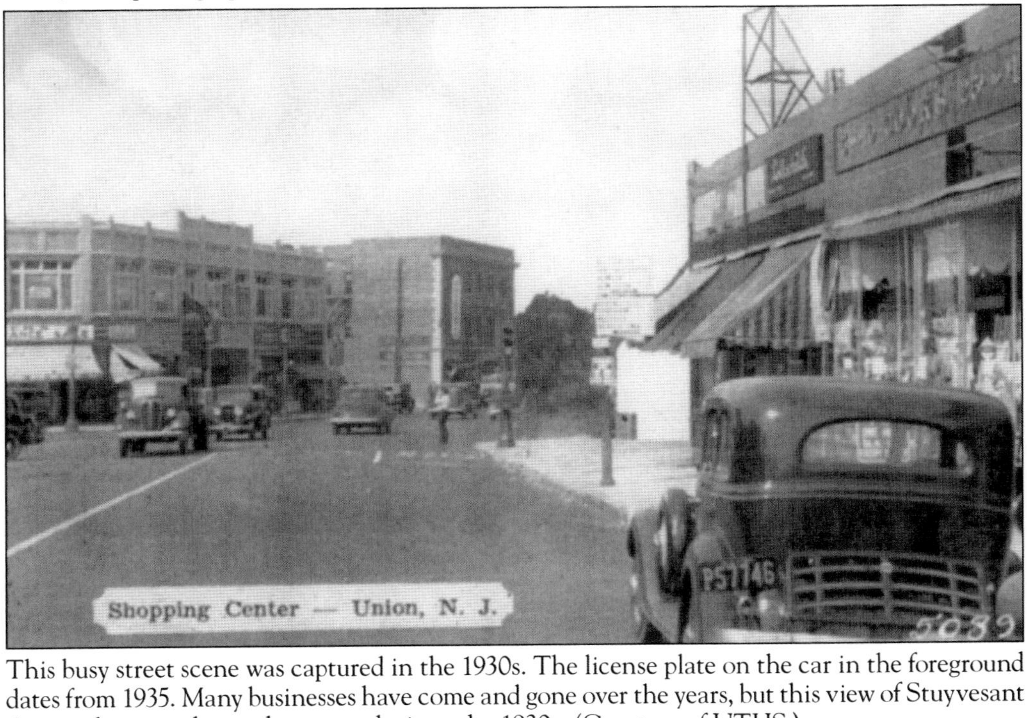

This busy street scene was captured in the 1930s. The license plate on the car in the foreground dates from 1935. Many businesses have come and gone over the years, but this view of Stuyvesant Avenue has not changed very much since the 1930s. (Courtesy of UTHS.)

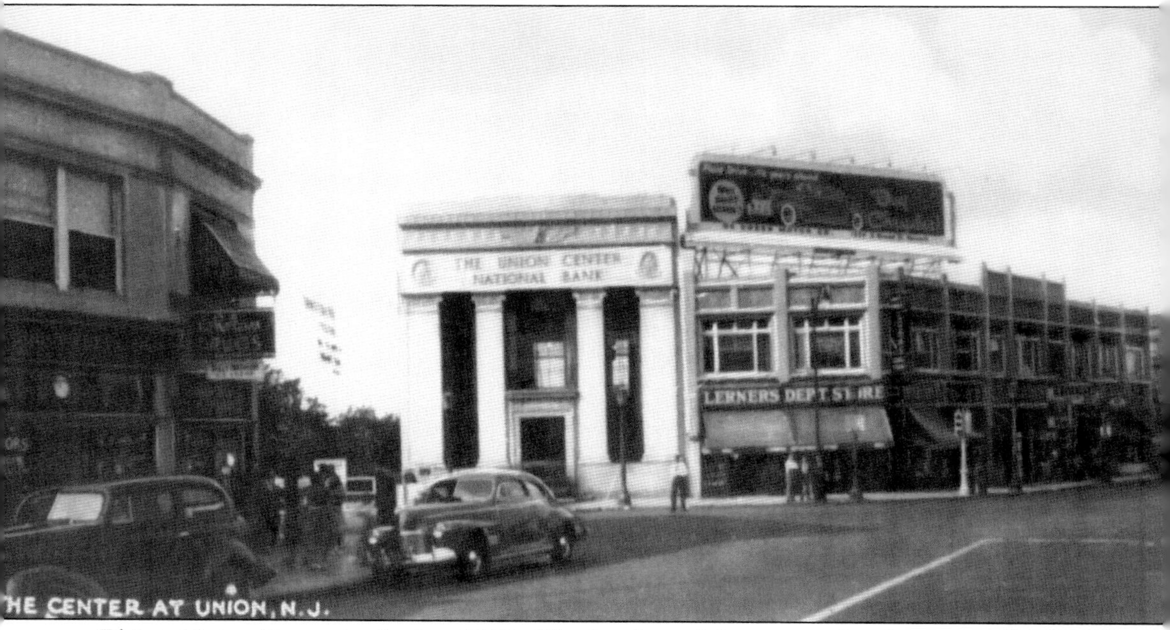

This is Union Center in the late 1940s. The last line of the caption has been cut off. The full caption reads, "The Center at Union, N.J. – Site of the Meeker Inn, Built 1755, Where General Washington Often Stopped." The Union Center National Bank occupies the site of the old Meeker Inn, although Lerner's Department Store probably featured Washington's Birthday sales every February. (Courtesy of UTHS.)

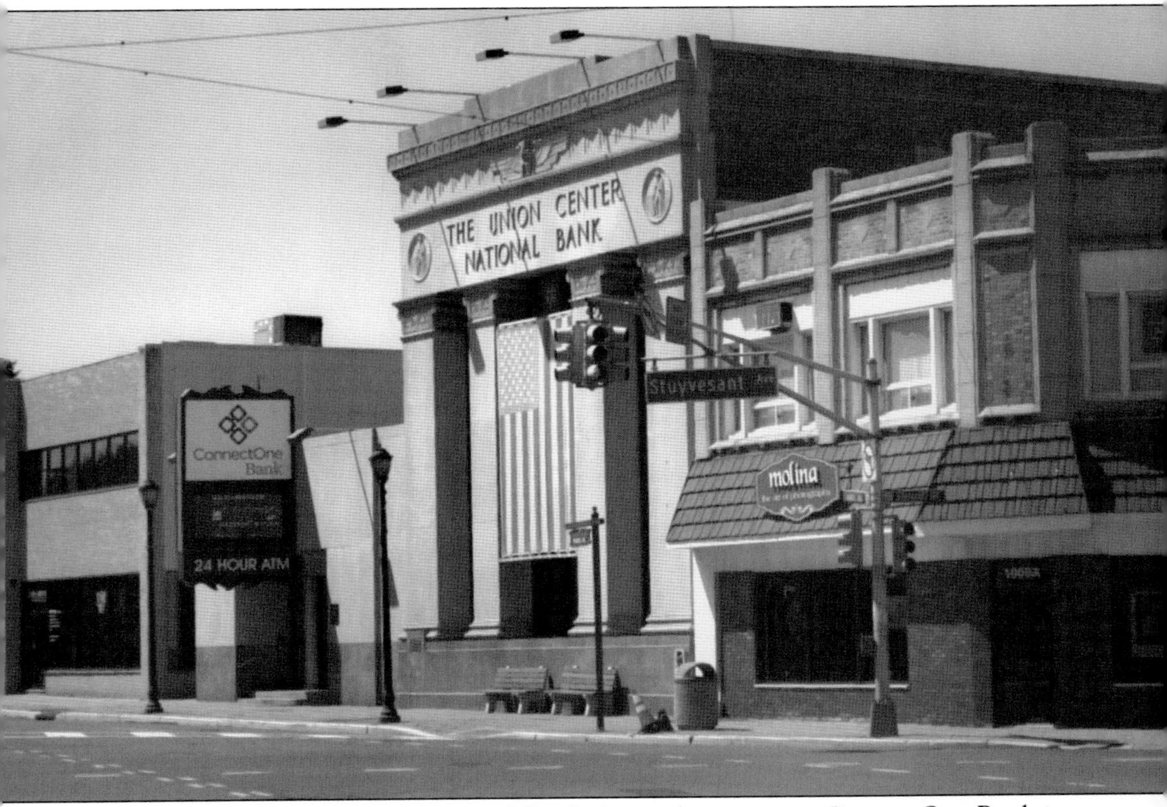

The venerable old Union Center National Bank changed its name to ConnectOne Bank in 2014. But the building itself still looks the same, and still has "The Union Center National Bank" emblazoned across its front. It will probably take an act of Congress, or an act of war, to have those words removed. The bank's digital clock and thermometer have been replaced by advertising. (Photograph by the author.)

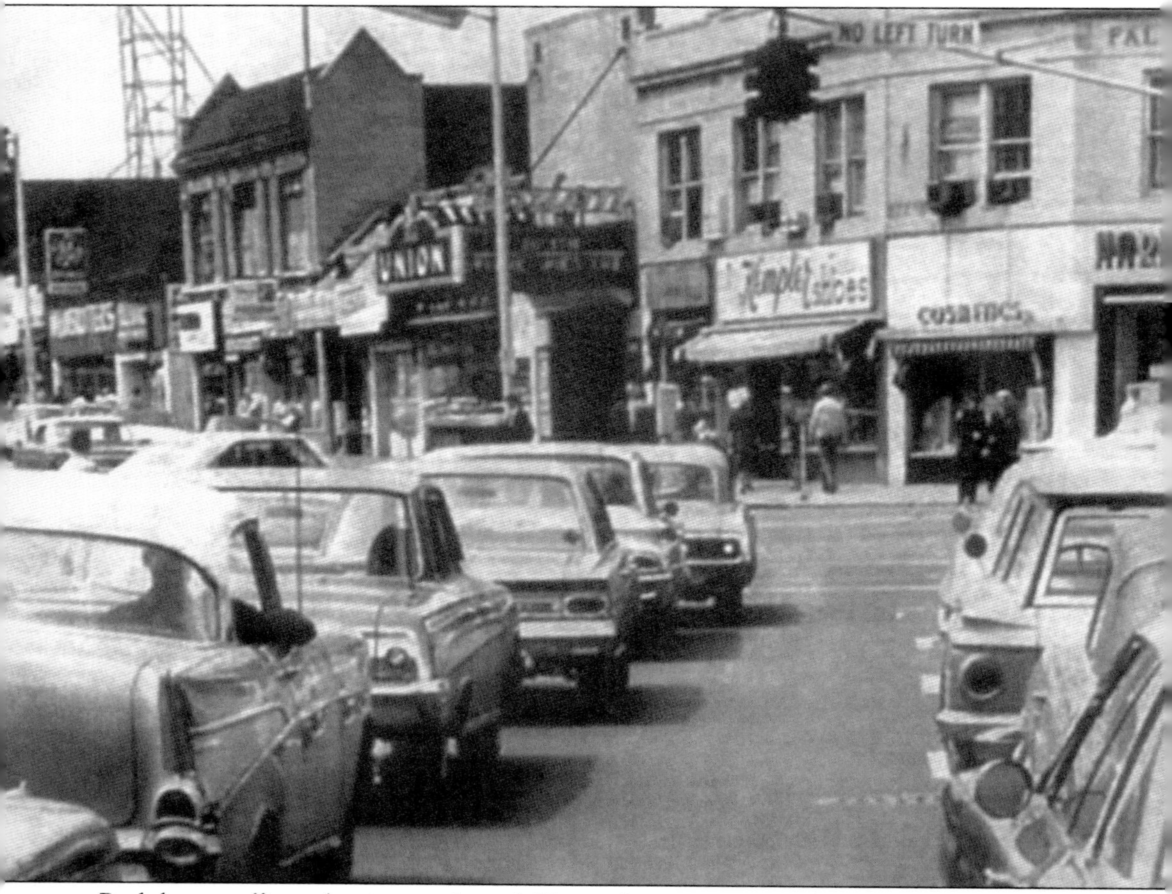

Rush hour traffic snakes its way through Union Center sometime during the early 1960s. (That is a 1957 Chevrolet in the lower left-hand corner.) Unfortunately, the film that is playing at the Union Cinema is not legible. Among the shops that have disappeared over the years is Wilderoter's, a few doors down from the Union Cinema. Among other things, Wilderoter's sold a full line of General Electric appliances. (Courtesy of UTHS.)

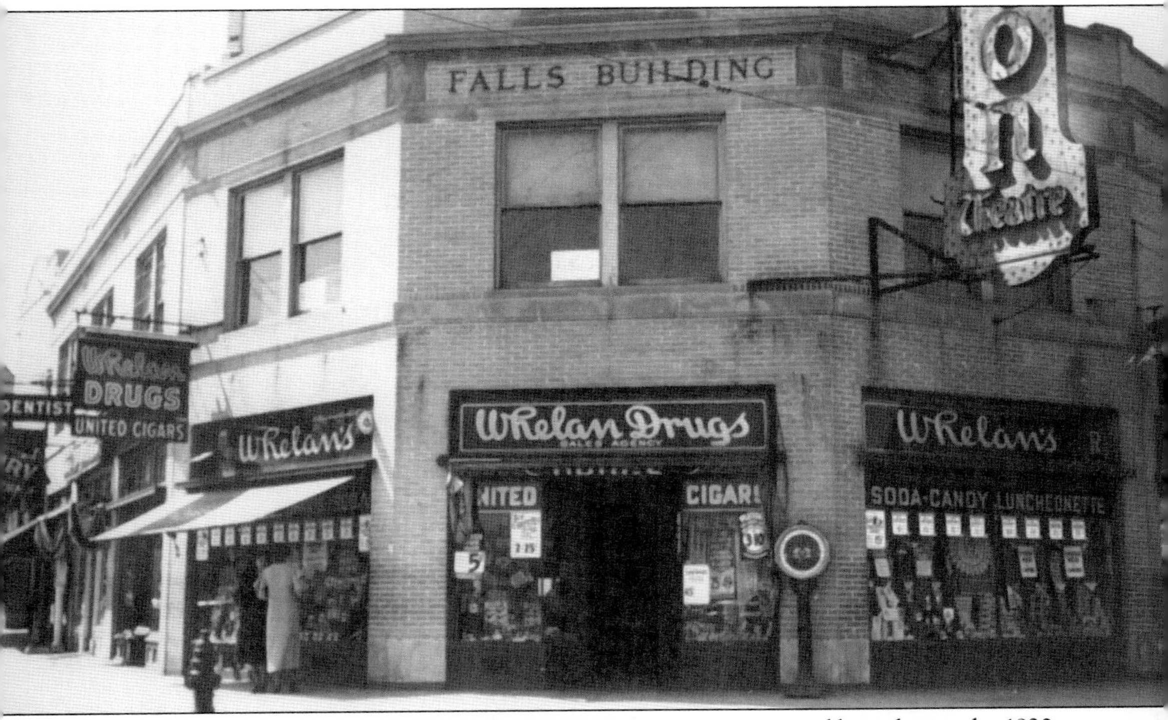

Whelan Drugs, at the corner of Morris and Stuyvesant Avenues, is pictured here during the 1930s. Although there are only three people in the photograph window-shopping (two under Whelan's awning), all the shop signs make the scene seem very busy. Overhanging the sidewalk on Stuyvesant Avenue are signs for a dentist, a dairy, and United Cigars. The bottom of the sign for the Union Theatre is visible at the upper right-hand corner. Years later, after the signs and the awnings came down, Harbro Drugs would occupy the same site as Whelan's. (Courtesy of UTHS.)

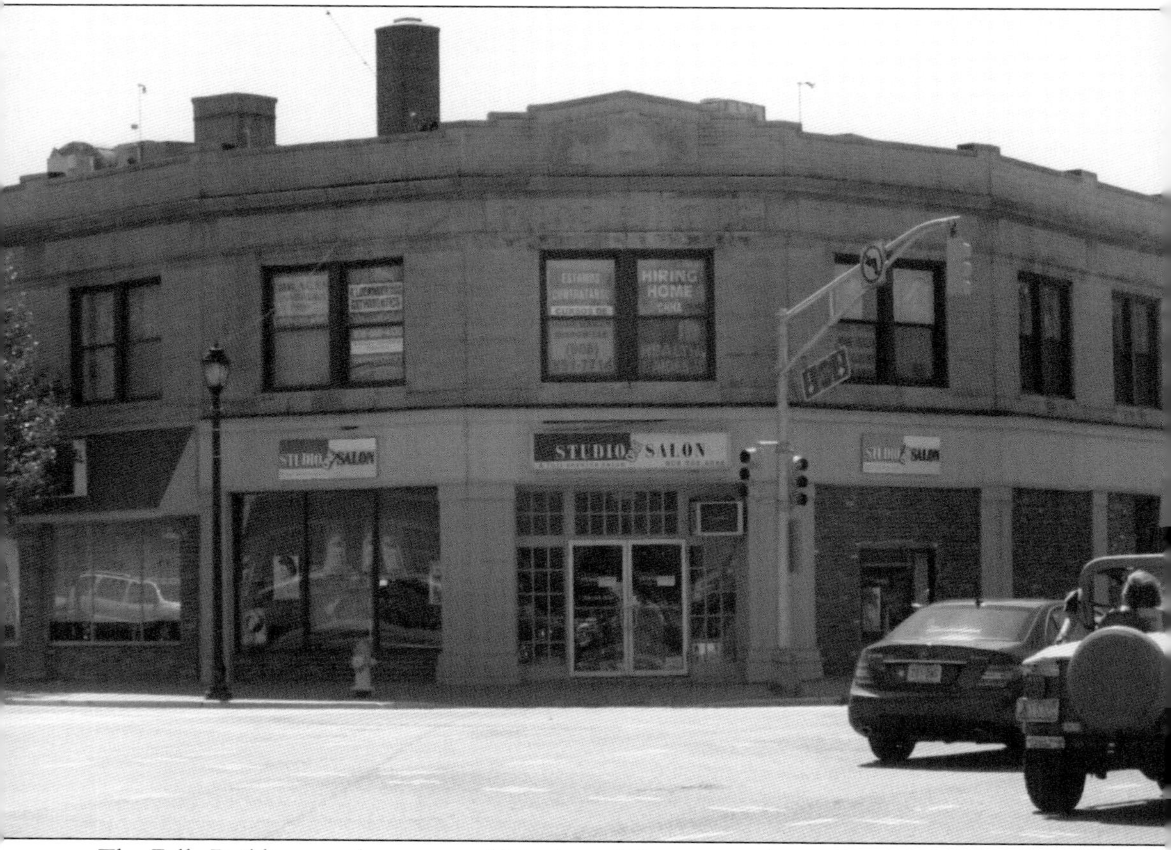

The Falls Building, at the corner of Morris and Stuyvesant Avenues, is pictured here in the summer of 2014. Whelan's Drugs has been gone for many years, replaced by a hairdressing salon, and almost all of the other shops have changed hands many times over the years. But the scene itself has not changed very much, and the building looks the same as it did back in the 1940s and 1950s. (Photograph by the author.)

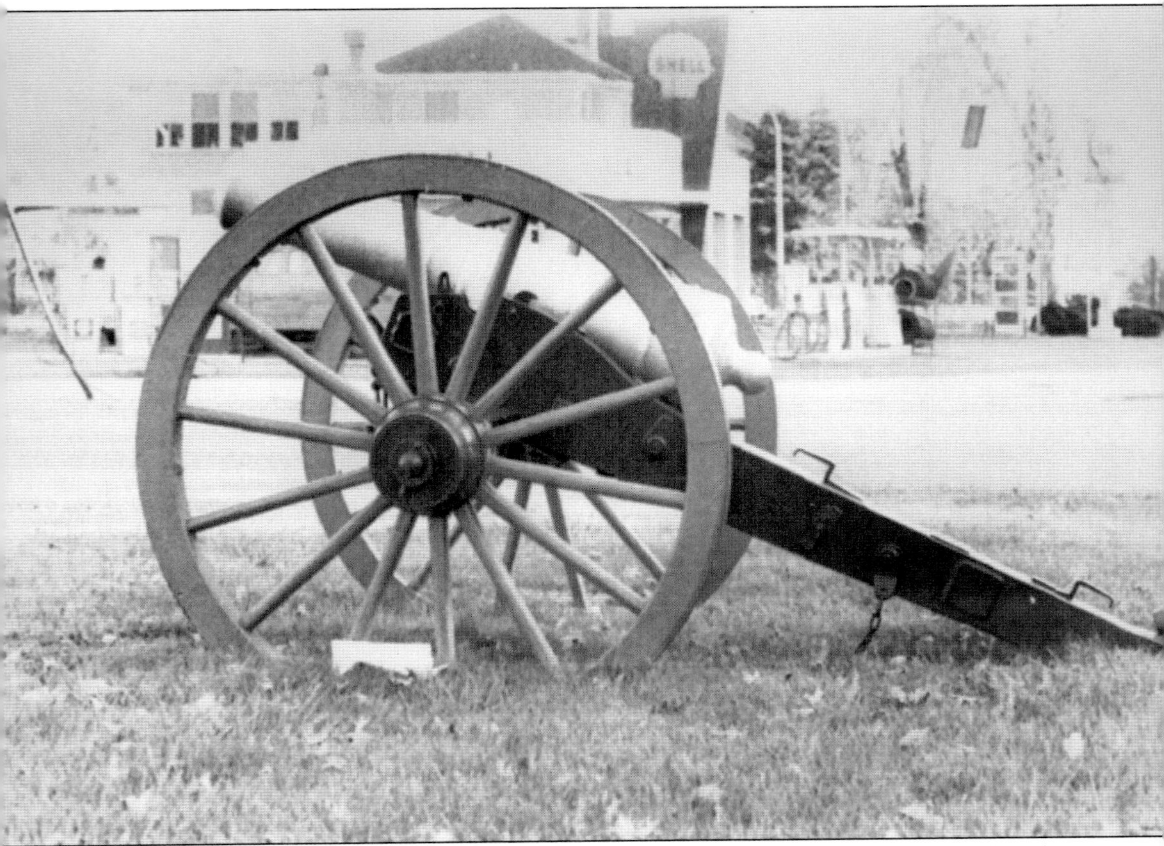

The cannon at the intersection of Stuyvesant and Elmwood Avenues is pictured here before the clock was installed on the plot of ground that is sometimes referred to as the island. Just across the street is Trimmer's Shell station, and up the street from the Shell station is the civic center. The civic center is gone, and so is Trimmer's Shell station, replaced by condominiums. But Union's famous cannon is still there, just as it has been for as long as anybody can remember. (Courtesy of Howie Frisch.)

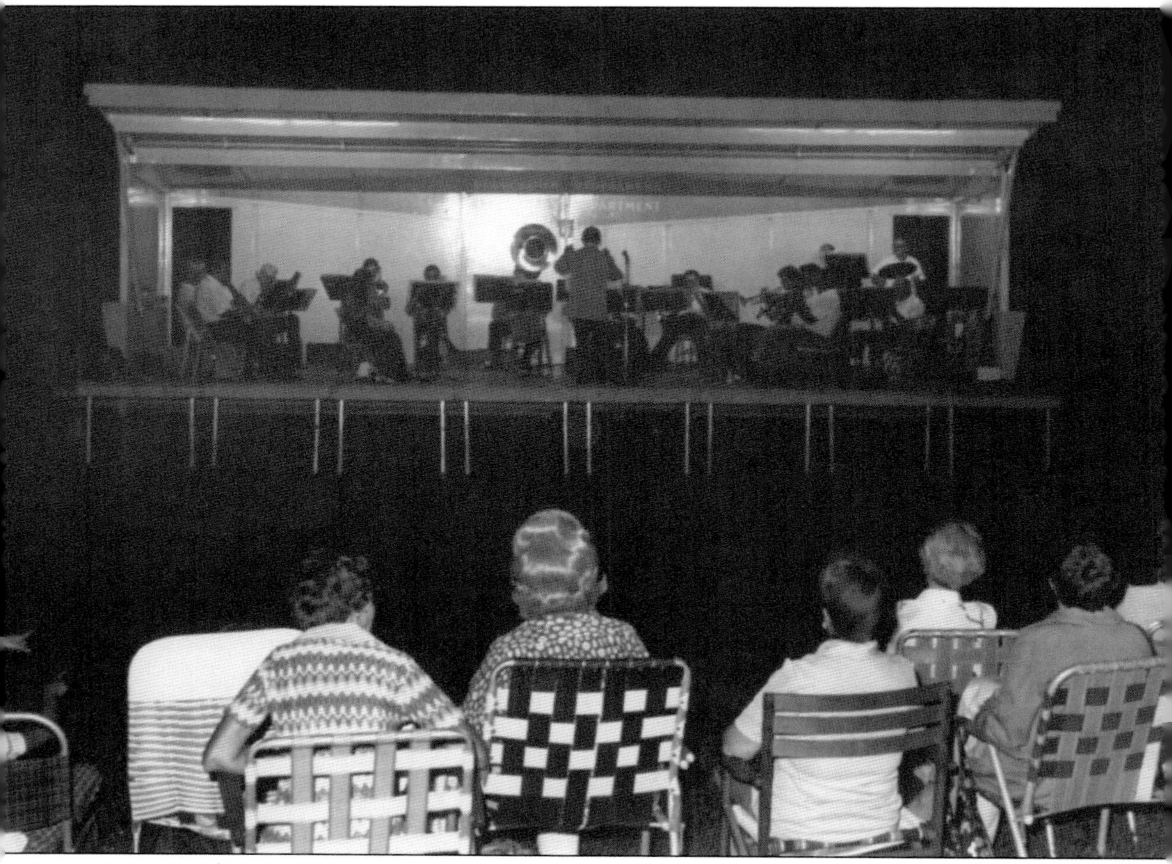

A group of Unionites enjoys an evening concert sometime during the summer of 1975. These concerts have been a summer feature in Union Township for many years, given at a portable band shell in Friberger Park, behind the municipal building. They are still given during the summer month, and are open to the public. If one decides to attend one of these concerts, all that is needed is a folding chair and some mosquito repellent. (Courtesy of Union Township.)

Two of Union Township's younger residents, Angela Seneca (left) and Patty McGeorge, paint the windows of the Café Mozart in October 1975. Cynics have referred to this Halloween ritual—painting the windows of Union Center's shops with Halloween decorations—as "supervised vandalism" and "legalized graffiti," but it has been a very popular activity over the years. The water-based paint washes off with soap and water and sometimes during a rainstorm. (Courtesy of Union Township.)

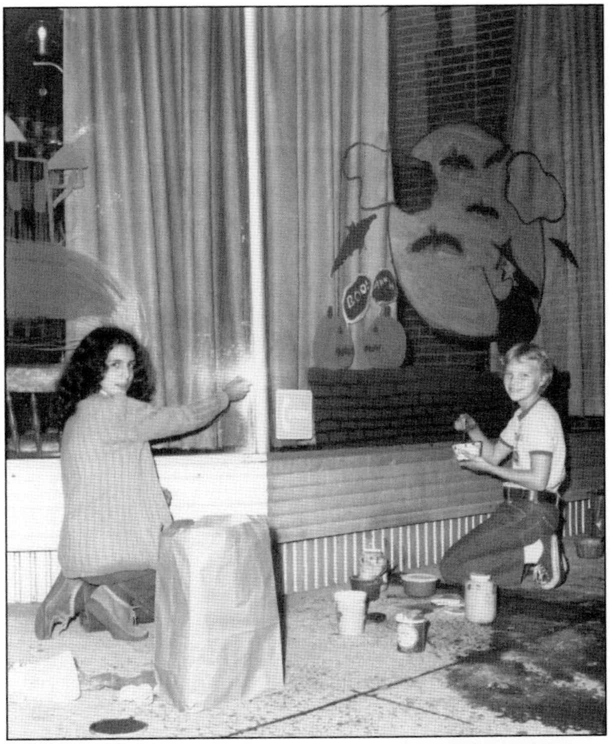

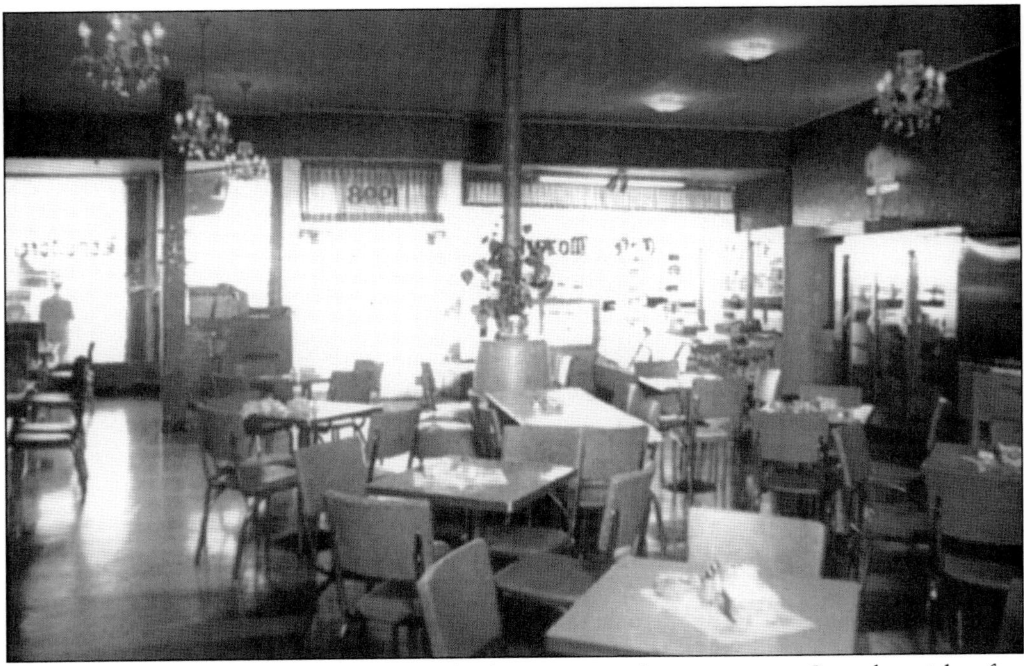

This is the interior of the Café Mozart, which was a nice place to go on a Saturday night after taking the Somerset bus back from New York. The café was a bit of old Vienna in Union Center. It was actually a konditorei, an Austrian pastry café or patisserie, specializing in German- and Austrian-style pastries along with coffee and hot chocolate. Café Mozart was not recommended for anyone on a fat-free or low-calorie diet. (Courtesy of UTHS.)

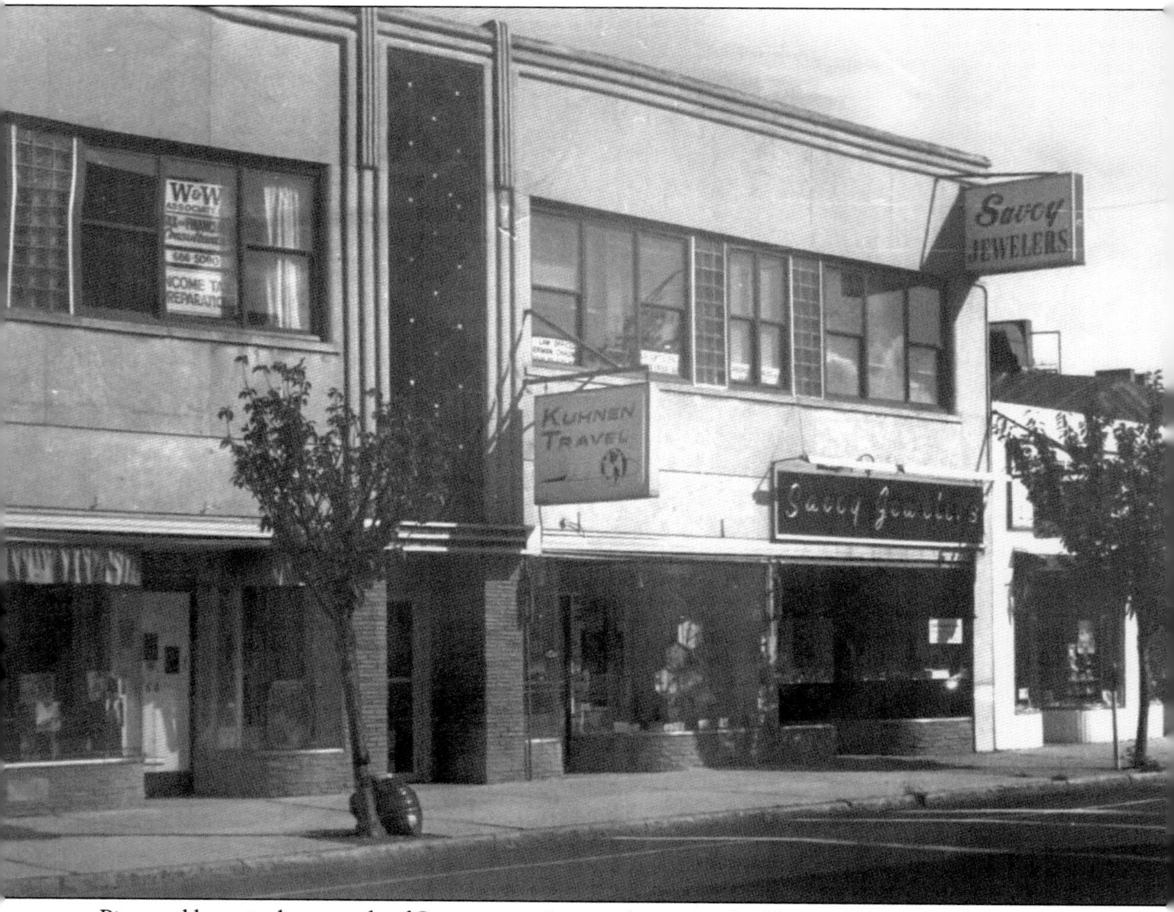

Pictured here is the stretch of Stuyvesant Avenue between the Union Cinema and the Elmwood Avenue cannon. The photograph is not dated, but it was probably taken during the 1970s. Kuhnen Travel and Savoy Jewelers were next-door neighbors at the time. Joe Kuhnen used to call himself "the vacationmaker," and he certainly did make a lot of vacations for a great many people over the years. (He booked the author's first flight to England in 1977.) Kuhnen Travel and Savoy Jewelers are both gone, but this particular section of Stuyvesant Avenue looks remarkably the same, 40 years later. (Courtesy of Tom Haggerty.)

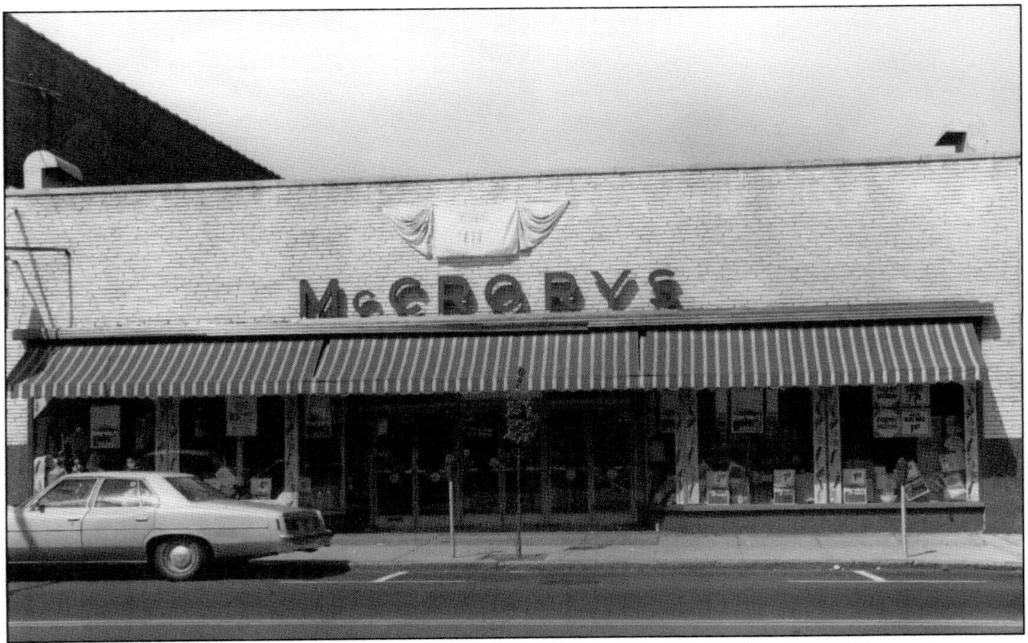

Pictured here is McCrory's five-and-dime in the late 1970s. In the 1950s, a nickel or a dime was still worth something, but few items cost 5¢ or 10¢ by the 1970s. Still, McCrory's was a good place to buy school supplies, hobby kits, and other incidentals. It also had a soda fountain and was a good place to stop for lunch if a person was passing through the center of town. A tuna salad sandwich and an ice-cream soda was always a treat for a young person who happened to be running errands in the area. (Courtesy of UTHS.)

Union Center Card & Gift Shop, the home of Hallmark Cards on Stuyvesant Avenue, is now the home of H&R Block income-tax specialists. The Center Camera Exchange is now the Lovely Nails Studio. Center Camera developed film and sold a full range of cameras and photography equipment. This was long before the digital age, when 35-millimeter photographs did not require a computer screen for viewing. (Courtesy of UTHS.)

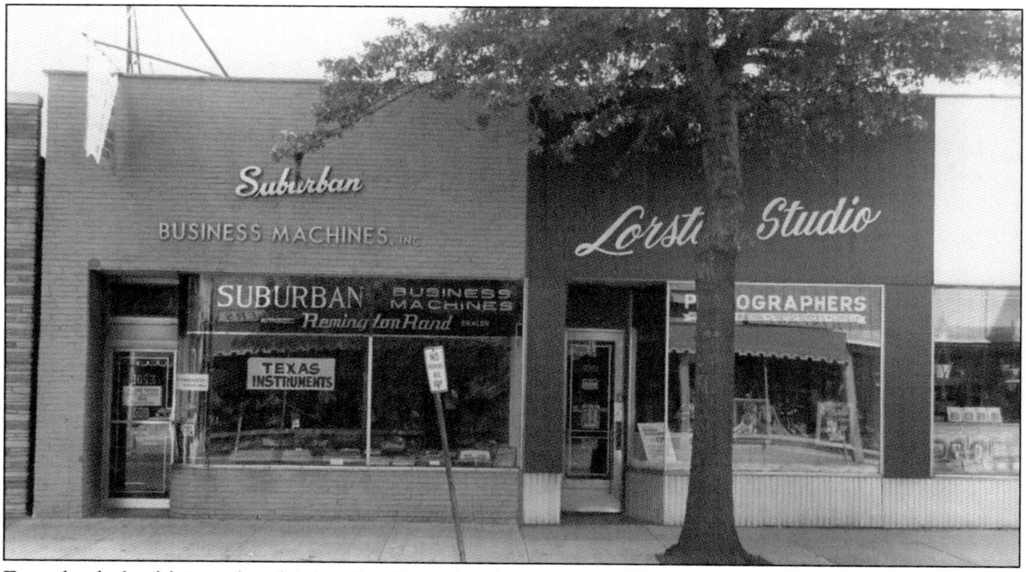

Everybody had his or her high school yearbook portrait taken at Lorstan Studio on Stuyvesant Avenue. Sitting for a senior portrait meant getting dressed up in a jacket and tie on a hot and humid July day before senior year began—which was a nuisance. But the studio's photographers knew how to make a fellow, or a girl, look good. And Suburban Business Machines was the place to get one's typewriter repaired, in the days before the word processor and printer. (Courtesy of UTHS.)

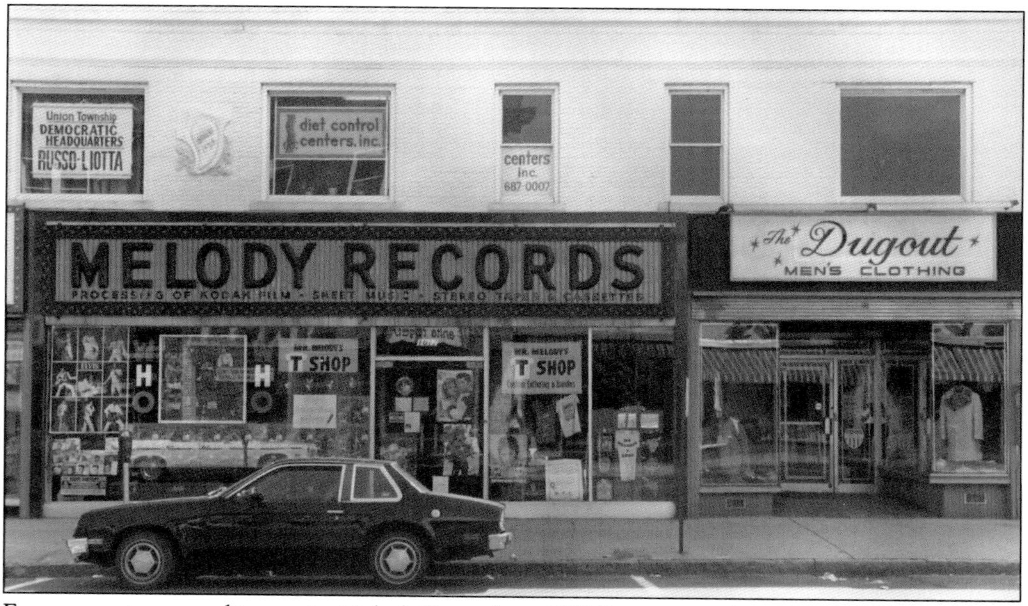

For anyone interested in music, Melody Records, at 1017 Stuyvesant Avenue, was a great place to go. The shop sold everything—from the latest 45-rpm pop hits to bluegrass, symphony, classical music, Broadway musicals, and motion-picture sound tracks. (A poster on the front door features John Travolta and Olivia Newton-John in the film *Grease*.) Inside, Mr. Melody would make T-shirts, complete with any photograph and message that the customer desired. The Dugout, the men's clothing store just to the right, sold nice jackets to go with the new T-shirt. (Courtesy of UTHS.)

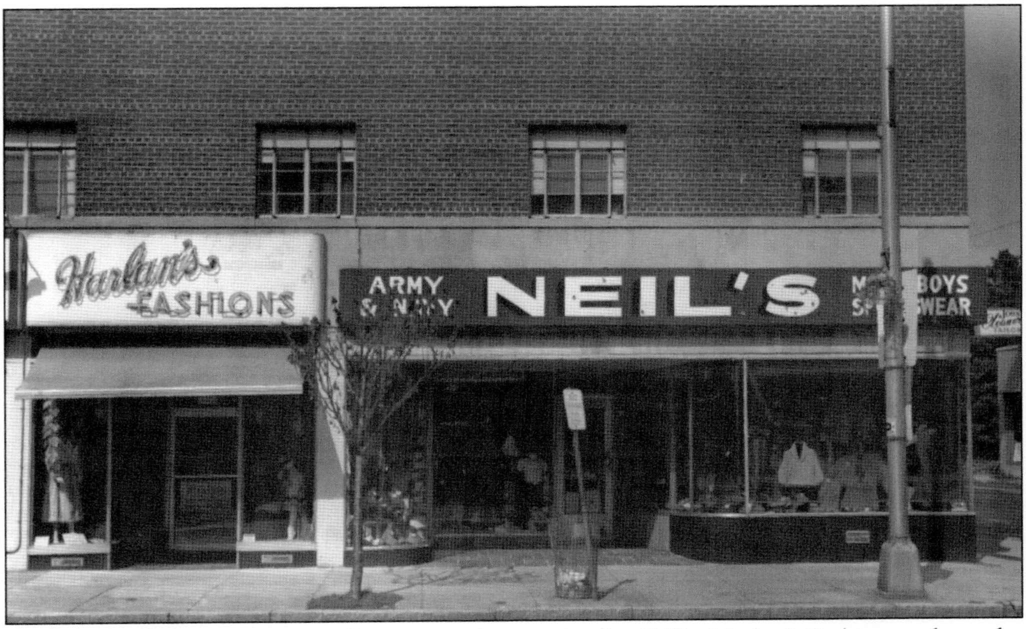

This is a study in contrasts on Stuyvesant Avenue in the 1970s: Harlan's Fashions, where the fashion-conscious shopped, and its next-door neighbor, Neil's Army & Navy, which catered to the blue jeans and casual set. Neither establishment exists any longer. John's Cleaners and Tailors, just around the corner on Emerson Avenue, is also gone. The entire row of shops was replaced by Army/Navy recruiting offices, which have also moved away. (Courtesy of UTHS.)

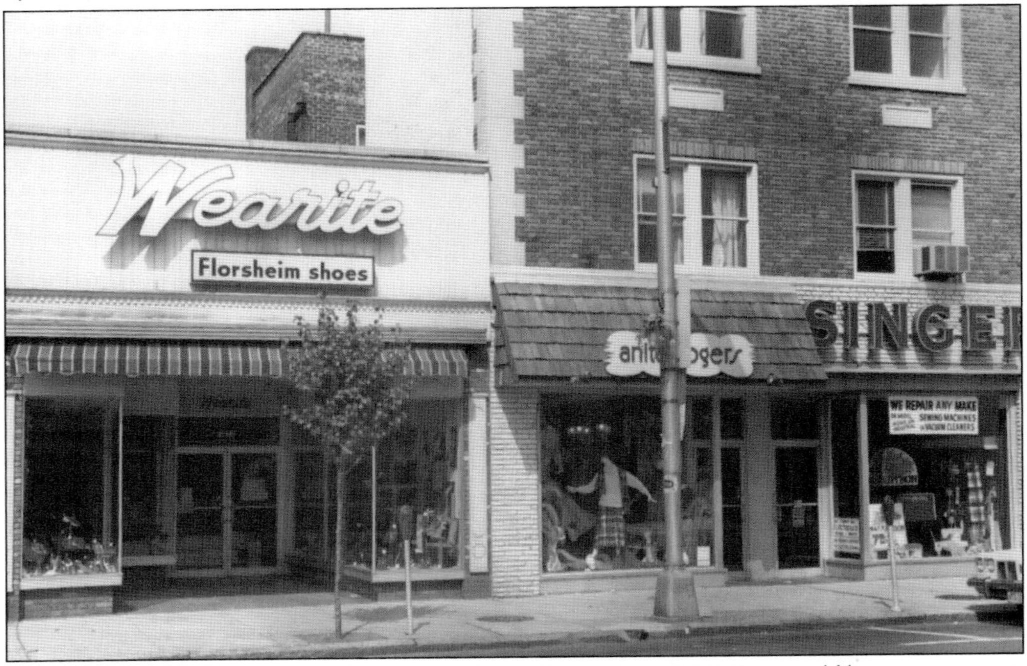

Numbers 1014–1018 Stuyvesant Avenue are pictured here about 1980. One could buy a snappy pair of Florsheim shoes at Wearite, pick up a smart new autumn outfit at Anita Rogers, and then go next door to have one's sewing machine repaired at Singers. Wearite has been replaced by Brooklyn Pizza, Singers is a sushi restaurant, and the shop in between is vacant. (Courtesy of UTHS.)

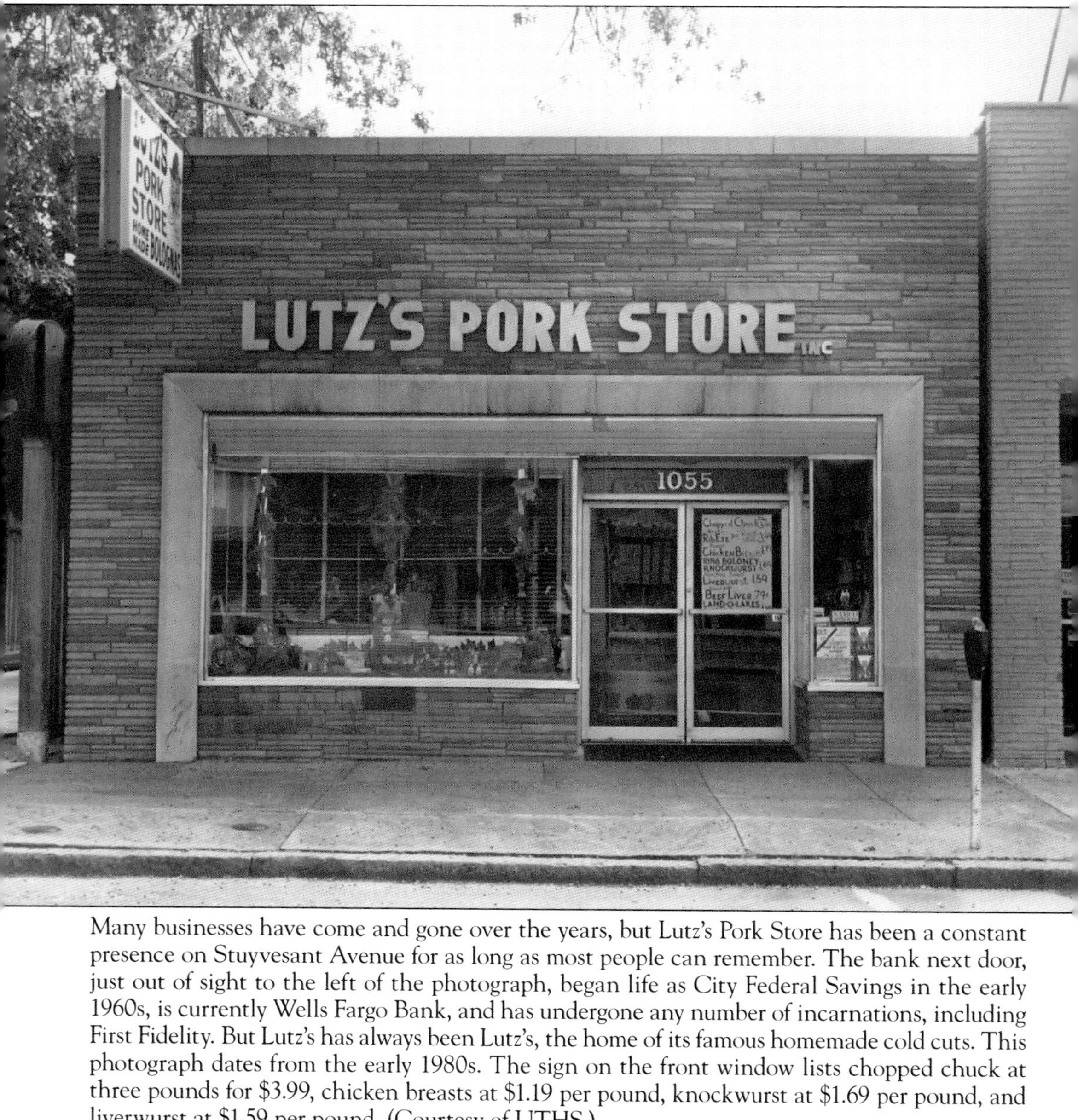

Many businesses have come and gone over the years, but Lutz's Pork Store has been a constant presence on Stuyvesant Avenue for as long as most people can remember. The bank next door, just out of sight to the left of the photograph, began life as City Federal Savings in the early 1960s, is currently Wells Fargo Bank, and has undergone any number of incarnations, including First Fidelity. But Lutz's has always been Lutz's, the home of its famous homemade cold cuts. This photograph dates from the early 1980s. The sign on the front window lists chopped chuck at three pounds for $3.99, chicken breasts at $1.19 per pound, knockwurst at $1.69 per pound, and liverwurst at $1.59 per pound. (Courtesy of UTHS.)

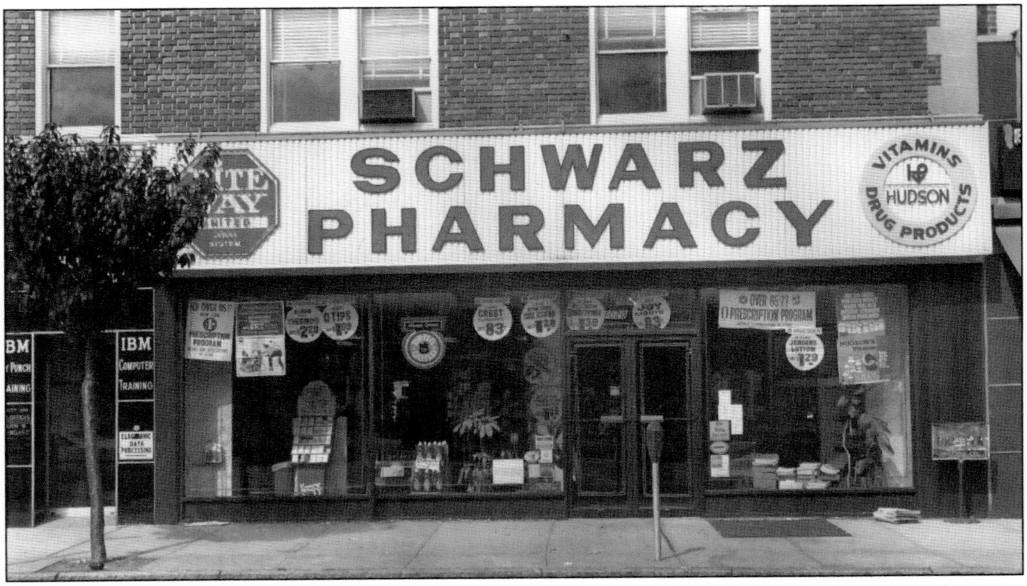

Schwarz Pharmacy had been on the "other side," the odd-numbered side, of Stuyvesant Avenue, for many years. In the late 1960s, it moved across the street to the even-numbered side. In addition to being a pharmacy, Schwarz sold everything from cosmetics to groceries and toys. Advertisements in the window are for Crest toothpaste at 83¢, Joy dishwashing liquid also at 83¢, and Jergens lotion at $1.29. Schwarz was eventually sold to a new owner, who ran the business successfully until competition from Rite Aid and Walgreens forced the establishment to close its doors permanently. (Courtesy of UTHS.)

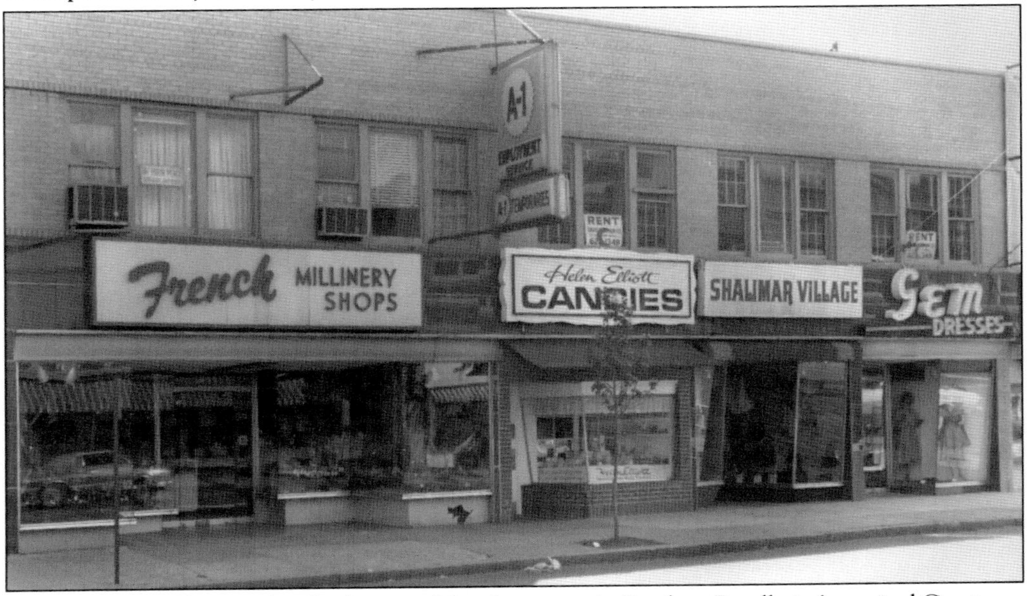

"Does anyone still wear a hat?" asks one of the characters in Stephen Sondheim's musical *Company*. Well, enough women wore hats to keep French Millinery Shops in business for a good many years. Right next door was Helen Elliott Candies, "Made Fresh Every Day, the Good Old Fashioned Way," at least according to the advertisement in the shop window. French Millinery and Helen Elliott have both disappeared, along with Shalimar Village, Gem Dresses, and A-1 Employment Service up one flight. (Courtesy of UTHS.)

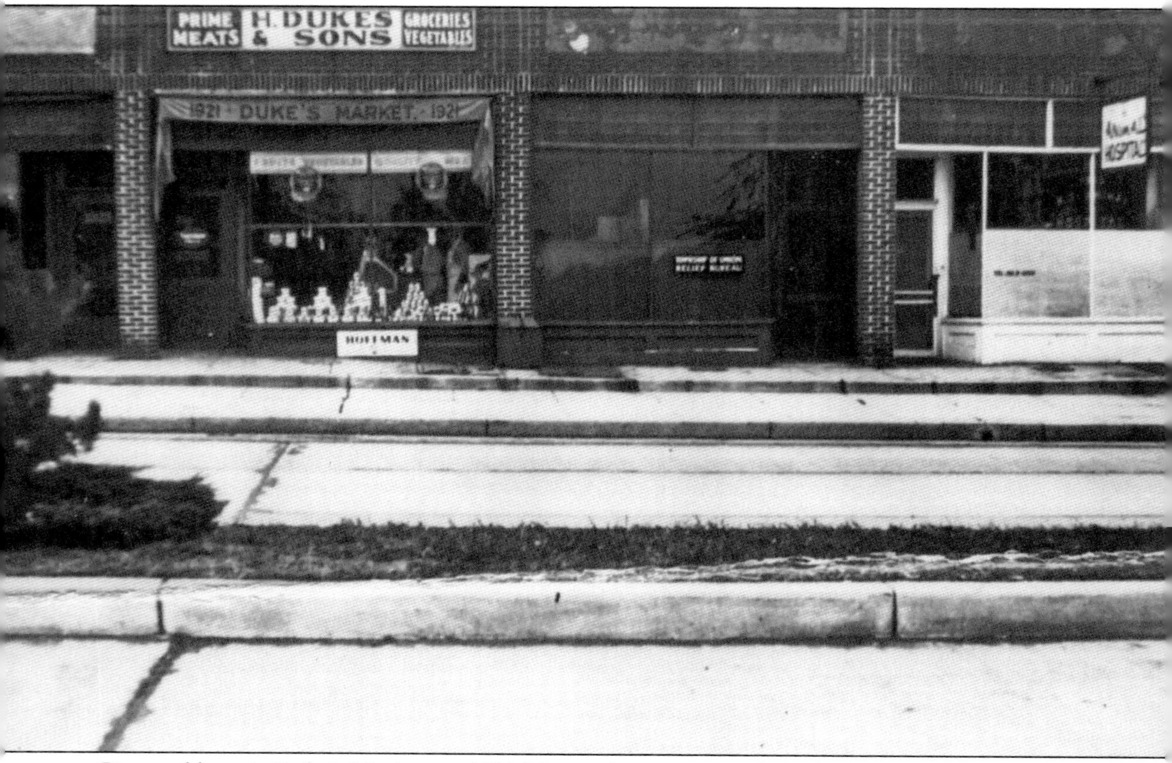

Pictured here is Duke's Market, at 1921 Morris Avenue, near Grandview Avenue. Homer Dukes ran an old-fashioned grocery store. He sold meat, eggs, fruit, vegetables, baked goods, and a full line of Hoffman sodas. He also would deliver grocery orders right to the house. There was an A&P within walking distance, over on Stuyvesant Avenue, but many people preferred the personal attention of small grocers to large and impersonal supermarkets. Dukes' Market went out of business at the end of 1960, when Homer Dukes sold the business. Next door, on the corner of Grandview and Morris Avenues, Ray Bell had his real estate office; his slogan was "To Buy or Sell, Ring Ray Bell."(Courtesy of Tom Haggerty.)

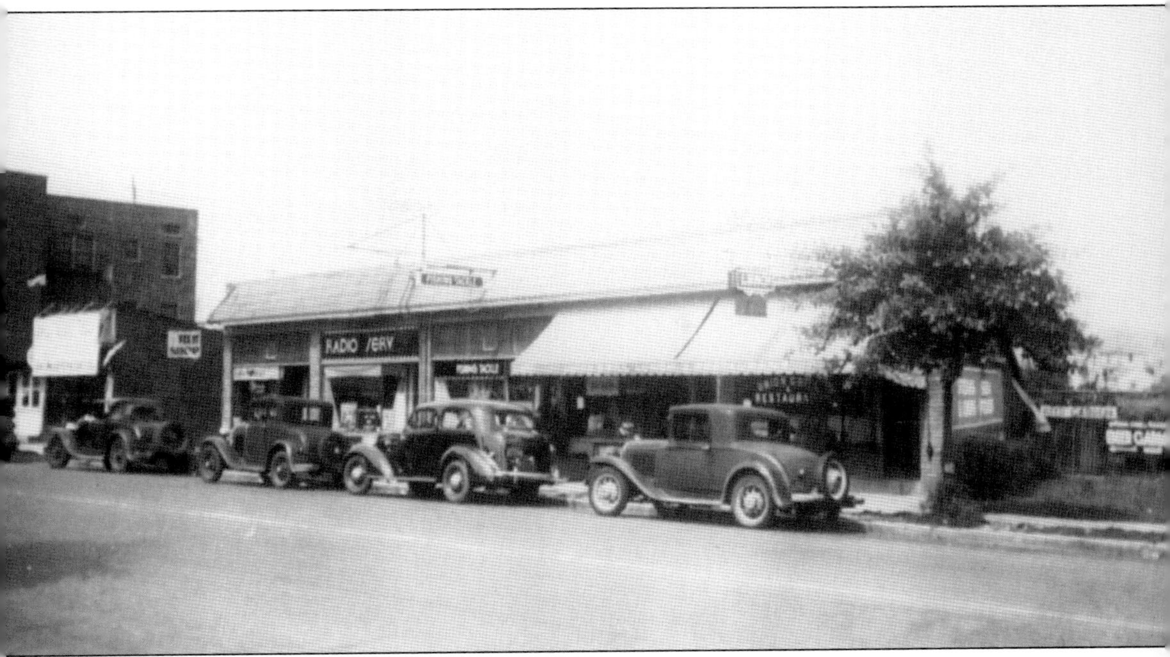

Stuyvesant Avenue, the main drag between Emerson and Morris Avenues, is pictured here in the 1930s, just down the street from what would be the site of McCrory's and much later, Dollar Tree. The row of shops includes the Union Grill & Restaurant, a fishing-tackle shop, a radio repair shop (which, in the days before television, was a very important establishment), and a Fix-It shop. A sign in the vacant lot on the right side of the photograph advertises a beer garden, and even features an arrow to point the way. At the time, many Union Township residents were either first- or second-generation Germans. A beer garden would have been very much a part of their background. (Courtesy of Tom Haggerty.)

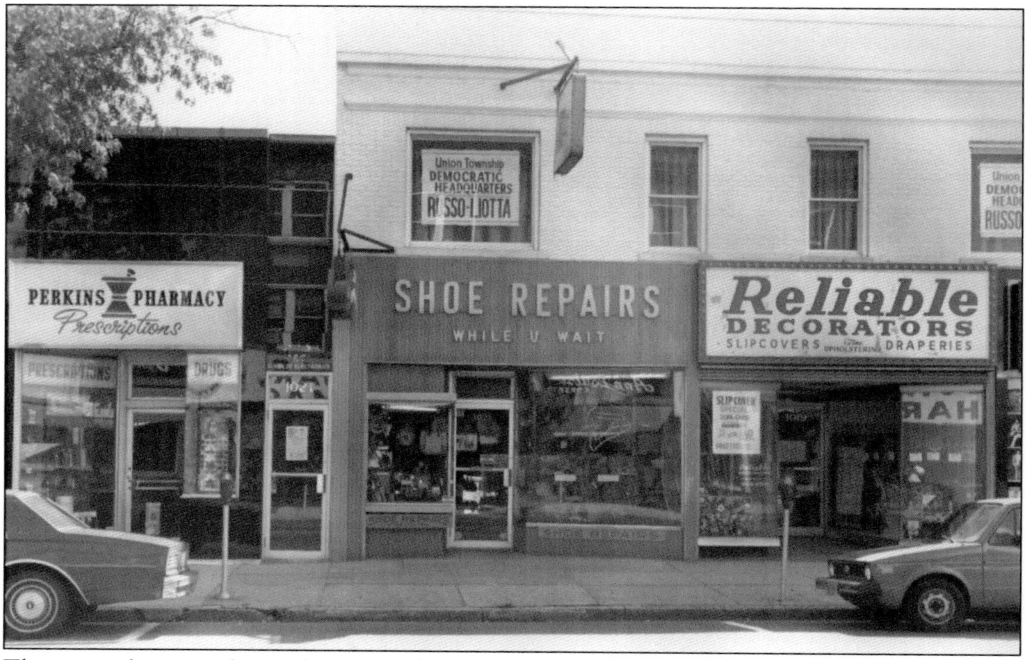

This scene has not changed very much over the years. Perkins Pharmacy is still going strong, and the shoe repair shop is still mending shoes. Reliable Decorators is gone, though, and the shop is now vacant. Perkins Pharmacy has been at this location for as long as most people can remember. (Courtesy of UTHS.)

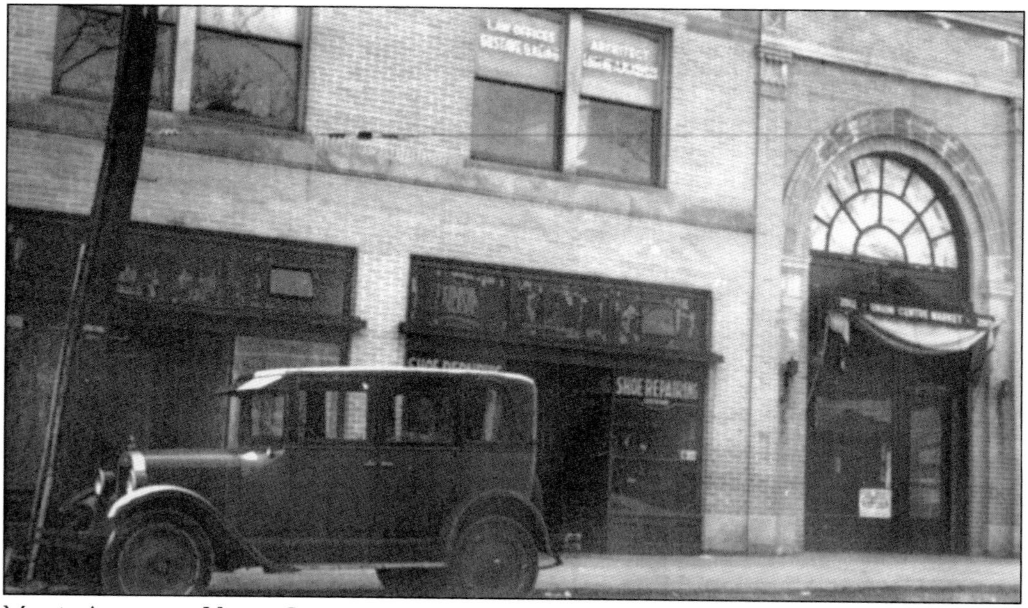

Morris Avenue in Union Center—2012 Morris Avenue, to be precise—is pictured here in the 1930s. The site had been occupied by the Union Centre Market, but was vacant when this photograph was taken, a small For Rent sign can be seen in the window. Whelan's Drugs is just a short walk up the street, just off to the left. A person could park his or her Ford sedan right on Morris Avenue in those days and not have to worry about being ticketed and towed away. The car in the photograph is a 1927 Chevrolet. (Courtesy of Tom Haggerty.)

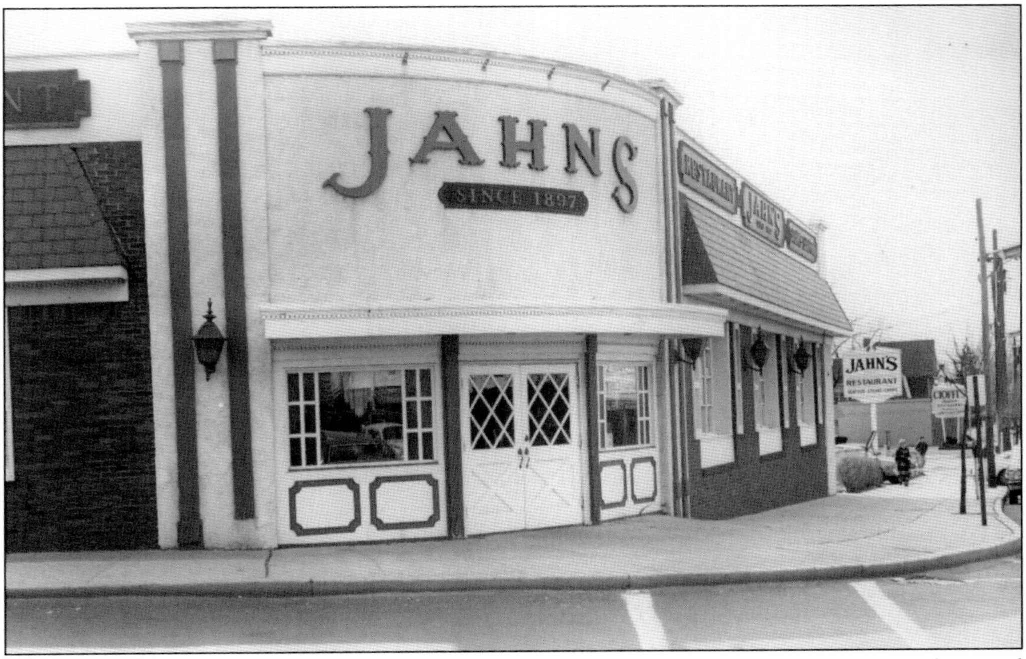

If the Café Mozart was old Vienna, Jahn's was strictly New Jersey. The restaurant never advertised itself as the home of good plain cooking, but that is what it was. There was nothing fancy about the menu at Jahn's; it featured items such as meat loaf and roast chicken. Before Jahn's, in the 1950s, the site was occupied by an A&P supermarket. (Courtesy of UTHS.)

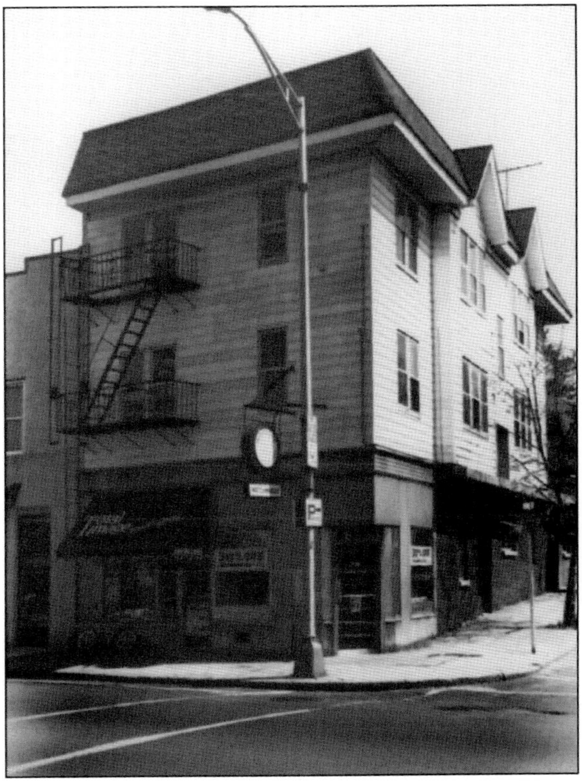

A watchmaker's shop has occupied the building on the corner of Stuyvesant and Rosemont Avenues for as long as anyone can remember. For many years, it was Woerdich's. In recent years, Gold Star Jewelers has been at the site. A Rite Aid, in the former Jahn's Restaurant, occupies the site on the other side of Rosemont Avenue, which is off the photograph. The building has looked the same over the past 50 or 60 years, regardless of occupant. (Courtesy of UTHS.)

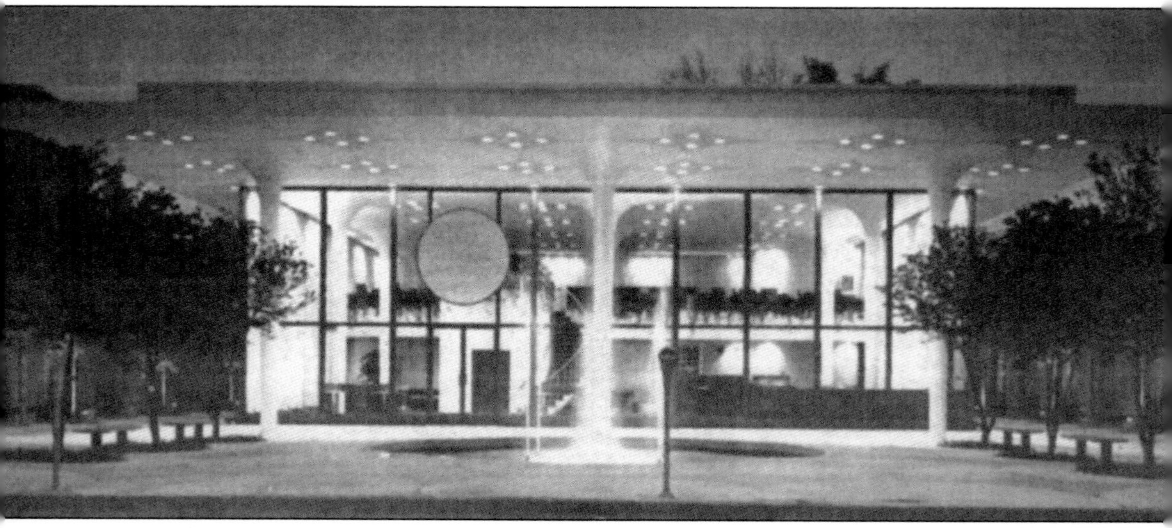

City Federal Savings Bank on Stuyvesant Avenue is pictured here during the early 1960s. The building was of such an advanced and unusual design that it received a write-up in the *Architectural Record*, the source of this photograph. The bank's best-remembered feature is probably the fountain that occupied the center of the plaza in front of the building. Once in a while, some bright young person would dump a box of washing detergent into the fountain. The resulting flood of soapsuds would cover most of the plaza and sometimes cascade onto Stuyvesant Avenue. Although the building has changed hands many times over the years, it has always remained a bank. Currently, it is a Wells Fargo Bank. (Courtesy of UTHS.)

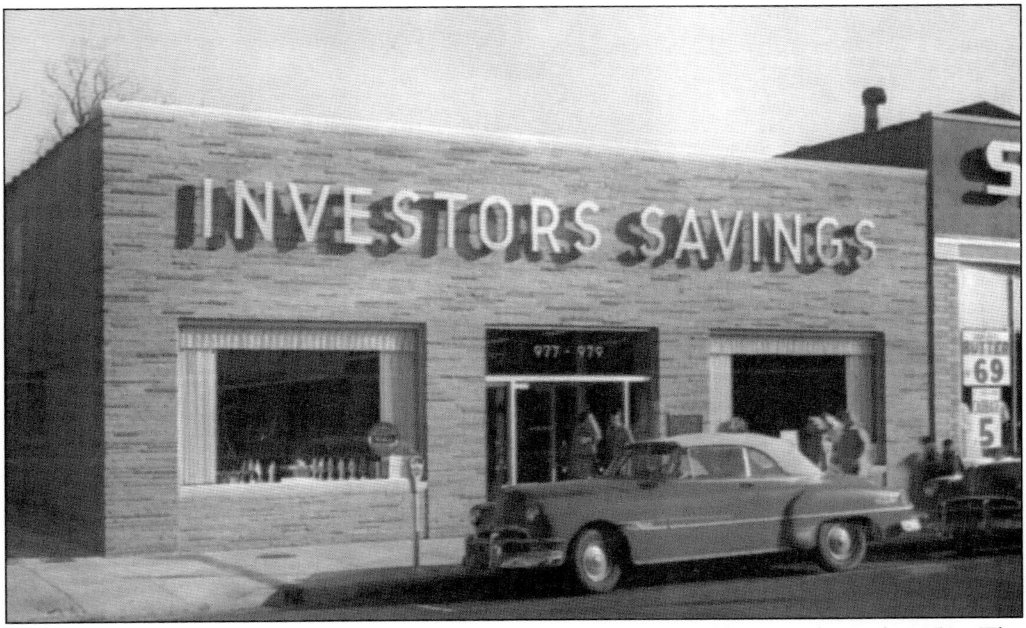

Investors Savings Bank, at 977–979 Stuyvesant Avenue, is pictured here in the early 1950s. The car parked out front is either a 1952 or 1953 Pontiac. The bank is now called Investors Bank, but that is about the only thing about the building that has changed over the years. A ShopRite supermarket was just next door. Signs in the window advertise butter at 69¢ per pound, and cabbage at 5¢ per pound.

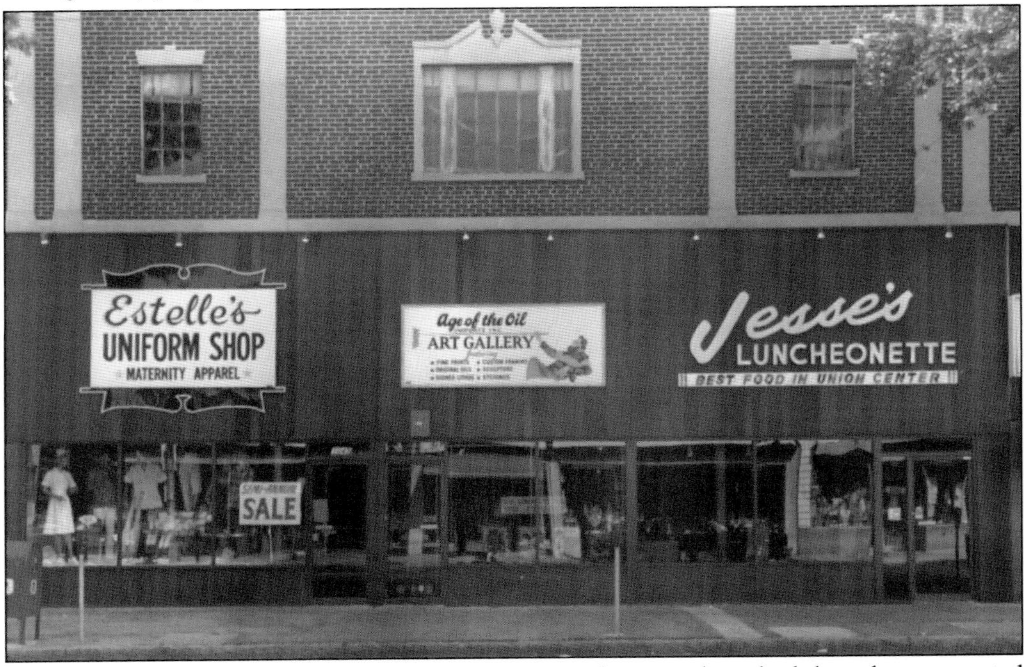

Estelle's Uniform Shop, Age of the Oil, and Jesse's Luncheonette have had their shops occupied by Bonchon Restaurant, Liberty Tax, and Barangay Restaurant, respectively. The owner of Age of the Oil—as in oil painting—used to be telephoned by homeowners who wanted to have their oil burners cleaned and serviced. (Courtesy of UTHS.)

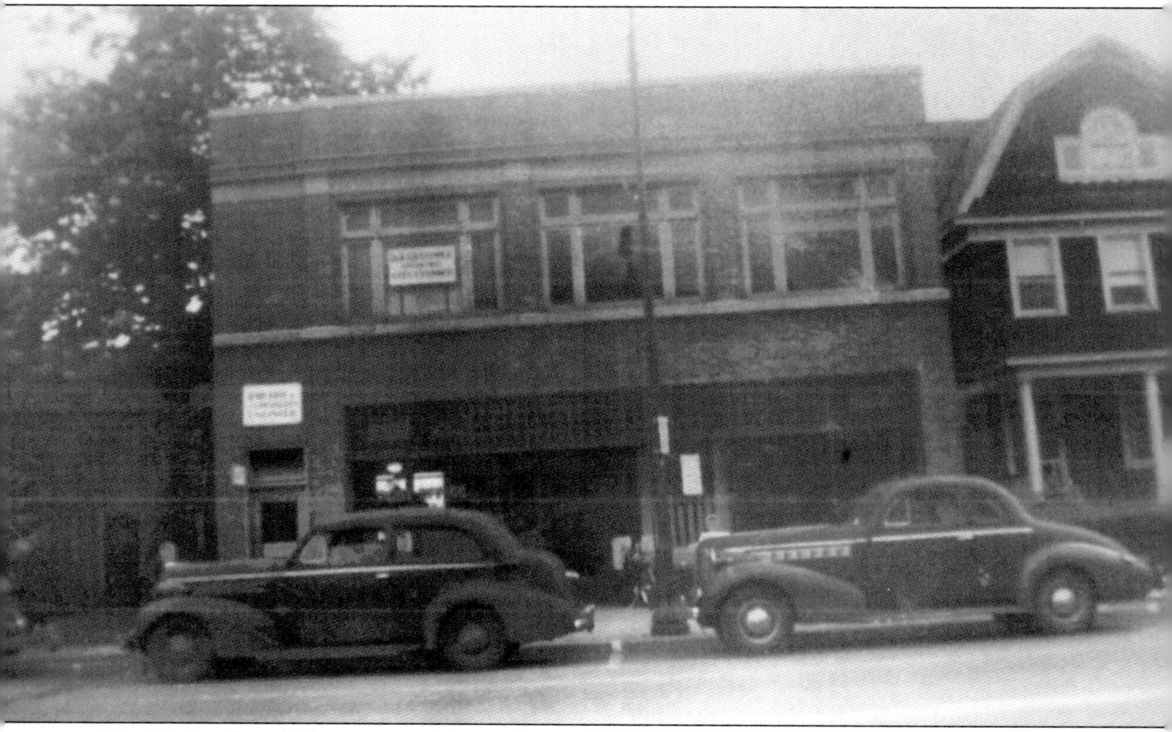

The Union Post Office was on Morris Avenue for many years, just down the street from Union Center National Bank. The photograph is undated, but the two cars are a 1936 Oldsmobile (left) and a 1931 Buick (right). Gaiser's Pork Store has occupied this site for as long as most Unionites can remember. The post office has moved several times since this photograph was taken, and the house to the right of the building has been pulled down, but Gaiser's is still there. (Courtesy of UTHS.)

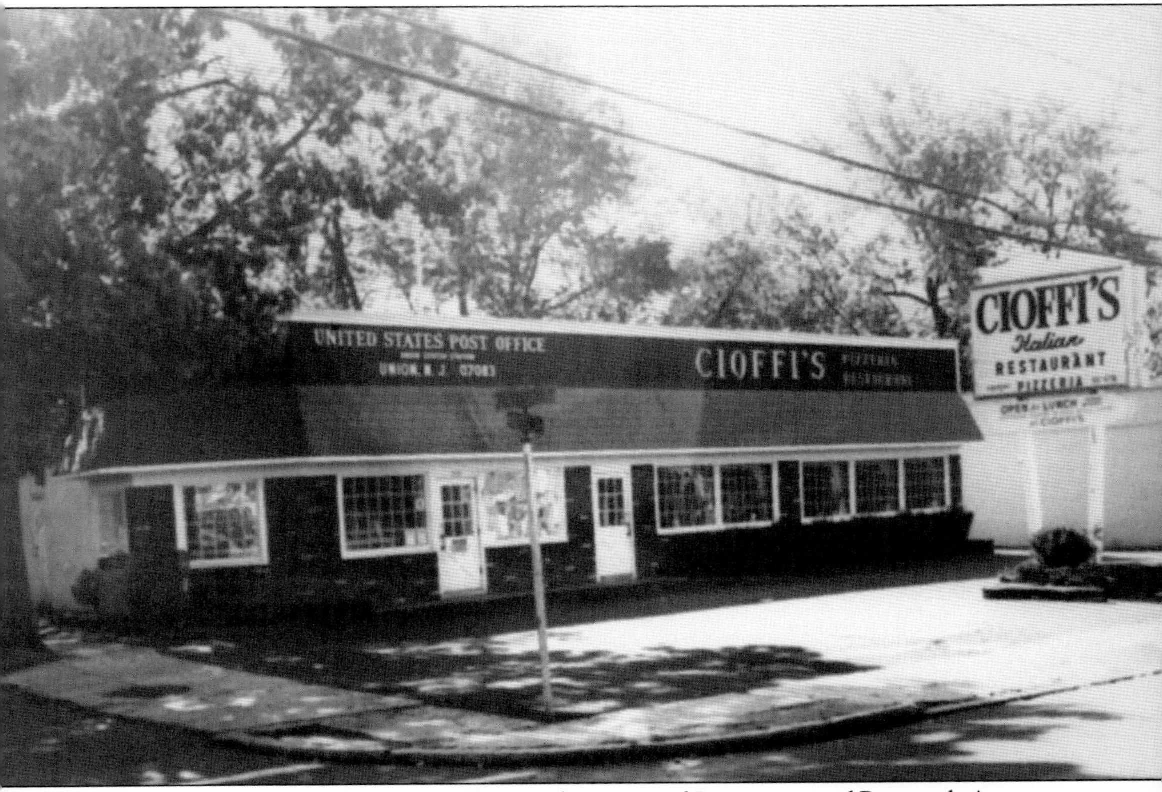

The Union Center branch of the post office, on the corner of Stuyvesant and Roosevelt Avenues, is pictured here about 1980. The post office had been just across the street, on the other side of Stuyvesant Avenue, but that site has been occupied by a series of banks for quite some time. The Union Center branch of the post office is now situated on Morris Avenue, just across the street from the municipal building. Cioffi's Restaurant and Pizzeria now occupies the entire building pictured here. (Courtesy of UTHS.)

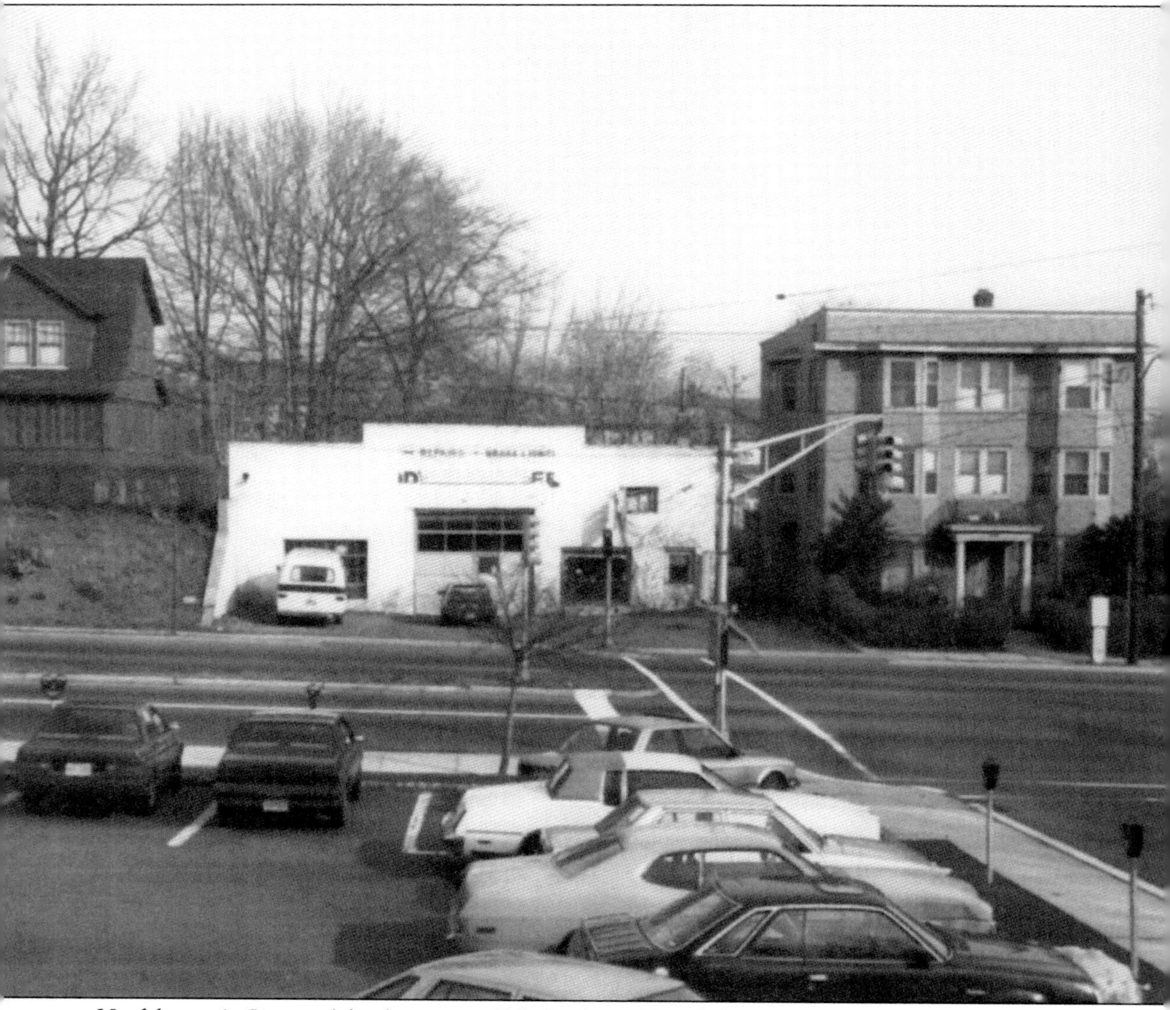

Hochberger's Garage (also known as Ed's Body and Fender), at 1945 Morris Avenue, is pictured here in the 1980s. Their motto was "You Bend 'Em, We Mend 'Em." The shop has since moved down the street to 1751 Morris Avenue. (Courtesy of UTHS.)

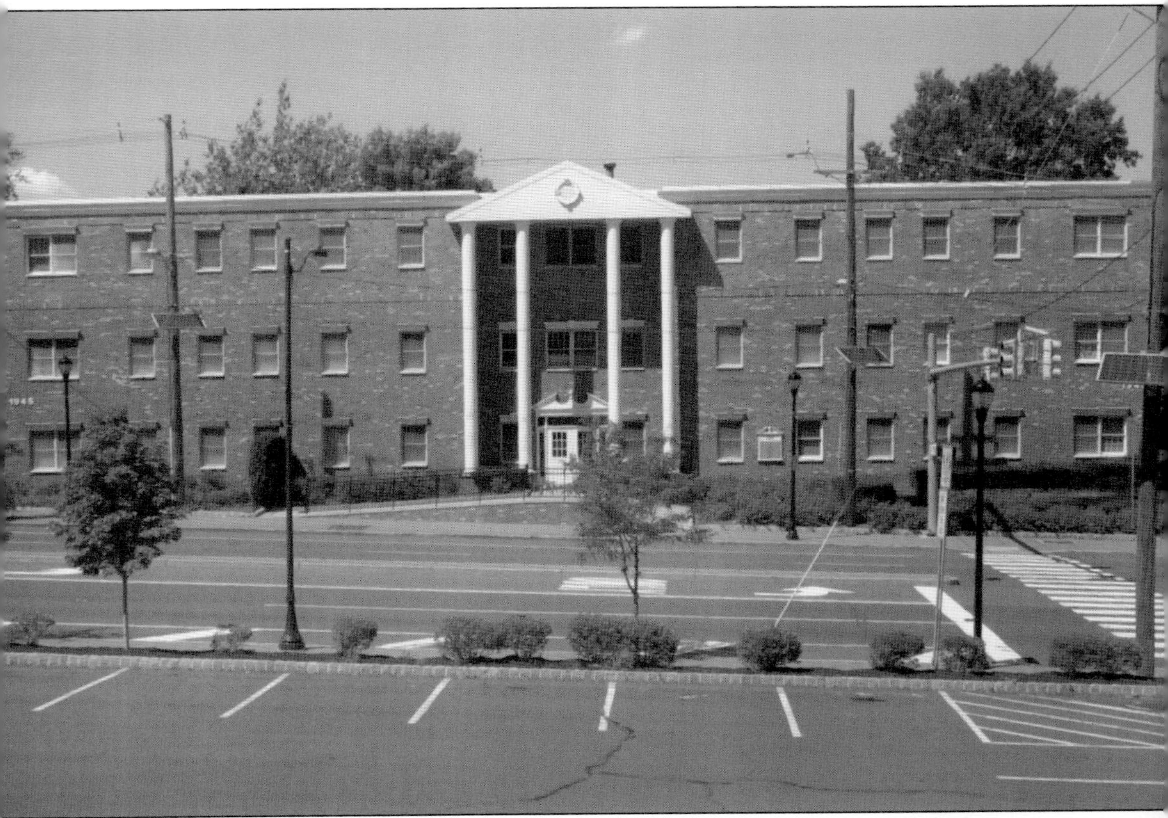

When Ed's Body and Fender moved down the street, a large professional building was constructed on the site. The building's white columns look slightly out of place on Morris Avenue—a visitor from out of the area once asked if Scarlett O'Hara used to live there. But even though it is not as romantic as it looks, 1945 Morris Avenue serves a utilitarian purpose, as the site for a number of doctor's and lawyer's offices, and even an Air Force recruiting office. (Photograph by the author.)

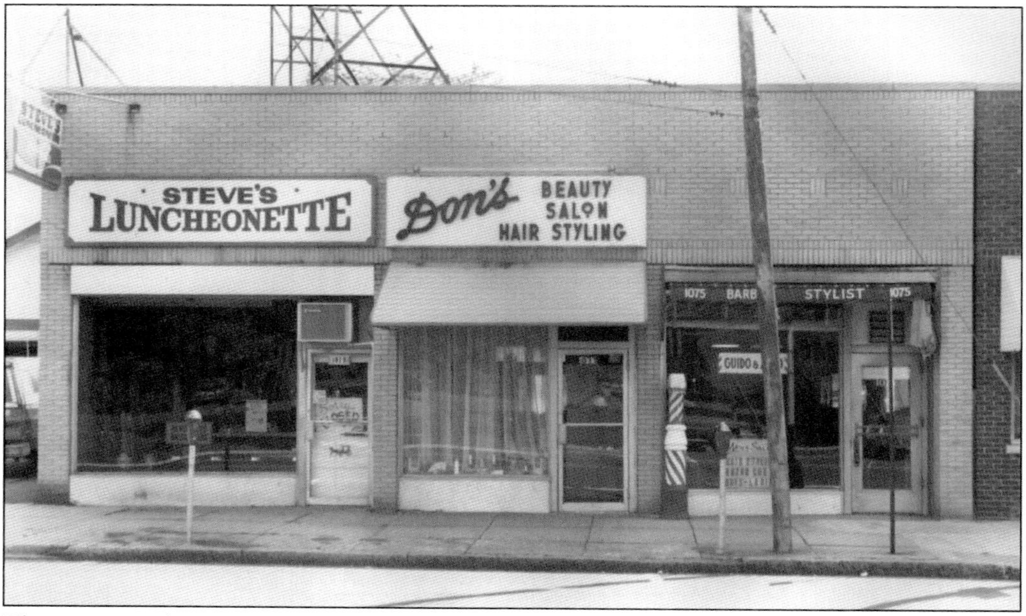

The sign over the entrance to Don's Beauty Salon has been changed since this photograph was taken in the early 1980s, but Don's is still located at 1077 Stuyvesant Avenue. Guido & Aldo's barbershop is vacant, and the site of Steve's Luncheonette appears to be vacant, as well. (Courtesy of UTHS.)

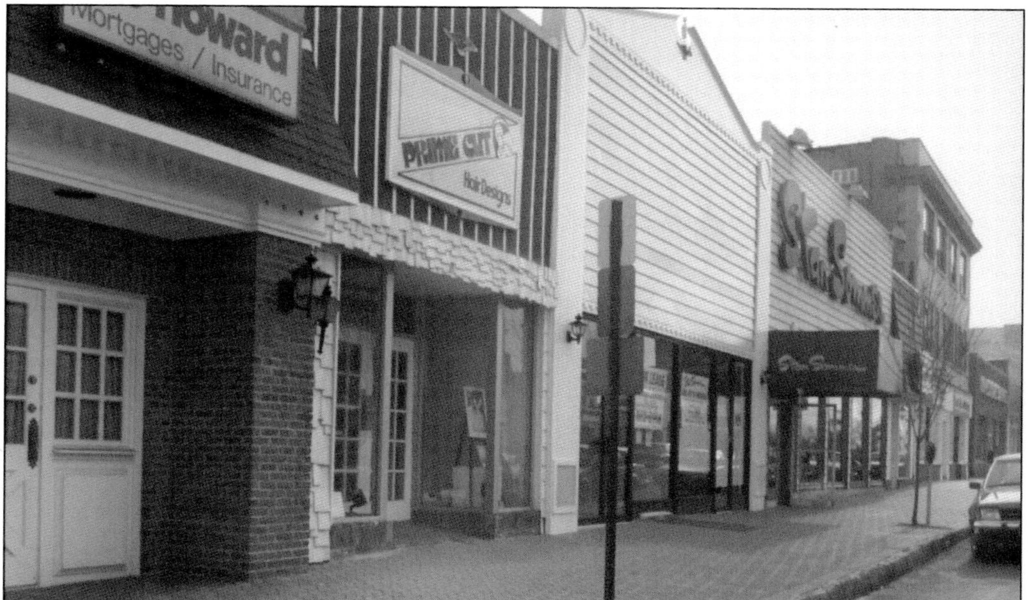

Stuyvesant Avenue was fairly quiet when this photograph was taken in the early 1980s. Still, it was great to be Howard powered, as the advertisements for the Howard Savings Bank used to say. The bank occupies the site that had been Gruber's men's shop for many years, and is currently occupied by still another bank. (There are many Unionites who predict that the town will one day be filled with nothing but banks and drugstores.) Prime Cut hairdressers have also gone, along with Stan Sommer, which had been a Stuyvesant Avenue fixture since at least the 1940s. (Courtesy of UTHS.)

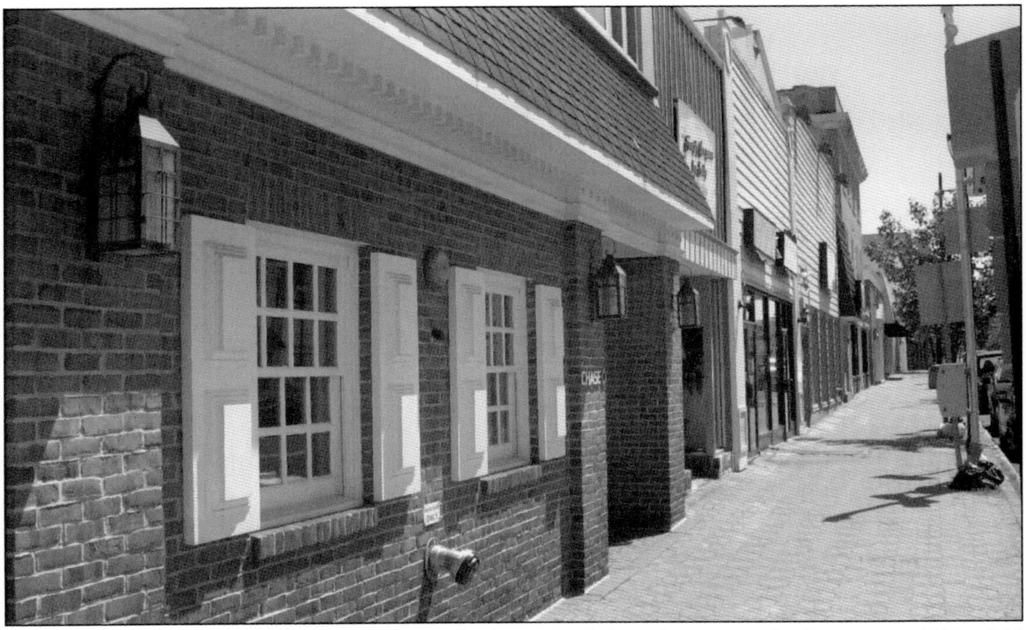

From next to the Chase Bank (formerly Gruber's men's clothing) in a view looking toward Rite Aid Pharmacy (formerly Jahn's Restaurant), other businesses have taken the place of Stan Sommer's neighbors. Besides the Chase Bank, this row of shops includes the Simply Gorgeous hairdresser, along with at least one other beauty salon, as well as Investors Bank and the 20th Legislative District headquarters. (Photograph by the author.)

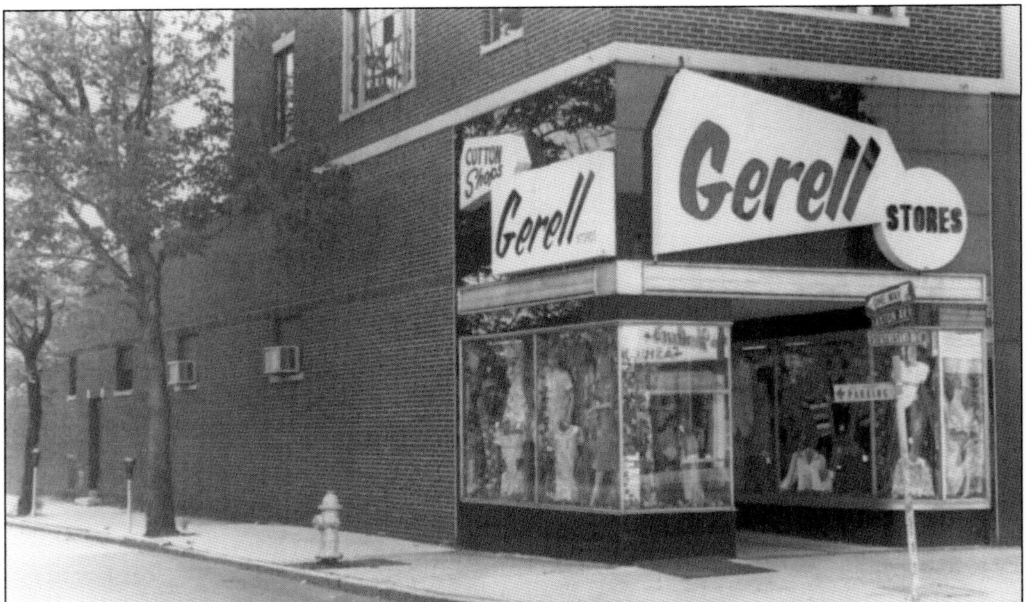

The corner of Stuyvesant Avenue and Axton Avenue is pictured here in the mid-1970s. The Shoe Box formerly occupied the premises, before Gerell's Cotton Shops took over the site. (The square section of the "Gerell" represented a shoe box at one time.) Gerell's has since disappeared, and the corner shop has been occupied by other enterprises, including a fish market and currently, a barbershop. Just across the street from Gerell's was Neil's Army & Navy. (Courtesy of UTHS.)

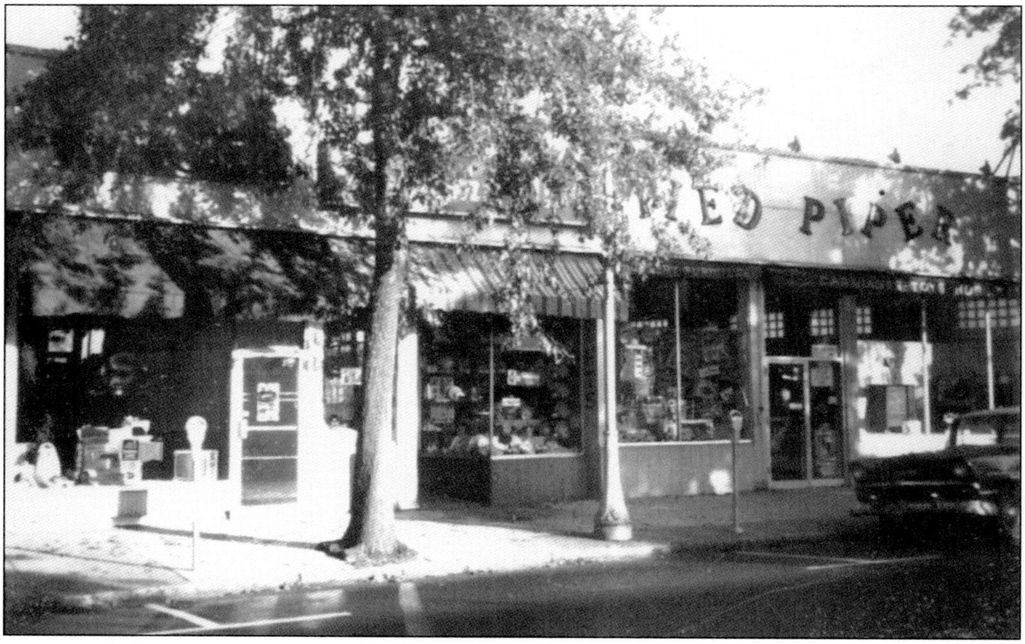

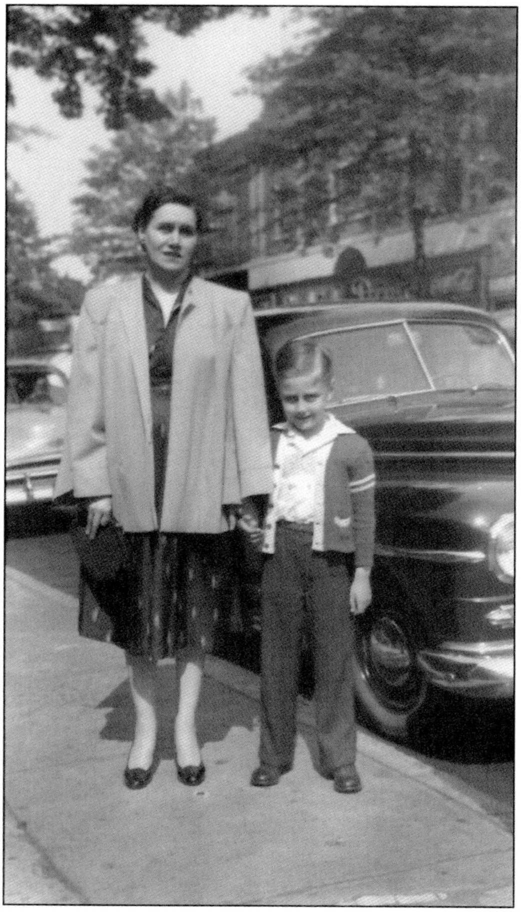

Before computer games were ever heard of, kids used to keep themselves busy with other things. They played board games such as Monopoly and also assembled model airplane kits. The Pied Piper on Stuyvesant Avenue, diagonally across from Lutz's Pork Store, sold everything needed to make a fellow's P-51 Mustang or P-47 Thunderbolt look authentic. When the electronic era took over, many hobby shops like the Pied Piper, along with the Play Fair, on the same side of Stuyvesant Avenue, past the Union Cinema, went out of business. (Courtesy of UTHS.)

Stuyvesant Avenue is pictured here on a Sunday afternoon in the spring 1957, across the street from Plaza Drugs. The author holds his mother's hand, while his father takes this photograph. (Author's collection.)

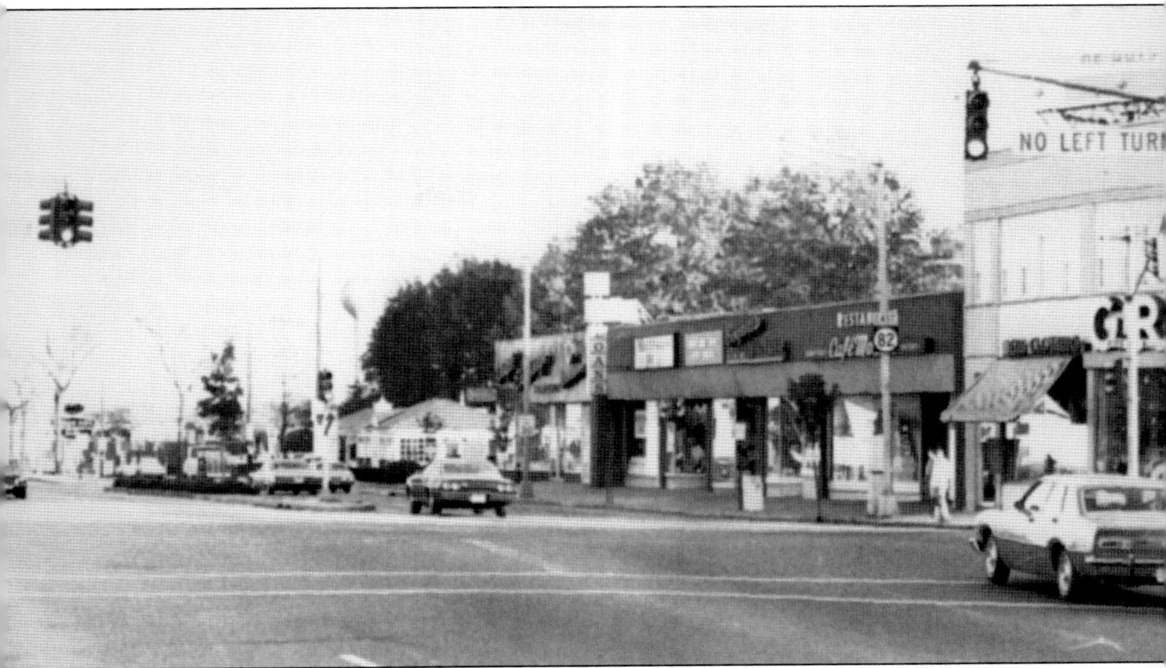

This is another view of Union Center the way it used to be, in this instance in the mid-1970s. Gruber's men's clothing is on the corner. Next door is the Café Mozart and then Bogart's Gifts. A few doors down, by the driveway leading up to the public library's parking lot, is the Lloyd Exchange travel agency. On the other side of the driveway is the Courtesy House, a place for people to get out of the rain while they waited for the Somerset bus to New York. Every one of these places has disappeared over the years, even the Somerset bus, which has been replaced by New Jersey Transit. (Courtesy of Howie Frisch.)

Consistent with our mission to preserve history on a local level, this book was printed in South Carolina on American-made paper and manufactured entirely in the United States. Products carrying the accredited Forest Stewardship Council (FSC) label are printed on 100 percent FSC-certified paper.

MADE IN THE USA